CHINESE CREATOR ECONOMIES

CRITICAL CULTURAL COMMUNICATION

General Editors: Jonathan Gray, Aswin Punathambekar, Adrienne Shaw
Founding Editors: Sarah Banet-Weiser and Kent A. Ono

Dangerous Curves: Latina Bodies in the Media
Isabel Molina-Guzmán

The Net Effect: Romanticism, Capitalism, and the Internet
Thomas Streeter

Our Biometric Future: Facial Recognition Technology and the Culture of Surveillance
Kelly A. Gates

Critical Rhetorics of Race
Edited by Michael G. Lacy and Kent A. Ono

Circuits of Visibility: Gender and Transnational Media Cultures
Edited by Radha S. Hegde

Commodity Activism: Cultural Resistance in Neoliberal Times
Edited by Roopali Mukherjee and Sarah Banet-Weiser

Arabs and Muslims in the Media: Race and Representation after 9/11
Evelyn Alsultany

Visualizing Atrocity: Arendt, Evil, and the Optics of Thoughtlessness
Valerie Hartouni

The Makeover: Reality Television and Reflexive Audiences
Katherine Sender

Authentic™: The Politics of Ambivalence in a Brand Culture
Sarah Banet-Weiser

Technomobility in China: Young Migrant Women and Mobile Phones
Cara Wallis

Love and Money: Queers, Class, and Cultural Production
Lisa Henderson

Cached: Decoding the Internet in Global Popular Culture
Stephanie Ricker Schulte

Black Television Travels: African American Media around the Globe
Timothy Havens

Citizenship Excess: Latino/as, Media, and the Nation
Hector Amaya

Feeling Mediated: A History of Media Technology and Emotion in America
Brenton J. Malin

The Post-Racial Mystique: Media and Race in the Twenty-First Century
Catherine R. Squires

Making Media Work: Cultures of Management in the Entertainment Industries
Edited by Derek Johnson, Derek Kompare, and Avi Santo

Sounds of Belonging: U.S. Spanish-language Radio and Public Advocacy
Dolores Inés Casillas

Orienting Hollywood: A Century of Film Culture between Los Angeles and Bombay
Nitin Govil

Asian American Media Activism: Fighting for Cultural Citizenship
Lori Kido Lopez

Struggling for Ordinary: Media and Transgender Belonging in Everyday Life
Andre Cavalcante

Wife, Inc.: The Business of Marriage in the Twenty-First Century
Suzanne Leonard

Homegrown: Identity and Difference in the American War on Terror
Piotr Szpunar

Dot-Com Design: The Rise of a Useable, Social, Commercial Web
Megan Sapnar Ankerson

Postracial Resistance: Black Women, Media, and the Uses of Strategic Ambiguity
Ralina L. Joseph

Netflix Nations: The Geography of Digital Distribution
Ramon Lobato

The Identity Trade: Selling Privacy and Reputation Online
Nora A. Draper

Media & Celebrity: An Introduction to Fame
Susan J. Douglas and Andrea McDonnell

Fake Geek Girls: Fandom, Gender, and the Convergence Culture Industry
Suzanne Scott

Locked Out: Regional Restrictions in Digital Entertainment Culture
Evan Elkins

The Digital City: Media and the Social Production of Place
Germaine R. Halegoua

Distributed Blackness: African American Cybercultures
André Brock

Beyond Hashtags: Racial Politics and Black Digital Networks
Sarah Florini

Race and Media: Critical Approaches
Edited by Lori Kido Lopez

Dislike-Minded: Media, Audiences, and the Dynamics of Distaste
Jonathan Gray

Media Distribution in the Digital Age
Edited by Paul McDonald, Courtney Brannon Donoghue, and Tim Havens

Digital Black Feminism
Catherine Knight Steele

The Digital Border: Migration, Technology, Power
Lilie Chouliaraki and Myria Georgiou

Digital Unsettling: Decoloniality and Dispossession in the Age of Social Media
Sahana Udupa and Ethiraj Gabriel Dattatreyan

Chinese Creator Economies: Labor and Bilateral Creative Workers
Jian Lin

Chinese Creator Economies

Labor and Bilateral Creative Workers

Jian Lin

NEW YORK UNIVERSITY PRESS
New York

NEW YORK UNIVERSITY PRESS
New York
www.nyupress.org

Library of Congress Cataloging-in-Publication Data

Names: Lin, Jian, 1991– author.
Title: Chinese creator economies : labor and bilateral creative workers / Jian Lin.
Description: New York : New York University Press, [2023] | Series: Critical cultural communication | Includes bibliographical references and index.
Identifiers: LCCN 2022030964 | ISBN 9781479811878 (hardback ; alk. paper) | ISBN 9781479811885 (paperback ; alk. paper) | ISBN 9781479811915 (ebook) | ISBN 9781479811892 (ebook other)
Subjects: LCSH: Cultural industries—China—Employees. | Arts—China. | China—Cultural policy.
Classification: LCC HD9999.C9473 C454745 | DDC 338.4/7700951—dc23/eng/20220818
LC record available at https://lccn.loc.gov/2022030964

This book is printed on acid-free paper, and its binding materials are chosen for strength and durability. We strive to use environmentally responsible suppliers and materials to the greatest extent possible in publishing our books.

Manufactured in the United States of America

10 9 8 7 6 5 4 3 2 1

Also available as an ebook

CONTENTS

Introduction: The Bilateral Creatives

A good cultural product should put social benefits first and at the same time should be a work that integrates social benefits and economic profits. Literature and art cannot become slaves of the market and must not be stained with the stink of money. Excellent works of literature and art, at their best, can gain ideological and artistic successes and be applauded on the market.
—Xi Jinping (2014)[1]

What strikes me is the fact that in our society, art has become something which is related only to objects and not to individuals, or to life. That art is something which is specialized, or which is done by experts who are artists. But couldn't everyone's life become a work of art?
—Michel Foucault (in Foucault, Rabinow, and Faubion 1997, 261)

In the second season of his talk show *Thirteen Guests* (*shisanyao* 十三邀)[2], host Xu Zhiyuan interviewed Ma Dong, producer and host of the popular Chinese online debating series *U Can U BB* (*Qipa Shuo* 奇葩说), whose name is derived from Beijing slang. Their conversation serves as a perfect metaphor for this book's subject: the multifaceted "subjectivity" of cultural workers in contemporary China. As an active Chinese public intellectual, Xu Zhiyuan graduated from Peking University in the late 1990s and worked as a columnist for the *Financial Times* and as Chinese editor and executive editor for *Bloomberg BusinessWeek China*. These publications featured his trenchant and nostalgic commentaries on Chinese culture and society. His writings from that time are saturated with a perennial fascination with Western classics and humanitarian values, alongside deep anxiety with the politico-cultural conditions of contemporary China. In 2005, he founded One-Way Space (OWS; originally named One-Way Library) in Beijing, which has become a landmark public cultural space in Beijing and an important media outlet for readers to access Chinese and international literary and intellectual works.

Ma Dong had quite a different life trajectory. He is the son of Ma Ji, one of the most famous Chinese *xiangsheng* (相声) comedians in the 1980s. Until 2013, Ma Dong was a successful producer and TV host employed by China Central Television (CCTV), the biggest state-owned media corporation in China. During his ten years with CCTV, he worked as host, producer, and director of several highly rated TV programs, notably *Challenging Hosts* and *Culture Interview*. He was also one of the chief directors of the CCTV New Year's Gala in 2009 and 2011. After resigning from CCTV in 2013, Ma joined the emerging Chinese content platform Iqiyi and later founded his own production company, Miwei Media, where he produced the comedic debating show *U Can U Bibi*. Despite the phenomenal success and popularity of Ma's new programs, Xu disparaged them for using "fancy language but discussing dated topics" (*Thirteen Guests*, 2017).

Compared with Xu Zhiyuan, Ma Dong seems to have experienced a more dramatic change in his professional career. He has moved from producing serious TV programs to commercial entertainment, and from working as a high-ranking manager in bureaucratic state-owned television to being a creative entrepreneur. In the eyes of Xu Zhiyuan, such a transformation is incomprehensible. In their interview, Xu denounces the vulgarity of today's entertainment culture, while Ma insists there is no intrinsic difference between *U Can U BB* in contemporary society and Shakespeare's dramas in his time. His target audience, according to Ma, is not the 5 percent intellectual elites like Xu but the 95 percent "ordinary public."

Xu's and Ma's philosophies are not as distant as this conversation implies, however. The scene in Mercedes in Xu's talk show is a reminder that Xu Zhiyuan is a cultural entrepreneur. In 2014, One-Way Space received its first investment from a Shanghai venture capital company, which helped Xu to expand his business into several segments: *dantan* (public cultural salon), *dandu* (bookstore and reading app), *danchu* (café), and *danxuan* (gift shop). He targeted "any industries that are possible" (Liu 2020). Building on Xu's personal influence, OWS became more of a media company, producing podcast and talk show programs in which Xu introduced his selected books, music, film, and interviews to an online audience. But the intersection of his multiple identities—entrepreneur, journalist, talk show host, writer, critical intellectual, and Chinese man—may have brought as many career opportunities as struggles to Xu's life. He often mocks himself on his personal WeChat account by writing things such as "an intellectual who tries to be a good product manager is not a good writer" (Xu Zhiyuan's WeChat post, 2019).

At the end of their conversation, Ma concludes that "essentially we are the same, just that you seem to have more anger while I feel more or less isolated" (*Thirteen Guests*, 2017). Xu is optimistic because he believes in a progressive society, which he aspires to advance through his OWS. By contrast, Ma seems to have been frustrated by his experiences (consider his history at CCTV and his decision to resign) and takes commercial entertainment merely as a way out of his mundane desolation.

Xu Zhiyuan's and Ma Dong's encounter in *Thirteen Guests* illustrates two routes to Chinese media business and entrepreneurship. From their shared experiences of doing commercial production with disparate cultural aspirations, we may detect a sense of "divided self" (Kleinman et al. 2011). Along with their nation's marketization reforms since the 1980s, Chinese people have had to come to terms with diverse and even conflicting factors—past versus present, state versus market, public versus private, and moral versus immoral—which have caused as much disjunction as coherency in their subjectivity in contemporary Chinese society. In the cultural field, this divided nature of governance and subjectivity may prove particularly relevant. Chinese cultural production has been continually affected by state-capital collusion, meaning that individual cultural workers seek a balance between their own cultural/career aspirations and the push and pull of the state and the market.

In this process, the cultural and media industries seem to provide a common, but temporary, solution: they bridge the divided status quo by generating new divided labor experiences. For those people with disparate backgrounds and interests, commercial cultural sectors offer career opportunities and promise creative autonomy, compared to the highly controlled production during the Mao era. As this book testifies, however, the cultural industries also create mixed and even paradoxical work and life experiences, which I refer to as the "bilateral creatives." People need to navigate and find a balance between state regulation, the market economy, and personal expressive and career aspirations.

How, then, is commercial cultural production organized in relation to the party state and creative people in contemporary China? While entrepreneurship (*chuangye* 创业) can appear desirable for cultural workers like Ma Dong and Xu Zhiyuan, it also brings unavoidable uncertainties and precarity. But what does precarity mean in the Chinese context for these different creative practitioners? In order to develop their creative Chinese subjectivities, how do they experience cultural work and creativity while coping with various driving dividing forces? How can this subjectification of cultural workers in China be distinguished from its Western counterparts? In other words, what does it mean to "be creative" (McRobbie 2016) in contemporary Chinese cultural economies?

I address these questions by examining the experiences—hopes, joys, struggles, frustrations, and anxieties—of people who do creative work in China. With this book, embedded in current scholarship on creative labor and subjectivity, I consider the distinctive politico-cultural-economic circumstances in contemporary China in which commercial cultural production is both promoted and circumscribed. My research into these labor conditions that form subjectivities is based on ethnographic data collected within a wide range of Chinese cultural sectors, mostly including television production, independent filmmaking, design, and the emerging social media entertainment industry. By engaging with specific conditions in contemporary China, I question the prevailing scholarly and policy assumptions about creative labor, which is predominantly studied and theorized within contemporary Euro-American contexts (Fung 2016; Alacovska and Gill 2019). The claim that labor conditions in contemporary cultural economies are becoming increasingly precarious (Gill and Pratt 2008; Curtin and Sanson 2016), for example, needs to be contextualized and nuanced by looking at the specific politico-economic conditions that induce such precarity, and the form such precariousness takes in non-Euro-American contexts such as China. As Anthony Fung points out, "In nonfree markets and nondemocratic states, many other factors [besides market and economic forces] shape, foster, or dictate the conditions of how cultural labor is produced, trained, and socialized" (2016, 206). The organization and governance of cultural production and creative labor must have their own shape in non-Western societies.

I explore not only how creative labor and production are organized and governed in China but also what creativity and culture do to Chinese individuals who see themselves as being creative. Creative work is often seen as aspirational, yet these aspirations are not merely illusionary (Duffy 2016). As Nixon and Crewe (2004) observe, not all cultural workers feel satisfied with their work or are able to realize their full creative potential. A passion for artistic or cultural creation often allows creative workers to ignore drawbacks such as low pay, long working hours, and precarious job security. In this sense, the discourse of the creative industries and self-realization acts as a mechanism of governance for cultural workers, leading to self-exploitation and self-blame (Ursell 2000; McRobbie 2002, 2016). At the same time, recognizing that aspirational creative workers may overlook or be willing to tolerate precarious work conditions does not necessarily mean that their aspirations or positive experiences are illusionary or driven by a misleading ideology. As Hesmondhalgh and Baker (2011, 221) note about cultural work in the British cultural industries:

> It is worth recalling that jobs, occupations and careers in the cultural industries rarely involve gruelling physical demands or tasks that endanger the person undertaking them. They hardly ever involve work of a kind that many others will find disgusting or disdainful (such as a nurse who has to care for incontinent patients, or a toilet attendant). In fact, cultural-industry jobs are often thought of as desirable and intriguing, even glamorous. They involve expressive and communicative forms of endeavour which are highly valued by many people in modern societies.

For those who work in China's cultural industries, where the regime of censorship is juxtaposed with precarious working conditions, the question becomes: What aspirations, joys, glamour, and self-fulfillment are generated by creativity? To what extent can this aspirational labor be distinguished from those studied in Euro-American societies? I thus investigate creative-labor conditions in China in terms of the precariousness these conditions generate, but I also consider the opportunities that creative labor offers to people from diverse social backgrounds. Adopting a critical media-industry approach (Havens, Lotz, and Tinic 2009), I combine a political economy of cultural production in contemporary China with an ethnographic cultural study of creative workers within state-owned cultural enterprises, independent filmmakers, international creative workers in Beijing, and the newly emerged digital creative class on social media platforms. While unveiling how politico-economic inequalities are concealed by the production of creative aspirations in China's cultural industries, I also highlight the inconsistency and paradox underlying the governance of creativity, work, and individual lives in a wide range of cultural and media sectors, including television, film, design, journalism, and social media. I argue that the governance of the creative economy in China has become "schizophrenic" and that creative subjectivity has become divided and multifaceted—creative workers in China are becoming bilateral creatives.

The vibrant network that consists of the media and the cultural industries in contemporary China both pushes and limits individuals' aspirations toward creativity and self-realization. As the following sections clarify, the governance of the cultural economy in China consists of a constant process of deterritorialization and reterritorialization: individual creativity and aspirations are incorporated into the large system of production, while the process also generates spaces for autonomy, negotiation, and even resistance. Creative workers must actively conduct self-governance, reaching a balance between their individual aspirations, the state's expectations, and the capitalist subsumption of their labor and creativity. The actual practice, as I will show, is imbued with numerous conflicts, negotiations, and paradoxes. The creative subjectivity found in the Chinese cultural economies becomes unstable. The state's expectation for a politically conforming and commercially cooperative creative subjectivity works with people's creative and career aspirations but is also challenged and resisted from within the everyday practices of being creative. The creative subjects studied in this book may work for the state but against it at the same time.

The Creative Class and Its Discontents

According to Jim McGuigan, all human labor is endowed with creativity (2010, 326). In the past two decades, however, the circulation of capital has delimited creativity, leading to the emergence of particular occupations in the so-called creative industries. Policy makers around the globe, following the British government of the 1990s, have embraced the creative-industries discourse. They have trumpeted cultural work for its bohemian spirit, autonomy, and playfulness. Cultural workers, often dubbed the "creative class"—most notably in Richard Florida's *The Rise of the Creative Class* (2002)—have been assigned a crucial position in creative city construction. They are widely considered to be a crucial force for boosting the creative economy (Howkins 2002). Unlike the capitalist sweatshops of the nineteenth and early twentieth centuries, present-day cultural production is usually organized in the form of microenterprises and small and medium enterprises (SMEs), characterized by a flexible managerial structure, creativity-driven growth patterns, and a "neobohemian" entrepreneurial character. As some scholars have indicated, this character has the potential to combine an avant-garde artistic lifestyle with entrepreneurship (O'Connor 2010; Lloyd 2010). In their view, cultural workers can enjoy autonomy, independence, and playfulness in the labor process. Instead of being exploited and suppressed, they often work for themselves, becoming artistically creative and entrepreneurial, reconciling work and life, as well as the arts and economy (Leadbeater and Oakley 1999).

This celebration of the creative class has sparked much criticism, most notably from scholars concerned by the working conditions and the formation of the workers' subjectivity within the cultural and creative arena (Gill and Pratt 2008; McGuigan 2010). Researchers of the cultural and media industries argue that creative labor is not so much an ideal occupation as a new precarious condition: creative workers suffer from problems including short-term contracts, uncertain career paths, inadequate insurance and retirement provisions, unequal earnings, and a lack of unions (Deuze 2009; Hesmondhalgh and Baker 2011; Curtin and Sanson 2016). According to some cultural studies researchers, cultural work in the West is now governed by a creative-industries discourse, which should be viewed as a typical example of neoliberal governmentality (Ursell 2000; McRobbie 2016). Discourses surrounding creativity function as elements connected by the "creativity *dispositif*" to implement job creation while also disciplining youthful populations to be creative (McRobbie 2016; Reckwitz 2017). As these critics indicate, the absence of responses to these problems in current creative-industry policies constitutes an intentional governmental tactic of neoliberalism. This tactic has grown a cult following among European and North American governments, rendering creative practices and institutions governable within the doctrine of the free market economy (Banks and Hesmondhalgh 2009). This creativity *dispositif*, however, produces vast inequalities within global creative workplaces.

Gender, intersecting with race, ethnicity, age, (dis)ability, and sexuality, results in forms of occupational segregation and unequal access to creative work and its reward system (Banks 2017). According to triumphalist claims about the "creative class" and the "creative city," the tolerance of cultural diversity and individual differences is crucial to cultivating creativity and a creative economy (Florida 2002). Yet the actual practices of the creative industries reinforce the marginalization of minorities and reproduce existing power relations and inequalities (Alacovska 2017; Finkel et al. 2017). Several individuals reap significant rewards from their creative labor, but a significant proportion of the population—such as women—still cannot access the most prestigious sectors of the cultural industries (Hesmondhalgh and Baker 2011, 232). The prevalence of informal recruitment and a networking culture in the creative industries often puts women in a more vulnerable position. They are subjected to sexism and inequalities, which are reinforced by the absence of collective workers' organizations (McRobbie 2009; Gill 2011; Conor, Gill, and Taylor 2015). These problems have surfaced among various creative professions across diverse sectors (Conor 2015; Leung, Gill, and Randle 2015; Scharff 2017). For example, Jones and Pringle's (2015, 46) study of New Zealand's film industry illustrates that film-industry work is highly gendered. It normalizes the "unmanageable" inequalities between women and men in terms of "pay, access to work, affirmation, [and] support systems." The hidden sexism in the neoliberal setting of film production causes disparate impacts for the "below-the-line" crew. Even Florida himself, in the second edition of *The Rise of the Creative Class* (2012, 392), admits that "a social safety net for the creative economy" is needed to compensate the risks brought by "the flexible, hyper-individualized and contingent nature of work" in the creative economy.

At the same time, contemporary capitalism values individuals' commitment to work and prioritizes work as the primary source for self-realization while downplaying other aspects such as family, friendship, and community that are of equal importance for human well-being. As Hesmondhalgh and Baker (2011, 228) stress, "For many people raising families, the demands of combining work and home life can feel close to impossible for much of the time. Societies need to recognize that such differences are always likely to exist and should not punish or reward these groups disproportionately." Creative justice (Banks 2017) thus lies in equally distributing access and rewards among diverse creative workers who not only aspire to work but also to live a fulfilling life. Creative-labor studies, following Hesmondhalgh and Baker (2011, 229), need to address the prevailing issue of inequality in the contemporary cultural industries and to explore what might constitute "good work," and how cultural work can be improved in modern societies.

De-Westernizing Creative-Labor Studies

The studies on creative labor mentioned above provide important references for this book's exploration of cultural work in contemporary China. One of the issues that arises in more critical approaches, however, is that most have been conducted in the contemporary Western, Euro-American context. Consequently, their analyses of labor and subjectivity tend to assume a neoliberal economy and a social-democratic institution. As Alacovska and Gill (2019, 2) note, "Creative labour studies are notoriously centred on Euro-American metropolitan 'creative hubs' and hence the creative worker they theorise is frequently white, middle-class, male and urban." The critical language of creative-labor studies often directs all discussions of inequality, precarity, and the "self-exploitation" of creative labor toward a critique of neoliberalism. Much critical scholarship thus implies that the informal economy and flexible employment are replacing the previously stable and unionized work patterns of the Western welfare state. These accounts of the neoliberalization and precarization of the social (Lorey 2015) may not accurately describe the politico-economic conditions in non-Western contexts such as Asia, Africa, and Latin America. Different social realities give rise to variations in the "discursive formation" of cultural-industries policy (Cunningham 2009; Flew 2013) and, consequently, affect labor conditions. Banks, Gill, and Taylor (2013, 6) similarly argue that there is a salient lack of a historical perspective in the current critical literature on creative labor; by considering "the specificities of socio-historic locations," they hope to "question the often-assumed neat boundaries and interchangeable referentialities of 'cultural work' as an object of inquiry, opening the possibility of multiple presents and a plethora of possible futures for both the work and the workers."

In addition to addressing this historical lack, I suggest that theorizing creative labor requires a geographically diverse approach that can contest the ethnocentrism of existing studies by taking into account different sociopolitical contexts. In Latin America, for example, policies on the cultural and creative industries have a strong focus on "cultural sustainability": social inclusion, cultural diversity, access, empowerment, and the well-being of citizens (Yúdice 2018). As shown by Leung and Cossu's (2019, 274) comparative research of digital entrepreneurs in Taiwan and Thailand, informal entrepreneurial labor acts as an alternative not only to traditional corporate life but also serves as a "subversion of collective struggle in times of political, economic and social difficulties." Although precarity is prevalent in the informal economies where entrepreneurs operate, such precariousness allows them to escape the rigid established corporate world and its discipline of normativity (Leung and Cossu 2019, 275).

In his study of creative labor in the Asian video game industry, Anthony Fung offers a valuable alternative perspective on creative labor to the Hollywood model, which often serves as a universal model underlying the global proliferation of creative industries (Fung 2016, 200–214). According to Fung, Asia's politico-economic diversity produces different models of creative-labor relations: "progressive artists" in South Korea, "skilled conformers" in Southeast Asia, and a "contented bourgeoisie" in China. As demonstrated by Fung's analysis, the global hierarchy of creative industries and the national political situation in different Asian countries differentiate the labor conditions and creative-worker subjectivity there from those in the Western neoliberal model (Fung 2016). According to Fung (2016, 212), cultural workers in Chinese video game companies "resemble industrial workers in their tastes, aesthetics, and lifestyles," despite the "creative" nature of their work. The exploitative system and the strict content regulation drive individual creators to focus more on the financial rewards of their work than on pursuing a bohemian lifestyle.

Likewise, in his study of single women doing creative work in Shanghai, Chow Yiu Fai (2019, 17) also accentuates that the Chinese political context distinguishes the politics surrounding creative workers and women in China from those in Western social-democratic societies. Severe state control and rampant capitalism dilute the possibilities for effective activism or revolution. While politics and individual resistance never stop emerging, they are trivialized and internalized into everyday work and life. Instead of creative single women only being marginalized and stigmatized, Chow (2019, 18) views them as people "who refuse to be pressurized into a life that is expected of them, with the seductions of security and predictability, and trepidations of contingency and precarity if lived otherwise." For these single women, to do creative work is to refuse "the advice by the state and by [their] parents to get married before it is too late, or the prospect of earning more money with jobs that are more lucrative than the creative ones" (Chow 2019, 18). The commitment to creative work in this sense is an affirmation of the self and its capacity to refuse and to care. Chow's analysis of the politics of care among single women in Shanghai demonstrates the need for creative-labor studies to diversify and complement the dominant Euro-American-centric approach to labor subjectivity and politics through careful contextualization.

Creative Labor in Contemporary China

This concern with contextualization is what has sharpened my focus on creative workers in contemporary Mainland China. Although China has set a goal of developing the market economy, the socioeconomic transformation it has undergone since the 1970s cannot merely be read as the result of the implementation of neoliberal ideology. In effect, the Chinese Communist Party (CCP) has never completely embraced a market-oriented model. The party state still holds a very powerful position in the distribution of economic resources (Liew 2005). Since 2000, the authorities have enacted policies to promote the cultural industries and to justify the entry of private capital into cultural sectors. The party state, however, has remained vigilant about foreign cultural goods and highly ideological sectors such as the media industry (Keane 2001; Wang 2003). According to Jing Wang (2001, 37), China's epochal transition in the post-Mao era should not only be accounted for in terms of economy (from state to market economy) and culture (from high to pop, from national to transnational), but also "in terms of the restructuring of the state ruling technology and the changing stock of its ideological practices." As Richard Kraus (2004, ix) pointed out almost two decades ago, the state has changed its role as "the sole patron of the arts during Mao's later years" and has now "been joined by individual consumers who purchase cultural goods and by a new class of arts angels who provide funding for cash-starved arts organizations."

This form of state power can be seen in the frequent endorsement of "soft power" and "national cultural security" discourses within China's cultural-industries policies (Keane 2013; O'Connor and Gu 2020), as well as through the enduring controversies around the terms "creative industries" and "creativity" (O'Connor and Gu 2006; Keane 2009).[3] In *The Rise of the Creative Class*, Richard Florida identifies three elements for evaluating and constructing the creative city, the famous "3 Ts": technology, talent, and tolerance. Florida argues that for a creative city to achieve real sustainable success, each T is necessary yet by itself insufficient (2002, 228–65). The third T (tolerance) calls for diversity and openness in terms of ideas, values, sexuality, and people. Of the three, this one is most problematic in China, given the country's pervasive censorship, the legal prohibition of homosexuality, and the CCP's longstanding functionalist approach to culture.

In China, creative labor as an occupation has experienced a profound transformation in its discourse and institutions. Before the launch of the reform and opening-up policy in 1978, artists, writers, actors, and media workers employed by state-owned cultural units (*wenhua danwei* 文化单位) were labeled as "literary and artistic workers" (*wenyi gongzuozhe* 文艺工作者). They enjoyed permanent contracts and relatively good welfare while being obliged to promote Maoist ideology. The tenet of their work was to serve "the broadest masses of people," which Chairman Mao Zedong defined as workers, peasants, and soldiers (Mao 1967). Cultural work, then, was politically oriented and kept under strict surveillance. Since 1978, this coercive system has gradually changed and, to some extent, disappeared. Decades later, cultural units have been transformed into state-owned commercial enterprises, and private capital is allowed to enter certain cultural sectors. Apart from those minorities who still have a tenure position (*bianzhi* 编制) in state-owned cultural companies, increasing numbers of cultural workers have only short-term contracts and make a living by competing with others in the market.

This marketization reform has created space for individual creativity and autonomy within state-sponsored cultural production, while the introduction of contract employment and market competition has simultaneously rendered cultural work increasingly precarious. The "state question" (Wang 2001) further complicates creative-labor precarity in China. While in the Western neoliberal context, flexible employment and the growth of the informal economy have led to the self-exploitation and self-governance of cultural workers, Chinese creative workers not only need to "be creative" for the market but are also required to "be creative for the state" and deal with the pervasive censorship and state regulatory regime in the course of their everyday work lives. Cultural producers now have the freedom to decide what to produce and how, albeit within certain parameters that are determined by government censorship and market selection. This situation allows the state to govern cultural production by using some neoliberal technologies without totally giving up its authoritarian regulations. As Jeffreys and Sigley (2009, 2) summarize, "China's adoption of market-based economic reforms has resulted in the emergence of a hybrid socialist-neoliberal (or perhaps 'neo-Leninist') form of political rationality, one that is both authoritarian in a familiar political and technocratic sense and yet also seeks to govern certain subjects through their own autonomy."

This distinctive system of cultural production and governance is what has prompted me to study creative-labor conditions and creative-worker subjectivity in today's Mainland China. Following the call for the "deimperialization" of knowledge production, and more specifically to "de-westernise creative labour studies" (Alacovska and Gill 2019), my approach adheres to that of Kuan-Hsing Chen (2010) in his book *Asia as Method* but adopts an "ex-centric perspective" to study creative labor in China. My aim is "not to reverse the binary relationships—west and east or north and south, coloniser and colonised, centre and periphery," but to displace or interrupt the "taken-for-grantedness of congealed knowledge claims" (Alacovska and Gill 2019, 3) in extant attempts to theorize cultural work. The primary objective of this book is to open up dialogue between existing scholarly concepts and theories and the empirical specificities of creative-labor relations discovered during my fieldwork in China.

By investigating the subjectivation of creative workers in relation to the complex and diversified labor conditions of cultural production in contemporary China, I engage with questions of governance, precarity, and subjectivity. The main questions I ask are:

1) How are cultural production and creative labor organized and regulated in contemporary Chinese cultural economy (*governance*)?
2) What are the working and living conditions of creative workers in the specific political economy of China's cultural industries (*precarity*)?
3) How do individual creative workers navigate the politico-economic system of cultural production in China (*subjectivity*)?

To explore these issues, I start from the aspirations, struggles, and negotiations of creative people in the Chinese cultural economies. Without overlooking the power relations and inequalities in the Chinese politico-economic context, I highlight the complexity of the contemporary cultural-production system and affirm the productive aspect of governance and the often trivialized politics[4] characteristic of the everyday work and life of the heterogeneous group of people called "Chinese creative workers."

The "Schizophrenia" of Cultural Governance and the Bilateral Creatives

The main focus of this book is the subjectivity of creative workers. As I discussed in the previous section, the authoritarian regime, in conjunction with a neoliberal market economy, has produced a new form of governmentality for creative workers in China. The collusion between the party state and capital affords cultural workers—who are often motivated by their passion for art and creativity—the sense of autonomy and freedom typically associated with the market economy. At the same time, flexible work arrangements have started to replace the socialist labor protection system, thus imposing a need for self-governance on creative subjects. Creative work in China has become a typical form of aspirational labor (Duffy 2016; McRobbie 2016); the promise of social, cultural, and economic capital attracts people to creative work, while the autonomy they expect is compromised by precarious employment, an uneven reward system, and pervasive cultural censorship.

My critical perspective on creative labor does not suggest that contemporary cultural workers (in both Western and non-Western contexts) are docile subjects and victims of "false consciousness" produced by the creative-industries discourses. Rather, I argue that the subjectivity of creative workers has become unstable and bilateral: it is always situated and contested within the vibrant interaction between individuals and the wider socioeconomic network of state institutions, global/local markets, organizations, and technologies. The governance of cultural production and creative labor is not only repressive but is also productive and processive, leaving space for individual agency and negotiation. This dynamic system of cultural production both promotes and limits individuals' aspirations to creativity and self-realization, resulting in a bilateral subjectivity among creative workers. The operation of the Chinese cultural economy subsumes and hinges on the vast energy and diversity of creative workers. Creatives' agency and life practices have become the crucial resource for the reproduction of a financially thriving but politically conforming cultural economy. But the process of subsumption is also contingent on the active participation of individuals, leaving space for autonomy and agency that ultimately contributes to the production of biliteral subjectivity: the lives and creativity of bilateral creatives are incorporated by the system but also open up negotiations that may escape, deviate from, or even undermine the dominant governance of cultural production in China.

In postsocialist China, the party state has arguably adopted a new form of governmentality that comprises both neoliberal tactics (a partial market economy) and disciplinary institutions (state censorship and surveillance). To achieve "good governance" of the population, the market economy is deployed as a desirable mechanism for the post-Mao party state. In this arrangement, the market economy reorganizes individuals, and collectives are reorganized into various institutions. Diverse research projects over the last several years have found this governmentality-oriented approach in population control (Powell and Cook 2000), college students' choice of profession (Hoffman 2006), tobacco control (Kohrman 2004), civic training in high schools (Culp 2006), and the disciplining of Olympic volunteers (Chong 2011).

Creative workers as individuals are also reorganized and made into "active subjects" by the market economy system. Unlike their predecessors during the Mao era—who were forced to be docile servants of the propaganda machine—creative workers in the postsocialist epoch have become self-governing subjects who must achieve a balance between market value and cultural value. In this process, the identities of artist and entrepreneur become blended as they are interiorized. It is the cultural workers themselves who take charge of and responsibility for what to produce and its consequences (being successful, being marginalized, or being banned).

Governmentality does not suggest a complete retreat of state power and sovereignty, however. Through marketization, the Chinese Communist Party has regained and renewed its ruling legitimacy while continuing to regulate and surveil the flows of culture and capital. This approach is how the party state can claim that "poverty is not socialism" while also striving for a "harmonious society" and "equality" in the official ideology (Brown 2012). Many prominent examples may be found in contemporary China of the exercise of disciplinary state power, such as ideological education, cultural censorship, and the repression of social dissidents. Through bans and censorship, cultural workers whose products the authorities deem harmful to society are deprived of their right to free expression. The existence of censorship and banning serves as an omnipresent warning for all cultural workers, who tend to discipline themselves by preemptively adjusting their creative products in acts of so-called self-censorship.

At the same time, the concept of governmentality does not refer to a static situation. Rather, it is always occurring, and its results are not always as expected. As Rose O'Malley, and Valverde (2006, 98) suggest, "Governmentality may be eternally optimistic, but government is a congenitally failing operation." In practice, China's governance of cultural production is not always successful, and government bodies need to constantly reform their techniques to fit changing socioeconomic conditions. As I will explain in chapter 1, although the state-market "discursive formation" of Chinese cultural-industries policy reflects the party state's instrumentalist configuration of culture and creativity, the Chinese state is not a unitary, static entity (Saich 2011; Pieke 2012). The bureaucratically fragmented administrative system and vested state interests in the economy significantly complicate the actual process of policy making and implementation (Gong 2006; Saich 2009), creating space for deviation, flexibility, and other expressions of agency. The state, furthermore, must constantly change and reform its policies and institutions to achieve an effective governance of cultural production. Chinese creative subjectivity, in this sense, is produced within the constant interaction between creative practitioners and the state/market power regime.

This contested system of governance created through both neoliberal and disciplinary institutions has exacerbated precarious labor conditions in the Chinese creative economy. As an analytical concept, however, precarity is always characterized by multiplicity and division (Neilson and Rossiter 2008, 55) between labor subjects from diverse social backgrounds in heterogeneous politico-economic contexts. For independent Chinese filmmakers, for instance, precarity refers to the insecure working and living conditions imposed by the party state's regulation of film production and market competition. For transnational creative workers in Beijing, in contrast, their precarity derives predominantly from the mobile, unstable life generated by the global/local creative industries. These precarious conditions are productive in terms of subjectivation, as they require subjects to constantly adjust their living strategies. This self-governance, Isabell Lorey states, "not only implies subjugation but is also incalculable and potentially empowering" (2015, 111). For example, I will argue in chapters 3 and 4 that the diverse aspects of precarity have created the potential for a caring community among indie filmmakers and for a "situated cosmopolitanism" among international creative subjects. The precarization of these creative workers thus not only leads to the governance of creativity and labor but also produces a creative subjectivity that is incalculable and refuses the subsumption of state-capital collusion.

Processive governmentality and productive precarity together make subjectivity always contested, multiple, and relational. Consequently, I understand the cultural workplace as a realm of difference, in which individuals from various backgrounds actualize their creative and personal potential in constant interaction with the techno-politico-economic system of the cultural industries. Cultural work, with its promised "cultural value" and potential for self-realization—no matter how difficult to achieve in actuality—seems to provide an alternative solution for diverse people seeking to survive in the face of social risks. For instance, in chapter 2, I show how cultural workers in Chinese state-owned media companies, frustrated by the omnipresent bureaucracy and their limited autonomy, have aspired to be part of the nonstate cultural economy and entrepreneurship as an imagined better workplace.

As described in chapter 3, discontent among Chinese youth with certain aspects of their previous lives—such as a lack of education, an unequal society, and the requirements of commercial production—has motivated them to choose filmmaking as a career and to identify themselves as independent film workers. In chapter 4, I outline how the thriving Chinese economy has propelled the transnational mobility of creative labor, making Beijing attractive for international creators confronted with precarious and competitive job markets in their home countries. In chapter 5, I show how thousands of migrant workers and young people from China's rural areas are giving up tedious manual labor to become an unlikely new creative class, enabled by emerging platforms and the social media (*wanghong* 网红) economy, which promises more fun, better pay, and improved class mobility. Becoming a (Chinese) creative worker requires what Deleuze and Guattari (1987) would call a "movement of deterritorialization" on the part of these people from diverse backgrounds, which consists of "freeing [one's] desire from the social and religious codes which have been placed on it, and liberating it from the territorial and national boundaries which have enclosed it" (Hickey-Moody and Malins 2007, 15).

Marketization reform in the Chinese cultural sectors has partly freed individuals and their creativity from the grid of the state propaganda machine. Cultural work in the market economy has granted state employees, indie filmmakers, international cultural workers, and video makers on Kuaishou (快手)[5] the possibility of deterritorializing themselves from their previous lives and work in order to pursue their desire for creativity, self-realization, and a better career. Simultaneously, becoming a creative worker also involves a process of "reterritorialization," which binds the subject into a new set of power relations. The movement of deterritorialization and the process of reterritorialization, according to Deleuze and Guattari (1983, 258), always exist simultaneously and are related, connected, and caught up in one another:

> [T]he movement of deterritorialization that goes from the center to the periphery is accompanied by a peripheral reterritorialization, a kind of economic and political self-centering of the periphery, either in the modernistic forms of a State socialism or capitalism, or in the archaic form of local despots. It may be all but impossible to distinguish deterritorialization from reterritorialization, since they are mutually enmeshed, or like opposite faces of one and the same process.

The desire for autonomy, self-realization, and a better career drives people to pursue creative jobs, yet the flows of these aspirations (or desires) are also captured by the flows of money and profit in the capitalist production system. This system, as I have already discussed, normalizes the precariousness and inequality of the creative workplace and generates new forms of organization to reterritorialize the creative subject. For instance, as discussed in chapter 4, the coming of international creative workers to China on the one hand deterritorializes China's cultural industries, while the lives and work of these transnational creators are also reterritorialized as part of the "Chinese creative workforce," which subjects them to the distinct precarity underlying the political economy of Chinese cultural production.

The interaction of deterritorialization and reterritorialization continues throughout the never-ending process of people "becoming creative." In *A Thousand Plateaus* (1987, 472), Deleuze and Guattari note that "the deepest law of capitalism" is that "it continually sets and then repels its own limits, but in so doing gives rise to numerous flows in all directions that escape its axiomatic." Capitalism, in this sense, not only decodes the flows of desire and reterritorializes them according to the market but also produces flows of desire that escape or go against the rule; extreme examples could be terrorism, drug use, and madness (Hickey-Moody and Malins 2007, 15–16). It is in this sense that "schizophrenia" is both the limit and logic of capitalism. As Deleuze and Guattari (1983, 34) explain:

> Capitalism, through its process of production, produces an awesome schizophrenic accumulation of energy or charge, against which it brings all its vast powers of repression to bear, but which nonetheless continues

> to act as capitalism's limit. For capitalism constantly counteracts, constantly inhibits this inherent tendency while at the same time allowing it free rein; it continually seeks to avoid reaching its limit while simultaneously tending toward that limit. Capitalism institutes or restores all sorts of residual and artificial, imaginary, or symbolic territorialities, thereby attempting, as best it can, to recode, to rechannel persons who have been defined in terms of abstract quantities. Everything returns or recurs: States, nations, families.

To achieve the maximum accumulation of capital requires that capitalism must push and pull in various movements of deterritorialization, which in turn unleashes flows of desire and energy that may challenge the existing system, thus reaching the "limit of capitalism." To avoid reaching the "limit" (the breakdown of the system), capitalism needs to constantly restore the power and apparatus of the "state, nations, families" that it deterritorializes at the same time. In this way, capitalism recaptures the escaping flows of desire and turns "revolutionaries into the criminal, the disorderly, the social outcast, the insane" (Hickey-Moody and Malins 2007, 16).

In postsocialist China, this schizophrenic capitalism is reproduced and complicated by the entanglement of the market economy and state intervention. The market economy legitimizes the rule of the Communist Party while constantly deterritorializing authoritarian social relations. Various regulatory policies, apparatuses, and institutions exist to counteract this deterritorializing effect of capitalism. The state and capital constantly support, collaborate with, and struggle against each other. This constant push and pull of schizophrenic state capitalism creates as much space for individuals to navigate as it generates conflicts and obstacles for them to overcome. Echoing Kleinman et al.'s (2011, 14) diagnosis of contemporary Chinese people, the socioeconomic transformation gives rise to the changing moral standards and subjectivities that "are divided by the political, economic, and cultural processes that constitute" China in the twenty-first century. To make cultural commodities valuable and marketable, for example, the system encourages creative subjects to experiment with diverse creative ideas and individual lifestyles. At the individual level, professional ethics, such as in journalism and intellectual writing, clash with people's aspirations for financial and social success; an increasing awareness of global values might conflict with localized lifestyles and nationalist sentiments. More importantly, these experiments also contain energy that can challenge the existing social order and mainstream values and thus need to be monitored and regulated by state apparatuses. This push-and-pull process never succeeds in creating a static "creative being" or "creative identity" capable of consolidating an existing lifestyle and work culture.

Cultural workers in China thus become "bilateral creatives" whose agentic work and life practices become valuable and marketable, while the flows of desire they release can also threaten and challenge the established social order and ruling system. These bilateral creatives are, in the extreme, working for and against the system at the same time. The independent Chinese filmmakers profiled in chapter 3 chose independent filmmaking because they hoped that it would allow them to balance their aspirations for career success and their discontent with their previous lives and the general state of society. Becoming "independent" in this sense refers to the active process through which these creative subjects actualize their experiences of discontent in a complicated network constituted by state regulation, domestic and global cinema, and various film-related devices such as cameras, tripods, and recorders. In one sense, the thriving domestic cinema economy and strict film censorship and licensing have precarized the lives and work of these filmmakers, pushing independent Chinese cinema toward a depoliticized "art cinema," but these filmmakers' insistence on "independence" and "difference"—reflected in the production, distribution, and aesthetics of their films—challenges the value system of mainstream Chinese cinema.

In claiming that these creatives have become bilateral, I do not suggest that every cultural worker in contemporary China shares the same identification and life/work experiences. Instead, by probing the everyday practice of creative labor, I seek to identify the moments in which cultural workers become bilateral, not only in how they are incorporated by China's governance but also in how they negotiate with, deviate from, and even undermine the systems of capitalism, neoliberalism, or postsocialism. My aim is to affirm the differences embodied by those labeled "Chinese creative workers" and their agency, without overlooking the larger power relations or reducing individual efforts to a result of "false consciousness" imposed by capitalist or state ideology.

Studying Chinese Cultural Work

This book focuses on the impact of the governance and precarization of creative labor in China on the formation of creative subjectivities. To address the main questions listed above, I adopt a critical media industries approach to investigate the dynamic relations of culture, political power, organization, and individual practices in the contemporary Chinese creative industries. According to Havens, Lotz, and Tinic (2009, 238), the use of a critical media-industry approach enables the study of the "micropolitics of institutional operation and production practices" and unites the concerns of political economy and cultural studies. Using this approach, I combine the methods of critical political economy and ethnography-based cultural studies to illuminate the governing and organizing system of creative production and labor in China. I leverage an intensive exploration of micropolitics at various production sites and workplaces to explore how individual creators act in such a system of governance and production.

Using political economy to study cultural production, as Aeron Davis notes, links "cultural outputs to the economic, industrial and political factors that shape the organizations and industries which then produce culture" (Davis 2008, 53). Such usage shows how different ways of financing and organizing can affect representations and behaviors in the field of cultural production (Murdock and Golding 2005; Hesmondhalgh 2019). In using this approach to study Chinese cultural production and creative labor, my aim is to investigate the complicated labor relations and governing system in which cultural production and cultural work are mobilized and organized.

My primary data for this political-economic analysis consists of the policy documents publicly issued by the Chinese authorities[6] (see Appendix II) and various industrial reports and statistics collected through interviews with practitioners and secondary sources (such as companies' financial reports, media reports, and other empirical academic literature). In the first chapter, I specifically analyze the genesis, development, and specificity of the policy and administrative institution of the Chinese cultural economy in the post-Mao era. The chapter introduces the specificity of the Chinese party state's approach to cultural production and underscores the potential contradictions that open up space for agency and negotiation by cultural producers. In the case studies that follow, I adopt political economy as an important method to illuminate the nuanced socioeconomic conditions and employment relations found in creative workspaces such as state-owned cultural enterprises, the film industry, and the digital platform economy.

At the same time, while political economy helps to illuminate the "structures, external factors and high-level decision-makers which come to influence and shape" cultural production (Davis 2008, 54), it is also essential to explore cultural production and cultural work from the perspective of those engaged in it, in terms of their experiences producing culture and their relations to larger politico-economic structures. To incorporate this perspective, I conducted ethnographical fieldwork in sites where Chinese cultural workers live and work, from their physical work and living spaces to the online spaces where they communicate with each other. I did this in order to "investigate some aspect of the lives of the people who are being studied [i.e., Chinese cultural workers], which includes finding out how these people view the situations they face, how they regard one another, and also how they see themselves" (Hammersley and Atkinson 2007, 3).

Between mid-2016 and early 2021, I conducted extensive fieldwork in Beijing, Shanghai, Hefei, and Amsterdam, interviewing over eighty practitioners involved in China's cultural industries. From these sites, I chose four groups of creative workers to serve as case studies: cultural workers in state-owned cultural enterprises (SOCEs), independent filmmakers, international creative workers in Beijing, and the newly emerging digital creative class. I selected these four case studies to investigate the process by which people from diverse organizational, ethnic, and class backgrounds—and of different genders and ages—become creative workers in the Chinese cultural economy. Following George and Bennett (2004, 5), each of these cases provides a "detailed examination of an aspect of a historical episode to develop or test historical explanations that may be generalizable to other events." I address my three research questions in these empirical case studies, which exemplify the production of bilateral creative subjectivity in contemporary China through four creative-work scenarios with different characteristics.

First, as the most dominant player in China's cultural industries, state-owned media plays a crucial role in the Chinese creative-labor market;

its bureaucratic managerial system alleviates job precarity while limiting autonomy. Second, independent filmmaking represents an alternative form of creative labor and production in China that is supposedly low-budget, politically sensitive, artistically avant-garde, and capable of providing autonomy and facilitating critical thinking (Berry and Rofel 2010). In practice, however, independent filmmaking is still associated with and precarized by China's thriving commercial cinema sector. Third, the booming economy has also made people from overseas view China aspirationally, as a place capable of fostering a creative career. The life and work experiences of international creative workers in Beijing epitomize the global dimension of the Chinese creative workforce while also exemplifying what I described earlier as "productive precarity." Fourth, the emerging Chinese digital and platform economy offers opportunities for the less educated, more marginalized population to participate as producers in China's creative economy. These "grassroots" people are becoming an unlikely creative class by actively using digital technologies and negotiating with platforms' governance systems.

I have adopted what Qu and Dumay call a reflexive approach to recognize "the subjectivity of both the interviewer and the interviewee and the socially constructed nature of interview accounts" (2011, 255). The research participants were recruited through snowball sampling, and interviews usually took place in informal settings such as restaurants, cafés, and the participants' homes. Before the actual interview, I usually arranged at least one informal meeting (for drinks or dinner), sometimes accompanied by the friend who had introduced me to the interviewee. To gain as much information about my research subjects as possible, I interviewed creators as well as other practitioners in the field, such as human resource managers, film producers, platform intermediaries, and algorithm engineers. When necessary, I arranged return visits and follow-up interviews (e.g., with Judie Deng, Chang Biao, Jian Haodong, Wang Hai, He Yang, and Even Yong).

While analyzing the data, I did not treat the interview transcript as a mirror of reality, "but rather [as] a text that needs to be subjectively evaluated" (Qu and Dumay 2011, 256). The research participants' subjective experiences of work and life in China's cultural industries offer crucial lenses to address the central concern of this book: the formation of subjectivity among cultural workers in contemporary China. I took these subjective experiences seriously in the analysis while also being aware of the larger social structure in which these creative-labor subjects worked and lived. For example, in this book I take "independent filmmakers" not as a fixed concept referring to the specific habitus of certain Chinese filmmakers but as a discourse that is frequently used by media, scholars, and some filmmakers. I know that their claimed independence is largely compromised during their actual filmmaking practice, but the concept of independent filmmaking is still useful in this book because it was favored by most of the filmmakers I interviewed, and because their persistent identification with "independents" or a "spirit of independence" was by no means mere illusion or deception. Similarly, my claim in chapter 4 about the cosmopolitanism that has arisen among transnational creative workers in Beijing is based on ethnographic observations and interviews, but I also clarify that this cosmopolitanism is situated and conditioned by certain techno-economic forces.

My analysis of subjectivity is further supported by other ethnographic data.[7] I conducted participant observation in spaces related to each case study. For example, to study international creative workers in Beijing, I frequented art events, hipster bars in traditional *hutong* (alleyways), galleries, and workplaces that were popular among my research subjects, either by myself or with interviewees. To gain a more balanced view of independent Chinese filmmakers, I visited the Song Zhuang Art Village, where several filmmakers reside. I also chatted and had dinner with local villagers, curators, art dealers, and media reporters. I visited the headquarters of CCTV (China Central Television) and the state-owned *People's Daily* newspaper to explore the working and living environment of creative workers employed by state media. I also followed most of my informants' WeChat profiles and joined a few selected WeChat groups (focused on or featuring indie film screenings, Beijing expats, and script writers in Shanghai) to observe their online activities. To study the social media platform Kuaishou and its creator culture, I combined a digital walk-through method (Light, Burgess, and Duguay 2018) with multisited ethnography[8] (Marcus 1995) to illuminate Kuaishou's model of operation and governance, and its specific creator subjectivity.

The Shape of the Book

Chapter 1 investigates the policy and institutional context of commercial cultural production in contemporary China. Based on a genealogical overview of Chinese cultural-economy policies, I show how the discourse of "cultural industries" was introduced and incorporated by the Chinese party state in the post-Mao era. The shift in the CCP's ideology to economic development in the post-Mao era, the national opening-up policy, and economic globalization together motivated the party state to carry out institutional reforms to provide space for the growth of commercial culture. But policy about China's cultural industries is never simply an economic plan to economize cultural and media sectors; the party state's ideological concern for social stability and national rejuvenation—recently translated into the idea of "Xi Jinping's Chinese Dream"—makes China's cultural-industries policy a "state discursive formation." The party state has adopted a functionalist, top-down approach to culture, viewing it as an economic asset and a crucial tool for wielding national and international soft power and for maintaining social and political stability. The cultural industries are thus supported and promoted by the Chinese authorities while also being subjected to strict surveillance and censorship.

Crucially, this top-down approach to controlling China's cultural industries and cultural production is imbued with contradictions, as becomes clear when we consider the institutional features of the Chinese political system and the process of policy implementation. The fragmented administrative system, the decentralized authoritarian regime, and the complicated relationship between state and commerce all profoundly affect the actual process of policy making and implementation in China's contemporary cultural sectors. The uncanny political system ultimately yields as many obstacles as opportunities for creative producers and other actors in the Chinese cultural sphere, thus laying the basis for a schizophrenic governance of cultural economies in China. On an everyday basis, the "state question" identified by Jing Wang (2001) in Chinese cultural production and popular culture thus not only refers to the state's ideological concern with cultural activities but is also connected to the intricate relationship between administrative power and institutions versus the various production workers. The crucial task for cultural producers in China is to find ways to negotiate and "play" with state power, which is contested, nonunitary, and exists on multiple levels.

Chapter 2 examines creative labor in Chinese state-owned cultural enterprises (SOCEs). According to official statistics, by 2015 there were 1.37 million employees in Chinese SOCEs (Ministry of Finance 2016). These state-owned companies, transformed from state-controlled "cultural work units" (*danwei* 单位), are now the most powerful players in China's cultural industries. Aside from their privileged market position, Chinese SOCEs are required by the Chinese government to shoulder a double responsibility to achieve both social and economic benefits (Central Committee of the CCP and State Council 2015; Ministry of Finance 2015). The need to balance the political and the commercial within cultural production causes a basic paradox that troubles creative workers in Chinese SOCEs and distinguishes them from the more autonomous workplaces in the Euro-American creative economy.

Based on the empirical analysis of fieldwork data, chapter 2 explores the governance of creative labor in Chinese SOCEs through an analysis of the condition of autonomy and the discourse of self-realization within selected Chinese state-controlled media companies. The autonomy of creative work within the system is contingent on the party state's ideological regulation, which results in a highly bureaucratic management system that restricts creative and workplace autonomy. Nevertheless, the various welfare benefits and career opportunities provided by the SOCEs also motivate state-employed creative workers through the discourse of self-realization—to "be creative for the state." In practice, however, contradictions are inherent in such a state-sponsored system of cultural production. Illustrated by the cases of loafing on the job, multitasking, and the "wave of resignation" (in the case of CCTV), these contradictions in governance can enable creative people to become a typical form of bilateral creatives: they exploit the system for their own interests and deviate from the expected subjectivity of "being creative for the state."

In chapter 3, I examine independent Chinese filmmaking as a form of creative labor. Independent Chinese filmmaking—compared with "main melody" film production[9] and commercial film production—is low budget, politically sensitive, artistically avant-garde, and seeks relative autonomy and to promote critical thinking (Berry and Rofel 2010). Such filmmaking is also supposed to occupy a position of high cultural capital in the field of Chinese film production (Nakajima 2016). Researchers and others are apt to generalize when characterizing independent Chinese film, assigning filmmakers to special categories or identities that disregard their underlying distinctiveness. This situation explains the terminological ambiguities surrounding the terms "independence," "independent film," and "Chinese independents" (Berry and Rofel 2010; Jiang 2012; Sniadecki 2013), since every given definition runs the risk of overlooking differences among the subjects it designates. Without getting embroiled in this debate, for the purposes of this study, I simply explore "independent filmmaking" as a discourse employed by Chinese creative workers to designate their filmmaking practice.

My ethnography has shown that people often choose to become independent filmmakers because they expect that doing so will allow them to balance their aspirations for career success and their discontent with their previous lives and the general state of society. Once they become practitioners in the industry, however, these filmmakers soon find that their creative labor is precarized in the existing "three-legged" system, which consists of "the party-state apparatus, the domestic market economy, and overseas connections" (Berry 2006, 115). The heavy censorship of films and the thriving state-supported domestic cinema industry prompt filmmakers to accept cooptation and depoliticization in their productions. Certain international film festivals and institutions, at the same time, encourage these Chinese filmmakers to identify themselves as "dissenting/artistic independents" by offering them funding and screening opportunities. This process of precarization steers independent Chinese cinema toward a depoliticized "art cinema," while filmmakers must deploy forms of self-governance such as multitasking, networking, and emotional management to maintain their optimism about the future.

This precarity and precarization also produces an informal, reciprocative community of caring among independent filmmakers to combat their career precarity. Animated by common aspirations for independence and freedom, this community not only helps alleviate living and work pressures by offering skills training and screening opportunities but also encourages a more open understanding of independence and independent filmmaking. This more inclusive and fluid conception of independence in turn allows for differences to emerge between the community's members, who are no longer circumscribed by rigid identities such as "politically dissenting" or "noncommercial."

In chapter 4, I shift the research focus from local Chinese creators to international creative subjects in China. While China has long been regarded as an emigration country, the "rise of China" is now also reversing trends in the transnational mobility of labor and migration. The economic opportunities engendered by the flourishing Chinese market have attracted people from overseas to appreciate China as an aspirational place for work and life. The global proliferation of the creative-industries discourse and creative workers' uneven prosperity around the globe have propelled the global mobility of creative labor, including into China. The country's emerging cultural industries and the existing gap between its cultural economy and that of its Western competitors have translated into a thirst on the part of the Chinese authorities and Chinese companies for "creative know-how," which has fostered job opportunities for international cultural workers. These international professionals are expected to enable the future success of China's cultural industries and to contribute to the image of Beijing as a global creative city, as well as to China's hope for an economic transformation "from made in China to created in China" (State Council 2016). But the career opportunities brought by China's emerging creative economy are also accompanied by risks and precarity; China's limitations on migration and the country's precarious working conditions, political restrictions, and socio-environmental problems all call for effective self-governance among transnational creative workers in China.

The presence of international workers in Beijing has broadened the geopolitical conception of "Chinese creative labor" and "Chinese creativity." The precarious life produced by the mobility and flexibility demanded of international creative workers in Beijing also fuels interaction and mutual understanding between local and global subjects, which then provides the conditions for a cosmopolitan subjectivity. It is through such everyday dealing with precarity that these international creatives in Beijing develop their bilateral subjectivity; this subjectivation of international cultural workers may transcend the Chinese authorities' expectation of a conforming and profitable creative workforce. As such, this subjectivation exemplifies what Isabel Lorey (2015) terms the "incalculable" consequences of precarization and self-governance.

The stories of these international cultural workers in Beijing make clear that the precarity caused by the economic globalization of creative labor should not be seen as exclusively negative.

In chapter 5, I examine an unlikely group of creative workers enabled by the emerging *wanghong* economy in China: creators of short videos on the social media platform Kuaishou. When thinking about the creative class, one tends to think of urban elites, an educated group of predominantly young people who work in the cultural industries. Yet the emerging *wanghong* and platform economy also offers opportunities for people from lower social classes to participate as content creators in China's digital creative economy. This new trend in China's creative industries can be seen in the popularity of Kuaishou, which attracts hundreds of millions of people in China, both from the countryside and from more peripheral second- and third-tier cities. Since 2012, Kuaishou has grown into one of the most popular video-sharing platforms in China. The platform allows its users not only to watch, make, and distribute short videos but also to become "complementors" (Nieborg and Poell 2018): active participants in the content production and monetization of the platform business.

Under the policy agendas of "internet+" and "mass entrepreneurship and innovation," discussed in more depth in chapter 5, the Chinese party state's strategy of economic restructuring has shaped the Chinese digital creative economy. The complicated state-corporate relationship renders Kuaishou's platform business increasingly "contingent," driven by the state's concern for economic transformation, cultural regulation, and social stability. Considering this analysis of the political economy, in the second part of chapter 5 I use Light, Burgess, and Duguay's (2018) walkthrough method to further explore how this state-platform contingency is encoded in Kuaishou's algorithms. These algorithms allow for maximum creativity to be expressed by grassroots users, but they also keep the system and its immense database largely invisible to them, thus contributing to the subsumption of individual vernacular creativity.

These algorithms do not make Kuaishou's new creative subjects passive, exploited "prosumers" (a portmanteau of "producer" and "consumer"). Neither do they reduce their work to exploited, free "platform labor," as some critical political economists would claim (Ritzer and Jurgenson 2010; Fuchs 2010; van Doorn 2017). By actively utilizing

Kuaishou's digital system, grassroots content producers are also empowered to develop a digital entrepreneurship within which creativity, life, and individuality are constantly recalculated according to an accounting of costs and profits. This digital entrepreneurship, in conjunction with the governance and censorship of the internet, contributes to the growth of China's digital economy, the production of social stability, and a conforming digital culture. I argue, however, that it also engenders a social mobility that deterritorializes hidden class and urban-rural divisions. The stories of these digital creators, together with the wide aesthetic range of videos, constitute a "silly archive" (Berlant 1997) in which the vernacular, the ubiquitous, and the banal are articulated. It may well be in such articulations that these Kuaishou creators resonate with the other bilateral creatives studied in this book. We can find moments of play, if not resistance—moments in which the official narrative of the "Chinese Dream" is juxtaposed with multiple dreams from actors who hardly ever get a face or a voice in mainstream Chinese media.

Starting with the ongoing COVID-19 crisis and its implications for China's cultural industries, I consider the future of China's creative industries and creative labor in chapter 6. China's newly issued "Fourteenth National Five-Year Plan" (covering 2021–25) has placed digitalization, smart technologies, and globalization at the center of Chinese cultural-industries policy. The early adoption of artificial intelligence (AI) and automation technologies in China's journalism and creative-design industries hints at a possible future of automation in creative production. A move toward automation has the potential to transform certain forms of creative work from symbol-based production to sign-based production, reducing complex human experiences into algorithms and unequivocal signs. The celebratory discourses of liberation and efficiency, however, obscure the future possibilities for creative labor. In China, we might witness the rise of digital Taylorism juxtaposed with a sophisticated surveillance system, promising efficiency and political security.

The massive scale and vibrancy of China's digital economy have also pushed Chinese tech and media companies to go global. The increasing presence of Chinese social media platforms such as TikTok and Kwai on the global internet suggests that the future might be characterized by "platformization from China," in which the technological innovations, business ecologies, and creator cultures developed within the Chinese internet infiltrate and disrupt the global internet and platform society. The new generation of social media platforms, thanks to their innovative technology and business ecology, appear to have gained more credibility and "communication capacity" (Sun 2009) than traditional media and cultural organizations such as CCTV and *People's Daily* in the process of the "going-out" (*zouchuqu* 走出去) of Chinese culture.

But the challenge for Chinese platforms that go global lies in their figurative "Chinese-ness," defined by the operative platform logics embedded in their creator practices, online culture, and governance. As also shown in chapter 5, such platform logics maximize the exploitation of labor and creativity from diverse backgrounds and circumscribe labor and creativity by ensuring that they are financially profitable and politically secure. In liberal societies, a discursive call for an open internet contradicts part of the "Chinese" platform logics. Chinese platforms are forced to adopt a "parallel platformization" strategy to establish their business in the two distinctive markets, distance themselves from their Chinese origin, and localize and diversify their platform governance. As a result, the digital economy and platformization from China incorporate momentum that can potentially deviate from the state's agenda of cultural "going-out," where platforms join creative workers in becoming bilateral.

After building on these case studies of the bilateral subjectification of creative workers in China, I conclude this book by highlighting the schizophrenic nature of Chinese creative economy as both industrial organization and governing system. It may still be too early to lament or celebrate these new developments surrounding the discourse of "the rise of China." If there is a postpandemic future to come, it may be equipped with similar dilemmas, frustrations, and aspirations.

1

Understanding China's Cultural Industries

Developing the cultural industries is a crucial way within the socialist market economy to meet the diverse spiritual and cultural needs of the people. In doing so, we must adhere to the direction of the advanced socialist culture and always put social benefits first while uniting the social benefits with economic benefits. We must be in line with the national goal of building a comprehensive, balanced, and sustainable economy; promoting leapfrog development of the cultural industries; and making them the new growth engine and pillar industry of the nation's economic restructuring.
—Central Committee of the Chinese Communist Party (2011)

To meet the people's expectations for a better life, we must offer sufficient spiritual food. We must deepen cultural-system reforms. . . . We need to develop modern cultural industries, innovate our production and market system, revise our cultural-economy policies, and cultivate new cultural sectors.
—Xi Jinping, Nineteenth National Congress of the Chinese Communist Party (2017)

Introduction

Before examining the experience of working in China's creative industries, we should first understand how creativity and cultural production have been configured by the Chinese authorities. During the Mao era, culture and aesthetics served as propaganda tools, while professional cultural production was kept under strict state surveillance. How was the discourse of "creative/cultural industries" translated into Chinese state policy and implemented in the postsocialist era?

As a policy discourse, the term "creative industries" was first coined by the British Labour government in 1997 while establishing a Creative Industries Task Force (CITF) as the central activity of the new Department of Culture, Media and Sports, or DCMS (Flew 2012, 9). Shortly after, the DCMS released the Creative Industries Mapping Documents, which identified thirteen sectors as components of the creative industries and underscored their contribution to employment creation, economic growth, and national export. Over the following years, discourse on the creative industries, with adjustments and modifications that I will discuss later, continued to drive the national policy of the United Kingdom and was taken up by many other countries around the world. In the UK context, this discourse signals the "New Labour" government's top-down approach to cultural economy, which attempts to align arts and media policies with economic policies and, more importantly, increase the engagement of arts and media with intellectual-property-based information technology (Garnham 2005; Flew 2012).

The DCMS's "creative industries" approach has generated widespread criticism. The conflation of the arts with economic discourse "overrides important public good arguments for state support of culture, subsuming the cultural sector and cultural objectives within an economic agenda to which it is ill-suited" (Galloway and Dunlop 2007, 17). The marketization of culture and Richard Florida's (2002) recipe of the "creative class" also run the risk of normalizing the neoliberal paradigm that manifests precarious labor conditions (Ross 2009; McGuigan 2009). According to Nicholas Garnham (2005, 15), the DCMS's creative-industries approach draws too much from "the prestige and economic importance attached to concepts of innovation, information, information workers and the impact of information and communication technologies." As a result, the approach strengthens intellectual property protections that benefit the major media conglomerates in "copyright industries" such as software, media, and entertainment. Strengthening these protections shifts media-industry practices from distribution and consumption to creating human capital by promoting and aggregating precarious employment conditions (Garnham 2005). The creative industries, according to Garnham's critique, become a "Trojan horse" that brings "the intellectual heritage of the information society and its technocratic baggage into the realm of cultural practice" and aligns it with "inappropriate bedfellows such as business services, telecommunications and calls for increases in generic creativity" (Cunningham 2009, 375).

Nonetheless, in full awareness of these critiques, it should be acknowledged that the creative-industries discourse has become diversified during its worldwide travels. As Stuart Cunningham (2009, 376) points out, instead of being a Trojan horse, creative industries have become "a Rorschach blot"; as creative-industries policies have been adopted worldwide, they have reflected different interests and explanatory schema. For example, the British top-down approach was not copied in the United States and some parts of Europe, where creative-industries policies were mostly regional- and municipal-development strategies based on place (Cunningham 2009; Boix et al. 2016). Compared to the British government's emphasis on economic growth and innovations in information and communications technology (ICT), the European approach to creative industries generally tends "to stress a greater degree of communitarian benefit and strategies of social inclusion" (Cunningham 2009, 378). Similarly, in poorer countries of the global south, the approach to the creative economy is often associated with poverty alleviation, cultural heritage, and basic infrastructure (Cunningham 2009).

In contemporary China, the discourse of the creative industries has also developed in a particular way. Cultural and media creativity (*chuangyi* 创意) and ICT innovation (*chuangxin* 创新) have been integrated into the national top-down agenda to transform the national economy "from made in China to created in China" (Keane 2006; State Council 2016). But what distinguishes the Chinese creative-industries approach from other international approaches is that behind the economic and commercializing discourse lies a political agenda. Chinese policy aligns culture and media with economic policy—as seen elsewhere—but also with ideological control and social governance. One might argue that, in most cases of the transnational diffusion of creative-industries policy, the Trojan horse and the Rorschach blot are in fact different sides of the same coin; both the "economization of culture" and the "culturalization of the economy" use market reasoning to dissociate culture and media from sociopolitical concerns (Hesmondhalgh 2008; H-K Lee 2016). Yet, for the Chinese party state, creativity, which is not problematic in the West, becomes the "thorniest question" due to its promise of "individualism" and "creative destruction" (Wang 2004, 13). China's marketization of culture is accompanied by a clear political concern where culture and creativity are treated as important tools for achieving social stability—as well as for catching up with the West—by the exercise of national soft power (O'Connor and Gu 2006; Su 2015).

In this chapter, which delves into the existing literature on the creative-industries discourse and its Chinese ramifications, I look at policy documents and governmental institutions to explore: 1) how the discourse of "creative/cultural industries" was translated into Chinese state policy in the postsocialist era; 2) how creativity and cultural production were configured in these policies; and 3) the features of the institutions responsible for implementing these policies. To accomplish these goals, I describe the policy and institutional context of commercial cultural production in contemporary China. I have collected and analyzed any policy documents related to the terms "cultural industries" and "cultural economy" issued by the central government since the late 1980s (see Appendix II).

The following sections provide a genealogical overview of Chinese cultural-economy policies to show how the cultural-industries discourse was introduced by the Chinese party state and incorporated into the post-Mao era. Following this historical review, in the second section I analyze the party state's approach to China's cultural industries. During the promotion of China's commercial cultural sectors, the country's cultural-industries policy has distinguished itself from the Western "neoliberal approach" by adding a specific "state discursive formation" to its configuration of cultural production. The mixture of state and market discourses in China's cultural-industries policy epitomizes the party state's instrumentalist configuration of culture and creativity. Given the dual role of culture as ideology and commodity, the state deploys the market economy and cultural industries as a new form of social governance.

Shifting the focus from state policy to institutions, the final section of the chapter examines the political system in which state policy is translated into concrete policies and implemented. Importantly, I argue that this translation creates space for flexibility, agency, and negotiation on the part of diverse actors in the Chinese cultural sphere.

The Advent of the Cultural Industries in China

Although the terms "cultural industries" and "creative industries" were not officially introduced to China until the early 2000s, the Chinese authorities had already started endorsing the idea of a cultural economy and commercial cultural production by the late 1980s. In February 1987, the Ministry of Culture, the Ministry of Finance, and the State Administration of Industry and Commerce together issued a policy document titled "Interim Provisions on the Administration of Cultural Institutions Conducting Commercial Service and Activities" (MoC 1987). The release of these provisions was the first time since the opening-up starting in 1978 that the party state officially acknowledged and legalized commercial cultural production in China. As the document asserts (MoC 1987, n.p.):

> To better meet the needs of the people for cultural life and to strengthen the development of cultural units, in recent years many cultural units have started providing commercial services and have obtained extra financial returns by means of their different expertise and equipment. These commercial activities will be beneficial for transforming our cultural units from nonprofit service suppliers to commercial service providers. These activities will benefit our socialist spiritual civilization, enable cultural units to provide diverse, high-quality services, and will make our cultural and art undertakings prosper (*shiye* 事业).

In the media sectors, state endorsement had already arrived. Even earlier, in 1979, the Publicity Department of the Central Committee of the CCP authorized Chinese news outlets—including newspapers, radio, and television—to run commercial advertisements (Chen 2011). In 1988 the state allowed newspapers, other periodicals, and publishing houses to provide commercial services (see below) to the public (SAPP and SACI 1988). These early cultural-economy policies initiated a "dual-track" (*shuangguizhi* 双轨制) reform within state cultural units (*danwei* 单位) such as performing arts groups, news presses, television and radio stations, cinemas, and theaters. Contracted employment was introduced, along with the approval of limited commercial production, without abolishing the preexisting state-controlled system.[1] This dual-track system allowed cultural units to establish a different personnel system for those hired for commercial business, whose salaries would be paid by the state cultural units instead of by the state. Although most staff still held tenured positions, the state allowed these units to give temporary labor contracts to a small number of employees.

This early approval of marketization by the state had a limited scope. Only the cultural units (the state-owned public cultural and media entities) were licensed to offer commercial products and services, which were limited to supplemental activities. For example, according to the "Interim Provisions" (MoC 1987), theaters, art groups, and libraries were allowed to conduct commercial businesses:

> Related cultural business (*yanshen yewu* 延伸业务): document copying, printing, and scanning; art consulting, public lectures, arts education, dance parties, music concerts, video screening, sales of calligraphy and paintings, instrument repair, theatrical costume renting, hairdressing and beauty services, commercial photography, public performance, and sports.
>
> Convenience services (*bianmin yewu* 便民业务): convenience stores, canteens, and hotels; production and retailing of musical instruments, audiovisual products, stationery, reproduction of cultural relics, advertisements, and stage costumes and props.

News presses and publishing houses, under the regulations of the State Administration of Press and Publishing (SAPP) at this time, were allowed to provide commercial advertising, consulting, printing, and professional education (SAPP and SAIC 1988). All these activities were "supplemental services" (*buchong fuwu* 补充服务), while core businesses such as content production (news, film, television, and art) and distribution were still protected from commercialization. Together with this limited authorization came strict licensing and content regulation of commercial activities (SAIC 1987). Nonstate-sponsored forms of cultural production, such as independent film and popular music, were not yet allowed to enter the market and were stigmatized as "underground" and "illegal." De Kloet (2002) has revealed that a primary reason for the decline of Chinese rock music in the mid- to late 1990s was the strong hold of the state on music production. Although record companies contracted musicians and organized music production, the distribution of albums had to go through state-owned publishing houses, which received 60 percent of the revenue (de Kloet 2002, 97).[2]

But this dual-track reform was also the result of the party state's response to the profound transformation of the Chinese cultural field since the late 1970s. After the end of the Cultural Revolution in 1978, the ruling ideology of the Chinese Communist Party shifted from Mao's political experiment with socialism and alternative modernity to Deng Xiaoping's reform and opening-up policy. Economic development, rather than political struggle, became the objective of the PRC (Brown 2012). This change was welcomed by the Chinese public in the 1980s and facilitated the marketization reform and growth of nonstate sectors. In 1992, the Fourteenth National Congress of the CCP defined the objective of Chinese economic reform as establishing a "socialist market economy." In this economy, the law of value and nonstate forms of ownership would play a greater role, while state-owned enterprises would remain the "leading force" in the national economy (Jiang 1992).

Although still dominated by state-owned units and not freed from propaganda responsibility, the cultural and media sectors thus started to embrace the market in postsocialist China. Their embrace of the market was precipitated by financial need and increasing competition from the "underground" cultural market—the influx of Western cultural products and the rise of local popular culture (de Kloet 2010). The financial burden of state-owned cultural enterprises and the potential contribution to the national economy finally motivated the government to legalize commercial cultural production.

Another factor that influenced China's cultural reform was the intensification of economic globalization. The building of special economic zones (SEZs) in the 1980s brought in foreign investments and global commercial popular culture, including pop music, film, and television. Simultaneously, China's joining of the World Trade Organization (WTO) in 2001 required the country to commit to allowing a relatively open market and free trade in many areas, including the cultural and media sectors (Ministry of Commerce 2006). To meet the challenge posed by international competitors, the Chinese government sought to boost the local economy and restructure it from an unsustainable reliance on export-based manufacturing to an innovation-driven, environmentally friendly, and added-value model. At the same time, the government also reformed existing economic policies and institutions in line with international standards and practice (*yu guoji jiegui* 与国际接轨).

It is within this political-economic context that a policy discourse about the cultural/creative industries was introduced to China. In August 1998, the Ministry of Culture established its Division of Cultural Industries as the first national administrative office for cultural industries. In 2000, the term "cultural industries" (*wenhua chanye* 文化产业) was used for the first time in the "Tenth Five-Year Plan for National Economic and Social Development," which stated that "in the coming five years, the government will enact cultural-industries policies, propel the construction and effective regulation of the cultural market, and promote the cultural industries" (State Council 2001).

Developing Strategies

After 2000, the Chinese central government officially adopted the cultural industries as a national strategy for economic development and enacted a series of industrial policies to promote and regulate the cultural economy. From 2001 to 2017, China's central government issued dozens of promotional and planning-policy documents for the cultural industries (see Appendix II). In 2003, the Ministry of Culture released its "Opinions on Promoting the Development of Cultural Industries" (MoC 2003). This document defines China's cultural industries as those "commercial sectors that produce cultural products and provide cultural services" (MoC 2003). As commercial and market-driven sectors, "cultural industries" (*wenhua chanye* 文化产业) are distinguished from "cultural undertakings" (*wenhua shiye* 文化事业), which are nonprofit public enterprises mostly financed by the government. Crucially, both cultural industries and cultural undertakings constitute Chinese socialist cultural development (*wenhua jianshe* 文化建设). The ministry recognized art and theater, the film and television industry, the audio-video industry, cultural entertainment, cultural tourism, the online cultural industry, publishing, arts education, and the art trade as the primary sectors of China's cultural industries (MoC 2003).

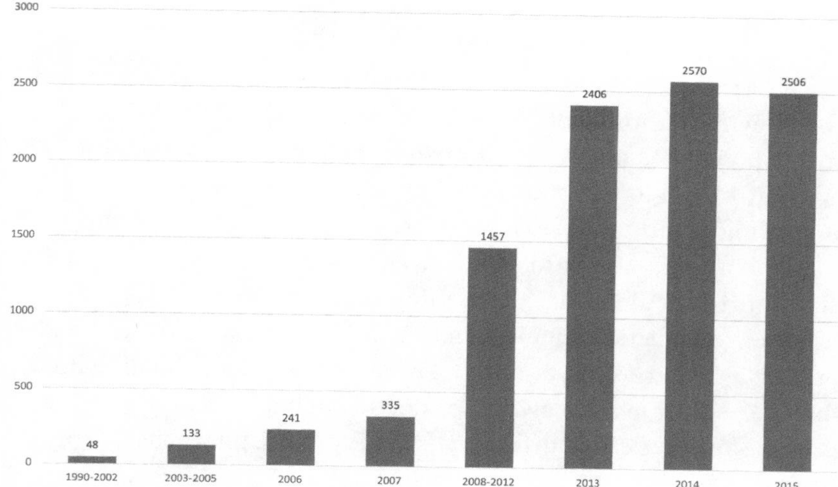

Figure 1.1. Number of cultural-industry parks in China (chyxx 2016).

The Chinese government took a top-down approach to implement its development agenda. Its first strategy was to incubate competitive market entities. To do so, the government initiated an enterprise reform within state-owned Chinese cultural units. In 2003, the State Council released its "Regulations on Supporting the Development of the Cultural Industries and the Enterprise Reform of Cultural Units" (State Council 2003). The regulations were first announced as a five-year pilot project, then were reformulated and extended in 2008, 2014, and 2018. These documents promote enterprise reform in Chinese state-owned cultural entities, formulating a series of regulatory and preferential policies in asset management, land disposal, financial support, income distribution, tax reduction, tax exemption, and social welfare (State Council 2003, 2008, 2014, 2018a). As I will show in more detail in chapter 2, to achieve the so-called scale economy, the government has encouraged state-owned cultural enterprises to merge into large cultural corporate entities. Following the logic of the scale economy, the state also formulates policies and allocates funds to promote national and creative clusters known as "Cultural-Industry Parks" (*wenhua chanye yuanqu* 文化产业园区). By 2015, China had over 2,500 cultural-industrial parks (see Figure 1.1); over 350 of these parks had "National" in their name and were funded by the central government, while the rest were constructed by regional governments.[3]

The state situated the nonstate cultural economy as an indispensable constituent of China's cultural industries. In 2005, the State Council issued a policy document to authorize and regulate the contributions of nonstate capital to the cultural and media sectors (State Council 2005). According to this policy, local and foreign nonstate capital could be invested in art, museums, libraries, internet cafés, art education, art agencies, tourism, animation, the gaming industry, advertising, film and television production, cinema, and the retail of books and audio-video products. Such capital was also allowed to have a shareholding of less than 49 percent in state-owned production and distribution companies in publishing, advertising, film, and television. The final objective of this strategy was

> to fully mobilize society to participate in the cultural construction and development of advanced socialist culture; to guide and regulate the entry of nonpublic capital into the cultural industries; to form a cultural market structure in which state-owned cultural enterprises play the dominant role, with the nonstate cultural economy as an important force; [and] to enhance the overall strength and competitiveness of China's cultural industries. (State Council 2005)

Apart from pursuing enterprise reform and ownership diversification, the state also deployed other strategies such as supporting key sectors, media convergence, digital information technologies, and "cultural going-out," or exports (*wenhua zouchuqu* 文化走出去). Special funds and preferential policies were established to support companies in specified "key sectors" (*zhongdian hangye* 重点行业), including animation, the television and film industry, digital content, publishing, performance and entertainment, and cultural tourism. These sectors, as I will explain in the next section, are the "core cultural industries" that are of great ideological importance to the state. The government believes that the development of these sectors will not only lead to the prosperity of commercial popular culture in China but will also help the country to accumulate soft power and improve its national cultural security.

The government has also viewed ICT as another crucial driving force for the Chinese cultural economy. New technologies, as one policy asserts, will transform and upgrade traditional cultural industries, giving birth to cutting-edge industries such as platform and AI economies. These economies can "develop value-added cultural products that combine world-leading technologies and independent intellectual property with national characteristics" (MoC 2003; State Council 2009). The "Thirteenth Five-Year Plan of China's National Economic and Social Development," covering the 2016–20 period (NDRC 2016), recognizes "digital creativity"—along with next-generation information technology, new-energy vehicles, biotechnology, green and low-carbon technology, and high-end equipment and materials—as strategic "emerging industries" (*xinxing chanye* 新兴产业). Compared with the Twelfth Five-Year Plan, the renewed development objective of the cultural industries was newly defined as "accelerating the development of modern cultural industries" (NDRC 2016, n.p.). The document emphasizes online audiovisual, mobile media, digital publishing, animation, and games as sectors for the digital creative industries and the integration of culture and technology (NDRC 2016, n.p.). As Flew, Ren, and Wang (2019) note, the plan's emphasis on the "digital creative industries" has replaced the "creative clusters" approach as the top priority in the national agenda of cultural-industries development. The state's ambition has shifted from the legacy media and cultural heritage sectors to strengthened digital-services industries, which can challenge the hegemony of Silicon Valley internet giants. More recently, the Fourteenth Five-Year Plan, covering the 2021–25 period, reiterated and elaborated on this national goal (NDRC 2021, n.p.). The "digitalization of the cultural industries" (*wenhua chanye shuzihua* 文化产业数字化), according to the plan, is the top strategy for constructing a modern cultural-industries system (*xiandai wenhua chanye tixi* 现代文化产业体系). This strategy aligns with the government's "Digital China" initiative, which aims to "welcome the digital era, stimulate the potentials of digital data, and build a strong cyberpower. Our goal is to accelerate the development of the digital economy, digital society, and a digital government—to advance the reform of production modes, lifestyles, and governance through digitalization" (NDRC 2021, n.p.).

Finally, the state formulated a series of promotional policies on cultural trade and export to promote the "going-out of Chinese culture."

Local artwork, exhibitions, films, television dramas, animation, internet games, publications, folk music and dance, acrobatics, and other cultural products that had "national characteristics" received support for export. Aside from various preferential tax and funding policies, China also launched several international cultural fairs to function as stages for China's cultural industries' "going out." These fairs included the International Cultural Industries Fair (Shenzhen), the China International Film and TV Program Exhibition (Beijing), and the Beijing International Book Fair. This globalization approach also aligned with the state's "digitalization strategy." According to the "Fourteenth Five-Year Plan for the Cultural Industries" (MCT 2021, n.p.), one of the national goals from 2021 to 2025 will be to cultivate and exploit the "competitive advantage" of Chinese digital cultural industries and support a group of "outbound Chinese cultural enterprises to produce products and services that represent Chinese characters but also can gain popularity on the international markets."

As a result of these policies, the Chinese cultural economy experienced rapid growth in the first two decades of the 2000s. According to official statistics, China's cultural industries maintained an average growth rate of 20 percent from 2004 to 2017 (see Figure 1.2). The economic value added by the cultural industries reached 4436 billion RMB (663 billion USD) in 2019, constituting 4.5 percent of Chinese gross domestic product (GDP). One source has reported that the cultural industries are becoming the new growth engine and "pillar" industry of the Chinese economy (Zhang 2018).

These policy documents and statistics show clearly that the Chinese party state has developed an aggressive plan to boost the creative economy. The shifting ideology of the CCP to economic development in the post-Mao era and the national "opening-up" policy and economic globalization together motivated the state to carry out institutional reform to provide space for the growth of commercial culture. But this enthusiastic national endorsement does not mean that the Chinese government has embraced the creative industries in the same way other countries have. As I will demonstrate in the next section, Chinese cultural-industries policy is never simply an economic policy that economizes cultural and media sectors. Rather, the state's ideological concern with social stability and national rejuvenation—recently translated into Xi

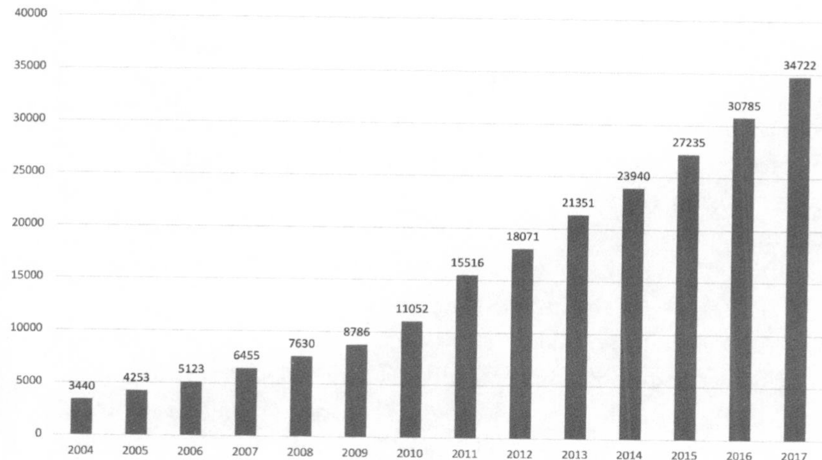

Figure 1.2. 2004–17 value added of the cultural industries in China (1 billion RMB, 0.15 billion USD). Created by the author; sources: *Guangming Daily* 2015; *Minyinzhiku* 2017; NBS 2018; MCT 2021.

Jinping's Chinese Dream—complicates the discursive formation of the cultural industries and distinguishes them from their counterparts in the rest of the world.

State Discursive Formation

Although political struggle and communist ideology were partly abandoned in postsocialist China, the state's instrumentalist interpretation of culture endured. Most importantly, media and art still need to support, or at least be in line with, the absolute rule of the Communist Party (Su 2015, 518). As President Xi Jinping (2014) has asserted, "the party's leadership is fundamental to the development of socialist culture and arts."

Even though the justification for the cultural industries lies in their potential to contribute to the restructuring of the Chinese national economy, their authorization is also premised on the party state's configuration of using culture as a tool for social governance—in the official language, "advanced socialist culture" or "social benefits." This stance can also be seen in the state's reluctance to use terms like "creativity" and "creative industries," as developed by the UK's Blair government in

1997. In 2005, when the discourse on the creative industries (*chuangyi chanye* 创意产业) arrived in China, the central government insisted on using the older term "cultural industries" (*wenhua chanye* 文化产业) in policy documents. One crucial reason for not using the term "creative industries," according to Wang Yongzhang—the former director of the Cultural Industries Division at the Ministry of Culture—was that the "cultural industries" in China not only refer to the economy and commodities but also have an ideological character (*yishixingtai shuxing* 意识形态属性). According to Wang, the creative industries "mainly focus on design and individual creativity . . . if we use 'creative industries' in our policy documents, there would be a risk that certain cultural sectors would fall out of the state's ideological control" (Wang 2007, n.p.).

Conservative Chinese officials and cultural traditionalists are suspicious of the "individualism," "change," and "creative destruction" promised by the international "creativity" discourse (Wang 2004; Keane 2009). In the West, debates around the term "creative industries" mainly have to do with the industries' latent neoliberalism and depoliticizing effects on culture and media (Galloway and Dunlop 2007; H-K Lee 2016). The term "depoliticization" also troubles the Chinese authorities, but in a different way. As Wang Yongzhang's remark illustrates, the state believes that the creative-industries discourse overlooks the "ideological character" of the cultural industries. The Chinese state worries that the discourse might lessen the state's role in the ideological regulation of social stability, national identity, and the moral order (Keane 2009; Tong and Hung 2012).

Along with the promotional policies on the cultural economy analyzed in the previous section, the Chinese authorities thus continued to configure the cultural sectors "in terms of what ought to be state-owned and what could involve the private sector—and thus influenced which content was defined as 'safe' vs. 'political'" (O'Connor and Gu 2006, 276). For example, in "Decisions on Allowing Nonpublic Capital into the Cultural Industries" (State Council 2005), nonstate investment had been allowed and was supported as part of the Chinese cultural and media economy. But the use of nonstate capital was still not permitted while setting up independent news agencies, publishing houses, and broadcasting networks, or for importing books, journals, film, television, and other audio-video products that were regarded as being ideologically important (State Council 2005).

These examples demonstrate that there is a "state discursive formation" behind China's cultural-sector marketization reform. Following Jim McGuigan, the state discursive formation emerges from the belief that "the modern nation-state should command the whole of society, regulate the economy and cultivate appropriate selves" (2004, 36). Under this discourse—shared by totalitarian regimes such as the former Soviet Union and Maoist China—cultural policy should function to "engineer the soul" of the public (McGuigan 2004, 36). Liberal and socio-democratic societies use this discourse to a lesser extent than the Chinese state's support for and promotion of high national culture (McGuigan 2004, 41). In contemporary China, the promotion of a commercial cultural economy is intertwined with a set of regulatory policies that attempt to shape the cultural industries, in accordance with the role of social-governance culture assigned by the party state.

Consider the two perennial discourses of "soft power" (*ruanshili* 软实力) and "cultural security" (*wenhua anquan* 文化安全). The party state has been eager to promote its national imagery to wield Chinese soft power on the global stage while expecting a conforming culture that ensures social stability and national unity. Coined by Joseph Nye in the 1980s, the term "soft power" has become popular in international diplomacy, with "cultural export" often touted as its key element (Nye 2005). This term has been embraced by the Chinese government over the last several years. The state made soft power one of the prime objectives of developing the cultural economy through the "going-out of Chinese culture" (*zhongguo wenhua zouchuqu* 中国文化走出去) (Keane 2010). According to President Xi Jinping, the building of Chinese soft power constitutes the "Chinese Dream"—as noted earlier, the great rejuvenation of the Chinese nation (Xi 2015). At the same time, China's joining the WTO officially opened up China's doors to foreign popular culture such as Hollywood movies, American pop music, and Korean and Japanese music. This cultural globalization still agitates Chinese cultural traditionalists, who fear the cultural invasion by the West and the loss of Chinese identity and traditional culture. The Chinese Communist Party has also been suspicious of Western cultural goods that purportedly camouflage the threat of "peaceful evolution."[4] As one policy document claims, "Opening up should be for our own use. We should not blindly copy the Western perceptions of culture and development. While learning and bringing in the best of foreign cultures, we also need to resist the unhealthy thoughts and cultures of the West to protect national cultural security" (Central Committee of the CCP and State Council 2005).

Such concerns have spurred the party state to incubate a competitive domestic cultural economy—especially in the state-owned cultural sectors—that can effectively protect the nation's cultural security from the forces of cultural globalization. To achieve this goal, the Chinese government categorizes cultural sectors into "core" cultural sectors and "related" cultural sectors. The core cultural sectors include six categories of cultural services: news information, content production, creative design, cultural distribution, cultural investment and operation, and cultural entertainment and leisure. The related cultural sectors support the core sectors and include copying and printing, stationery manufacturing, cultural agencies and intermediaries, and instrument manufacturing. According to the 2017 "Guidance on Foreign Investment in Chinese Industries" issued by the National Development and Reform Commission and the Ministry of Commerce (NDRC and MoC 2017), the party state only welcomes foreign investment in the related cultural sectors. The highly ideological core cultural sectors—such as news and information services, publishing, and the production and distribution of television, film, and digital content—are closed to foreign investment.[5]

The state discursive formation regulates the content of everyday cultural production. From television, film, and news to internet culture, a pervasive censorship regime functions to supervise commercial culture, in service of "the CCP's number one political agenda, maintaining social stability, and . . . contribut[ing] to the CCP's cultural agenda—i.e., stabilizing and re-energizing the dominant moral order" (Bai and Song 2014, 79). In this way, the thriving cultural market and vibrant commercial culture are made compatible with China's one-party ruling system. By assigning culture a dual role as ideology and commodity, the state can deploy the market economy and cultural industries as a new form of social governance.

Institutional Deficiencies and Flexibility

Governed by this state discursive formation, media industries and cultural workers in China need to meticulously manage their creativity between market needs and state regulation. But this does not mean that creative production in China is nothing but a propaganda apparatus. As I will argue in this section, Chinese administrative institutions complicate the process of policy making and implementation, which is always full of tensions and negotiations.

As Yu Hong (2017a, 10) states in her study of Chinese internet and communication policies, "Fragmented class interests, incompatible regional experiments, self-serving bureaucratic interests, and competing developmental visions are pulling the rebalancing in different directions." Although China has often been seen as an authoritarian party state, its political system is also characterized by resilience and adaptability, which allow for bottom-up policy changes and political-economic experiments. Heilmann and Perry (2011, 11), for example, note that "China's vast and bureaucratically fragmented political system is animated by policy processes that allow for far greater bottom-up input than would be predicted from its formal structures." The state system is characterized by complex and even conflicting relationships with the market and social governance. "Competing bureaucratic imperatives and vested state interests in the economy have created and continue to create nonaligned initiatives and diffused commitments," resulting in the nonunitary nature of the state (Hong 2017a, 15). I will argue that this nonunitary and even contested nature of the state is what creates spaces of agency in the Chinese creative economy.

To create spaces of agency, the fragmented government system first engenders discrepancies between different administrative departments. As Lieberthal and Lampton (1992, 8) point out, "China's bureaucratic ranking system combines with the functional division of authority among various bureaucracies to produce a situation in which it is often necessary to achieve agreement among an array of bodies, where no single body has authority over the others." This phenomenon, termed "fragmented authoritarianism" by political scientists (Lieberthal and Lampton 1992; Mertha 2009; Yang 2013), is a process of policy making and implementation in postsocialist China that involves constant bargaining and competition among government agencies with diverse and even contradictory interests. As a typical multisector industry, cultural production in China has been regulated by multiple governmental bodies, which—according to the recent reform of the State Council (2018b)—include the Ministry of Culture and Tourism (MCT), the China Film Administration (CFA), the National Press and Publication Administration (NPPA), the National Radio and Television Administration (NRTA), the Cyberspace Administration of China (CAC), the Ministry of Industry and Information Technology (MIIT), and the Publicity Department of the CCP).

The State Administration for Industry and Commerce and the Ministry of Finance also hold administrative power over cultural policies related to finance and the market. According to the official description, the Ministry of Culture and Tourism oversees heritage, art, and tourism; CFA, NPPA, and NRTA are responsible for the media sector; and the CAC controls the internet and digital sectors. The Publicity Department of the CCP, which is the highest authority for all propaganda and cultural affairs, supervises the other cultural governmental bodies. But with the increasing marketization and convergence between digital and traditional media, such a bureaucratic division—as I will illustrate below—results in overlapping tasks and a blurring of boundaries between different administrative bodies, causing deficiencies in policy implementation and market governance.

Cultural and administrative resources are spread over diverse departments—such as culture, media, tourism, education, finance, and technology—which renders the state's macroeconomic governance inefficient. In March 2018, for example, the Chinese government launched a new institutional reform of the country's cultural sectors. The major changes were that the previous Ministry of Culture became the Ministry of Culture and Tourism, and the State Administration of Press, Publication, Radio, Film and Television (SAPPRFT) was divided into three new government bodies: the State Administration of Press and Publishing (SAPP), the State Administration of Radio and Television (SART), and the State Administration of Film (SAF). The SAPP and the SAF, previously affiliated with the State Council, became divisions of the Publicity Department of the CCP (State Council 2018b). Although the reform was meant to "strengthen the party's leadership and boost administrative efficiency" (State Council 2018b), it exerted a negative impact on the gaming industry. Before this time, to launch a new computer game in China, game companies needed to first register at the Ministry of Industry and Information Technology, according to its "Procedures on Software Product Management." The second step was to go through content censorship at the previous Ministry of Culture (now the Ministry of Culture and Tourism), according to the "Temporary Provisions on the Administration of Internet Culture." After gaining approval, companies still needed a special license from the SAPPRFT, as required by the "Provisions on the Administration of Electronic Publications" (SAPPRFT 2015). Finally, before computer games could enter the market, companies had to register for copyright at the National Copyright Administration (NCA).

Within this complicated system, any slight change in an institutional or regulatory policy would have a huge impact on the whole gaming industry. But because the previous Ministry of Culture and the SAPPRFT were involved in the institutional reform of the State Council, the government simply stopped licensing new games in 2018. Statistics from 2017 (WallStreetCn 2018) show that an average of 770 new games had been licensed each month, and over 9,000 had been launched in the year. The institution reform of 2018 accordingly stopped thousands of new games from launching, which directly hurt the financial interests of Chinese game companies, especially small production firms. Although occasionally hindering companies, the fragmented governmental system also has given them leeway in negotiating state censorship. Chinese media producers have widely adopted the term *cabianqiu*, a popular Chinese slang term that literally means "the ball strikes the edge of the table," as a tactic "to test the boundaries of cultural policy" and to bypass censorship (Keane 1998; Cunningham, Craig, and Lv 2019). For example, in 2016, Hunan Television's popular show *Where Are We Going, Dad?* was banned by the SAPPRFT for its "overuse of children." In response, Hunan Television chose to move the show to its online platform, Mango TV, since the SAPPRAFT's ban only applied to television broadcasts (Nauta 2018, 182). The discrepancy in regulations between television and digital media thus opened space for television producers to evade censorship and continue disseminating controversial content.

Besides the fragmented governmental system, the complex relationship between central and regional government counts as the second most important feature of Chinese political organization that creates ambiguities. In China, the political administration is not a fully centralized authoritarian regime. As many scholars have noted, the *nomenklatura* system of personnel management[6] reinforces the authority of the central government and produces national unity (Naughton and Yang 2004; Chan 2004). At same time, the authority of the central government also lies in its power of fiscal administration (Ong 2006; Huang 2008). Beijing exercises its central authority over revenue collection and distribution (Kennedy 2013), which in theory balances local government budgets, thereby leveling the budgets of wealthier provinces and cities with those of poorer ones. In addition to these two centralization strategies, regional governments have significant autonomy in governing the subnational economy. According to Xu Chenggang (2011, 1078), "Regional economies (provinces, municipalities, and counties) are relatively self-contained, and subnational governments have overall responsibility for initiating and coordinating reforms, providing public services, and making and enforcing laws within their jurisdictions. This feature qualitatively differentiates the Chinese economy from a typical centrally planned economy."

This "regionally decentralized authoritarian" (RDA) regime—a term coined by Xu (2011)—is distinct from federalism, in that Chinese officials are not accountable to their constituents but to higher-ranked leaders. Simultaneously, this RDA is also distinct from the Maoist command economy. Ever since Deng Xiaoping embarked on China's marketization reform in the 1990s, GDP growth has become the basis for official promotions. To stand out in the regional GDP competition, local officials have embraced what Heilmann and Perry (2011) conceptualize as a "guerrilla policy-making style." Inherited from the CCP's wartime tactics, this "guerrilla approach" characterizes contemporary Chinese policy making, in the sense that the top leadership preserves the power to make decisions on nationwide strategies, while "operationalization and implementation require substantial latitude for local initiative and independence" (Heilmann and Perry 2011, 18). As a result, policy making is always in a process of continual improvisation and adjustment, with pilot efforts and practical experience preferred to abstract theories or models (Heilmann and Perry 2011, 18). Local guerrilla leaders are sometimes "dictatorial, opportunistic and ruthless" and sacrifice political accountability. Yet their approach also contributes to the adaptability, versatility, and flexibility of the party's rule and policy making. For example, van der Kamp, Lorentzen, and Mattingly's research (2017, 165) shows a discrepancy in the actual implementation of environmental policy between rich regions and poorer ones. More specifically, since revenue collection determines bureaucratic promotion, officials in "revenue-starved cities" tend to "protect highly polluting local industries," yet authorities in revenue-rich cities show more compliance with central mandates by "responding to popular demands for more transparency and cleaner industry, which the center also promotes." As a result, the local government's dependence on fiscal transfers from Beijing actually results in noncompliance with China's central policy.

The partial decentralization of the Chinese fiscal and administrative system not only contributes to economic growth but can also undermine other governance reforms (van der Kamp, Lorentzen, and Mattingly 2017). The RDA regime and the flexible policy style it produces empower subnational governments and officials in the realm of actual policy making and implementation. Under the supervision of the central government, "they initiate, negotiate, implement, divert, and resist reforms, policies, rules, and laws" (Xu 2011, 1079). In the cultural sectors, for instance, some local governments such Shanghai and Beijing introduced and embraced "creative industries" (later "cultural creative industries") as a policy discourse around 2005 (Keane 2009). Local officials welcomed this terminology precisely because it differed from the "cultural industries" term the central government used. The local government often frames "creative industries" as an economic policy; this avoids the ideological importance of cultural production, thus discursively reducing the resistance to the term from conservative parties.

The "Three-Year Planning of the Cultural Creative Industries in Shanghai: 2016–2018" (SACCI 2016, n.p.), for example, states that the "cultural creative industries are crucial for Shanghai to maintain economic growth and to achieve industrial restructuring. . . . The goal of our reform is to promote comprehensive innovation in industrial mechanisms, capital operations, and business models to stimulate the market and society while also maintaining a fair and just cultural market." In contrast to the central government's emphasis on the "dual character" of the cultural industries, the ideological importance of cultural and media production is notably absent from this document. Instead, the Shanghai government adopts a more technocratic discourse in its promotion of the creative industries, stressing the role of technology, capital, and creativity in industrial restructuring and economic growth.

Finally, the political system analyzed above also complicates the state-commerce relationship in China. The lack of transparency in regulatory requirements and capricious law enforcement gives authorities flexibility to govern the local economy while creating space for rent-seeking and corruption in state government. Given its nonunitary nature, the state plays multiple roles in the Chinese economy, from promoter and regulator to direct participant. As many researchers have noted, connections with the government are ubiquitous among Chinese-listed firms (Dickson 2003; Breslin 2012; Wang 2016). Having personal ties with certain government officials can effectively help companies negotiate with policy makers and dodge potential regulatory obstacles. This situation is even more common in the media and cultural sectors, as the state imposes even more regulations on the cultural industries because of their "dual responsibility." As the next chapter will show, state-owned cultural enterprises (SOCEs) are more privileged than private cultural companies due to their closer relationship with the state. This connection to the state government not only endows them with easier access to financing and the market but also brings greater influence on policy making and economic regulation.

For example, in the highly regulated and heavily censored film industry, state-owned film production companies—such as the China Film Group Corporation (中影集团) and the August First Film Studio (八一电影制片厂)—and private production firms that have personal ties with powerful officials have more power to negotiate with the China Film Administration about the licensing and censorship process. According to one of my informants,[7] most big Chinese internet and media companies have a department called "government relations," which, as its name indicates, directly deals with the authorities about censorship and business management. A ubiquitous yet unspoken strategy on the part of China's largest internet companies is to hire influential retired officials from central and local governments as consultants who can provide insider knowledge on policy as well as mediate between the company and the government.

The fragmented administrative system, the decentralized authoritarian regime, and the complicated state-commerce relationship all profoundly affect the process of policy making and implementation in China's contemporary cultural sectors. Instead of being a unitary entity, in practice the Chinese state functions as a network constituted of different, often conflicting, forces emanating from state administrative bodies, local governments, and market entities.

Conclusions

In this chapter I have examined the genesis, dominant discourses, and institutions of China's cultural-industries policies. The shifting ideology of the CCP toward economic development in the post-Mao era, the national opening-up policy, and economic globalization have together motivated the party state to carry out institutional reforms to provide space to the growth of commercial culture and to deploy the cultural industries as part of a national development strategy. This enthusiastic national endorsement, however, does not mean that the Chinese government has embraced the creative industries in the same way that many countries have in the West. The state discursive formation of Chinese cultural-industries policy reflects the party state's instrumentalist configuration of culture and creativity. Cultural production in contemporary China follows the market rule, while it also needs to promote social stability and reaffirm the dominant moral order.

In practice, China's political organization creates abundant space for agency, deviation from official policies, and flexibility for diverse actors in the cultural and media sphere. On an everyday basis, Jing Wang's "state question" (2001) in Chinese cultural production and popular culture thus not only refers to the state's ideological concerns about cultural activities but also has to do with the intricate relationship between administrative power and various production subjects. The crucial task for cultural producers in China is to negotiate and find ways to "play" with state power, which is contested, nonunitary, and multivariate.

Framed by this understanding of the development of Chinese cultural-industries policy and its complicated modes of implementation, the following chapters will explicate how the interaction and negotiation between the state, the market, and cultural producers work in different organizational contexts in contemporary China. The central questions that I will explore in the following pages are as follows: How do creative people actively negotiate with this state-market system to produce notions of creativity? How does this dynamic process of negotiation affect the formation of creator subjectivity and make creators bilateral? I will start this empirical investigation from the working experiences of Chinese state-owned cultural companies.

2

Being Creative for the State

The state-owned cultural enterprises are vital forces for developing the cultural industries and constructing an advanced socialist culture. We must endeavor to build up a modern corporate system with cultural characteristics to show the effects of uniting social benefits with economic benefits.

—State Council (2015c)

Introduction

China Central Television (CCTV), one of the largest and most influential media companies in China, seems to be losing appeal among its employees. Since 2013, a number of renowned hosts[1] have resigned from CCTV in quick succession in what has been called the "wave of resignation at CCTV" (*yangshi lizhi chao* 央视离职潮). Until recently, a job at China's most influential media company would bring popularity, social status, and a successful career. This situation raises the question: Why did these established television stars decide to leave, especially at a time when China's new-media and cultural industries were booming? According to media reports, the new jobs of those who left ranged from high-ranking managers in new-media and investment companies, university professors, founders of start-up companies, and housewives/husbands. Why would these cultural workers decide to give up the "iron rice bowl" (*tie fanwan* 铁饭碗)[2] provided by CCTV, which was far more secure than precarious positions at private companies? This question leads us to the various concerns about labor (including creative labor) in China's state-owned media companies that animate this book.

As I showed in the book's introduction, creative work in a globalized society is not always as autonomous, self-expressive, and fulfilling as imagined by creative-industry policies and scholars such as Richard Florida (2002) and John Howkins (2002). Instead, creative workers have become a creative "precariat" who suffer under precarious working conditions and are surrounded by problems such as short-term contracts, unequal earnings, and a lack of unions (Hesmondhalgh and Baker 2011; McRobbie 2016; Curtin and Sanson 2016). Discourses surrounding creativity and the seemingly autonomous managerial setting function as elements connected by the "creativity *dispositif*," which, as Angela McRobbie discusses, builds a "romance" of creative work and its translation into "a kind of *dispositif*, a self-monitoring, self-regulating mechanism" (2016, 38). Following Foucault, she regards creativity as holding a specific function in the current neoliberal economy: "Creativity is designated by current modes of biopolitical power, as the site for implementing job creation and, more significantly, labour reform; it is a matter of managing a key sector of the youthful population by turning culture into an instrument of both competition and labour discipline" (McRobbie 2016, 38).

As I revealed in the previous chapter, however, the creativity *dispositif* has a different form and connotations in contemporary China due to its "state question" (Wang 2001, 35–52): the state views culture not simply as commercial but as a tool for wielding soft power (Nye 2005) and propagating the ideology of the Chinese Communist Party. In China's cultural industries, a special form of work organization exists in the form of state-owned cultural enterprises (SOCEs). According to official statistics, by 2015 there were 1.37 million employees in Chinese SOCEs (Ministry of Finance 2016). Transformed from state-controlled cultural work units (Li and Wang 1996), these state-owned companies have become the most powerful players in China's cultural industries. In the few existing studies on Chinese SOCEs, Wang Weijia provides a historical and ethnographic review of the commercializing reform of China's state-controlled news agencies since the 1990s. She investigates journalist education and employment, labor control in Chinese news presses, and laborers' working and payment conditions (2011). From the perspective of organization studies, Wang investigates this commercial transition and its sway on cultural workers in a more concrete way by providing a comprehensive ethnography of CCTV's organizational culture and its practitioners' lives and work (Wang 2006). Fung and Zhang also studied the localization of the global television format at Hunan Television (2011). Apart from these insightful projects, questions about the power relations governing creative labor and their impact on creative workers' subjectivities in Chinese SOCEs remain underexplored.

In effect, SOCEs are required by the Chinese government to shoulder the "double responsibility" of simultaneously achieving social and economic benefits (State Council 2015c; Ministry of Finance 2016). As Zhu Ying states in her study of CCTV, "The pressures of generating revenue alongside conforming politically are frequently at odds with media practitioners' sense of duty associated with watchdog journalism and cultural enlightenment" (Zhu 2012, 9). The need to balance the political and the commercial in cultural production creates a paradox that troubles creative workers in Chinese SOCEs.

If creative workers in Anglo-American society are subjected to a neoliberal governmentality constructed by the creativity *dispositif*, what are the creative-working conditions in Chinese SOCEs? What kind of subjectivity is expected and produced through the governance of creativity and labor in Chinese SOCEs? Can we take the phenomenon of the "wave of resignation" as evidence of resistance to this governance and subjectivation? Finally, are there any other forms of resistance to the existing power relations within the workplace of Chinese SOCEs? To study these questions, I take my point of departure from conceptions of "autonomy" and "self-realization."

Autonomy, Self-Realization, and the Creativity *Dispositif*

In current discussions on creative industries and creative labor, autonomy has at least two connotations: "creative autonomy" and "workplace autonomy" (Holt and Lapenta 2010; Hesmondhalgh and Baker 2011, 40). Creative autonomy refers to the independence of art from other social forces such as religion and politics, an aesthetic idealism that originated from Kant's distinction between aesthetic, moral, and rational judgment (Hesmondhalgh and Baker 2011). In the creative industries, this form of autonomy is threatened by the capital's demand for "embedded instrumental rationality," or "reducing all value to exchange value by applying market principles to everything in a global cultural economy" (McGuigan 2004, 53). Workplace autonomy, in contrast, refers to "the degree of self-determination that individual workers or groups of workers have within a work situation" (Hesmondhalgh and Baker 2011, 40). The development of the creative industries and the post-Fordism they represent provides a large market for artists and cultural workers, who now have more opportunities to obtain financing through artistic production. The proliferation of deregulation in cultural companies has also endowed cultural workers with more "responsible autonomy," which "attempts to harness the adaptability of labor power by giving workers leeway and encouraging them to adapt to changing situations in a manner beneficial to the firm" (cited in Hesmondhalgh and Baker 2011, 41; Friedman 1977, 78).

Self-realization, according to the *Oxford English Dictionary*, refers to "the fulfilment by one's own efforts of the possibilities of development of the self" (cited in Hesmondhalgh and Baker 2011, 33). Compared to other forms of labor such as factory labor, it seems that creative labor, "at least according to creative workers, offers genuine possibilities for self-realization" (Hesmondhalgh and Baker 2011, 141). Various creative-industry policies issued by governments also tout the potential for self-realization in the creative industries. As one claims, "Just imagine how good it feels to wake up every morning and really look forward to work. Imagine how good it feels to use your creativity, your skills, [and] your talent to produce a film. . . . Are you there? Does it feel good?" (quoted in Nixon and Crewe 2004, 129). In reality, as Nixon and Crewe recognize, not all those working "there" feel good and can realize their creative potential (2004). Yet, as both Ursell (2000) and McRobbie (2002) argue, it is the passion and love for creative work that motivates people to choose creative professions as their career. All the drawbacks concerning pay, working time, and security can be ignored for the alluring promise that creative work will help them realize their creative potential—in McRobbie's words, "find the meaning of life in work" (2002, 110). Rather than celebrating such happiness and the possibility of self-realization, Ursell and McRobbie both recognize the articulation of "passion in work" as part of the governmental discourses of creative work (Ursell 2000, 810; McRobbie 2002, 109).

In summary, in the current neoliberal creative economy, creative labor may not be as autonomous and fulfilling as it claims to be. Furthermore, the discourses of autonomy and self-realization constitute core elements of the creativity *dispositif* (McRobbie 2016). The managerial setting of "responsible autonomy" fosters creative workers' aspirations toward self-realization, which is at the same time circumscribed and orchestrated to produce the desired creative subjectivity.

Given the "state question" (Wang 2001) haunting Chinese cultural production, as well as the special managerial structure of Chinese state-owned media, the condition of autonomy and the role of self-realization might manifest differently in this context, leading to different questions. First, to what extent is autonomy possible in an authoritarian cultural system that relies on censorship and propaganda? Second, under this condition of autonomy, how do the connotations and dysfunctionality of the self-realization discourse appear in the everyday work of creative workers at Chinese SOCEs? The goal of this chapter is not simply to examine the extent to which creative workers can achieve autonomy and self-realization but to illuminate the role that notions of autonomy and self-realization play in governing the subjectivity of creative workers in Chinese state media. This exploration offers an opportunity to see how the governance of creativity and creative labor functions in Chinese SOCEs, and how it is distinguishable from the Western creativity *dispositif*.

This chapter is based on fieldwork carried out in Beijing and Shanghai from July to October 2016. During this time I made ethnographic observations and conducted in-depth interviews with creative workers from the television, film, and new-media industries, including employees of state media and private cultural companies, as well as freelancers. I address the above questions mainly by analyzing ten in-depth interviews with state-employed creative workers and observations I made of their companies. As a point of comparison, I also refer to interviews with freelancers and creative workers in private cultural companies. I examine other sources as well, including cultural-industry policy documents, selected news reports, and online discussions about working in Chinese SOCEs. The SOCEs include three national and three provincial media companies involved in business genres ranging from film and television to the news press. The informants' names have been pseudonymized for security and privacy reasons. Given the diversity of Chinese SOCEs, I do not claim to present a comprehensive ethnography of creative production in SOCEs in this chapter. Instead, I outline some of the more common challenges faced by creative workers in Chinese SOCEs that can help to illustrate the question of how creativity discourses function in the governance of cultural workers in Chinese SOCEs.

Before moving on to a discussion of autonomy and self-realization, I will first introduce the historical background of China's cultural-system reform and its state-owned media. I suggest that the autonomy of creative labor within state media companies is contested and contingent on the problematic managerial setting of the system. The employment benefits offered by the system still attract creative workers to be creative for the state, especially those who aspire toward self-realization. By exploring the prevalent phenomena of "loafing on the job," multitasking, and the "wave of resignation," in this chapter I attribute the function of the self-realization discourse to the contradictory nature of the system itself. On this basis, I echo the call in the book's introduction to contextualize creative-labor studies and to devote more attention to different sociopolitical localities in order to facilitate a more differentiated theorization of creative labor and, in turn, of how the politics of creative workplaces might be reimagined.

From *Ganbu* to Employees: Cultural-System Reform and Chinese SOCEs

Before 1978, all Chinese cultural organizations—usually called *danwei* (单位), or "cultural work units"—were financed by and considered a part of the government apparatus. Their only responsibility was to serve the ideological propaganda of the Communist Party. Propelled by the economic reforms starting in 1978, China also launched a cultural-system reform in the late 1990s. To reduce the financial burden of competing with foreign cultural enterprises, some of these *danwei* were gradually transformed into commercial enterprises under the terms "industrialization" and "conglomeration" within China's cultural policy (State Council 2003, 2014; Keane 2013, 23). The commercialized cultural *danwei* include publishing and news presses, film studios, and television stations. To achieve economies of scale, formerly small cultural institutions with similar businesses were merged into large state-owned cultural conglomerates, such as the China Film Group Company and the Shanghai Century Publishing Group Corporation. Supported by the Chinese government, these SOCEs still hold a very privileged and powerful position in China's cultural industries. Through their close relationship with the government, they can influence policy making and industrial administration.

This reform has never completely relieved these state enterprises of their ideological duty of propaganda and education. Rather, Chinese SOCEs are now supposed to have a dual function as "cultural institution" (*wenhua shiye* 文化事业) and "cultural industry" (*wenhua chanye* 文化产业). As a cultural institution, they must produce "good social benefits" (*shehui xiaoyi* 社会效益) that contribute to a harmonious society. As players in the cultural industry, they should achieve commercial success in domestic and global markets, thus enhancing China's soft power. In the context of Chinese cultural-industry policy, however, social benefits have always had priority over commercial profits. The core of the cultural-system reform, as the government claims,

> is to enforce and improve cultural-economic policy and strengthen the regulation of state-owned cultural assets; [the goal] is to construct a mechanism that can ensure the pursuit of state-owned cultural enterprises for social benefits while uniting the social benefits with economic benefits . . . in order to advance the development and prosperity of socialist culture. (Central Committee of the CCP and State Council 2015)

The cultural-system reform also transformed the personnel system. In the prereform era, cultural workers were part of a cultural cadre (*ganbu* 干部; a Chinese term for CCP bureaucrats), who enjoyed permanent contracts and social welfare. They worked and lived within the *danwei* units, which for them were not merely workplaces but home-like units that provided a panoply of welfare benefits such as health care, housing, and education (Xing 1995). In return, *danwei* exercised a form of social control, "securing individual compliance, maintain[ing] collective order and normative consistency and deal[ing] with problematic and deviant situations" (Shaw 1996, xii). The main task of cultural work units thus centered on Maoist ideology at the expense of autonomy and critique. A central tenet of work was to serve "the broadest masses of people," which, defined by Chairman Mao, were workers, peasants, and soldiers (1967). Although such cultural labor was highly political and strictly overseen, the workers could still enjoy stable and secure working conditions.

Since the launch of the cultural-system reform, the *danwei* institution has gradually disappeared. The cultural units morphed into state-owned commercial enterprises once private capital was allowed to enter certain cultural sectors. According to an annual report, by 2015 China had more than 13,000 SOCEs, with over 1.2 million employees (MoF 2015). Apart from those workers who still have *bianzhi* (tenure), which is restricted to long-term, more experienced staff members, a major influence of this reform on creative labor is that most workers have become contracted employees and are now regulated under the "modern enterprise managerial system." Apart from the few senior workers who still have tenure, most workers have become temporarily contracted and are regulated under the enterprise managerial system.

This transition from *danwei* to enterprises is still underway and has caused many ambiguities. As Fu Caiwu indicates, a common route of SOCE reform is to replace the supervisor-oriented system with the sponsor-oriented system. In the supervisor-oriented system, central and local governments directly intervene in the management of companies, under strict plans formulated by the authorities. In the sponsor-oriented model, government authorities only retain ownership, while executive power is returned to the companies. The SOCEs thus enjoy more autonomy and flexibility in management and market competition. The key problem for cultural SOCEs, however, is that one of the central mandates they receive from the state is to serve the ideological agenda of the party. This mandate is often captured in discourses of protecting "national cultural security" (*guojia wenhua anquan* 国家文化安全), upholding the "main melody" (*zhuxuanlv* 主旋律), and prioritizing "social benefits" (Hu 2005). Government officials in charge of cultural and propaganda affairs are wary of losing control of the SOCEs. Deregulation might cause "political mistakes" in cultural production and thus constitutes a potential threat to their political careers.

To counter this threat, a strict regulatory and censorship system has been set up within these companies. For example, new employees receive special training not only for professional skills but also for cultivating their political and ideological sensitivity. This reluctance toward deregulation has resulted in an odd managerial system in which the "modern enterprise system" is articulated with a rigid bureaucracy teeming with rent-seeking and corruption. More specifically, the system of cadre promotion (*ganbu jinsheng* 干部晋升) and tenure employment (*bianzhi*) remains reserved for high-ranking supervisors in most state SOCEs, while junior employees are managed under a temporary contract and the modern enterprise system. For instance, Shen Haixiong, the incumbent head of CCTV, is also the deputy director of the State Administration of Press, Publication, Radio, Film and Television (SAPPRFT). In Chinese state-owned media, most leaders of state-controlled companies also hold important positions in the central or local government bodies, employed as the managers of state companies while serving as policy makers in the cultural industries. As Wang Weijia notes, this "marriage between political power and market" can produce a secure ideological network while giving rise to rent-seeking and corruption (Wang 2011, 240). Worse still, such an organizational hierarchy is based on the unequal distribution of power and welfare benefits between supervisors and subordinates, as well as between formally tenured members and temporary employees (Wang L. 2006; Wang W. 2011). As I will discuss in the next section, this problem of hierarchy and bureaucracy restricts the autonomy and self-realization of state employees.

The Crippled System and Contested Autonomy

CCTV employees are divided into four grades. The first level is "formal staff," which mainly consists of workers who were recruited in the 1980s and early 1990s, before the cultural-system reform. These people are still deemed *ganbu* (cadres) and enjoy tenure contracts, the best salary, and the highest status within the company. The second tier consists of people who are "employed by the station" (*taipin* 台聘), which refers to those hired during the period from the midnineties to the early 2000s. During this period there were no formal tenure positions available, because CCTV was undergoing its first institutional reform (Zhu 2012). But by now most of these "station-employed" workers have become formal staff and can enjoy the complete welfare system. The next rank is called "employed by the company." In this phrase, "company" specifically refers to Beijing Zhongshi Huicai Cultural Development Ltd., which is a subsidiary company of CCTV that was founded in 2003 and is responsible for the human resources of CCTV. All the employees in this rank are contracted workers. The last type of CCTV staff are called "program employed" and are hired by television program teams in CCTV. They do not formally belong to the personnel system of CCTV and, therefore, cannot enjoy as many welfare benefits as formal employees. The number of employees in the top two classes of staff is very limited, constituting only 20 to 30 percent of the workforce (*Huashangbao* 2014). Different ranks also represent different levels of wage and status. Within CCTV, staff ID cards are reportedly also divided into A, B, C, and D, representing the above four classes of employment (*Huashangbao* 2014).

This grading system is just the tip of the hierarchical iceberg of SOCEs such as CCTV. For employees, their supervisors' personality and words matter more than the work itself. The office heads perform all the evaluations and provide promotions and executive approval. To be qualified cultural workers, employees must first be "well-behaved" subordinates. As a result, this hierarchical structure poses a threat to creative workers' autonomy, a concept that is underscored by many policy makers and creative business scholars as a sine qua non of creative work (Florida 2002; Holt and Lapenta 2010). In their study of creative labor, Hesmondhalgh and Baker define autonomy as self-determination and not simply "freedom from all others," adopting it as a standard of good cultural work (2011, 40).

As explained earlier, one could argue that "responsible autonomy" is possible and even necessary within capitalist art commerce; only the survival of autonomous cultural work can maintain the continuous supply of originality and authenticity demanded by consumers (Banks 2010, 260). Within China's creative industries, such responsible autonomy has also been introduced into private commercial companies. For instance, according to my informants in conglomerates such as Tencent and Alibaba, and small production companies such as Canxing Production and Miwei Media, most of these companies have set up an efficient managerial structure through well-designed recruiting, incentive, and evaluation systems. Cao Jun is an executive editor of Miwei Media, which produced the successful online series mentioned in the introduction to this book, *U Can U BB* (*Qipa Shuo* 奇葩说). Before joining Miwei, Cao worked on the production of a local television show at Shanghai Media Group, a large SOCE in Shanghai. Compared to his previous experience,

Cao was amazed by the autonomy he enjoyed at Mewei. All the employees had shares in the company, and the friendly relationship between the boss and staff members created an enjoyable, homelike workplace. During the interview, Cao mentioned that one of his colleagues had been designated as one of the editors in chief of *Qipa Shuo* when he was still a college student. The youngest chief director of Miwei was only twenty-eight, while those holding the same position in state media usually have more than ten years of experience. For private companies such as Miwei, employees' creativity rather than their age or social experience appears to be what matters. As Cao Jun, editor of Miwei Media, told me, "We trust young people! Because they're creative and understand the audience."

Chinese SOCEs have tried to incubate such responsible autonomy. In 1993, CCTV launched an institutional reform called the "producer responsibility system" (PRS). Under the PRS, producers are entitled to more autonomy in terms of "personnel, finance, and production management within their own teams" (Wang 2006, 60). They can hire contracted employees and organize production by themselves. As a result, CCTV produced several successful news programs such as *Horizon* (*Dongfang Shikong* 东方时空) and *Focus* (*Jiaodian Fangtan* 焦点访谈), the first Chinese TV programs to conduct watchdog investigative reports on current affairs. According to Ying Zhu, however, the success of PRS reform owes much to Yang Weiguang, the then president of CCTV, who was open minded, courageous, and had strong connections with high-standing officials in the CCP. Local provincial media followed CCTV and adopted the PRS. But the complexity of SOCEs is such that the PRS system was an expedient response to the contradiction between employment quota restrictions and the increasing manpower needs caused by rapid business expansion. Later, local provincial media also adopted the PRS, but this adoption was similarly less a measure to deliberately promote autonomy than a temporary response to the tension between employment quota restrictions and their increasing manpower needs.

A similar reform can be traced among other state cultural enterprises, usually under the name of cultural-system reform.[3] Company A,[4] one of the CCP's official news presses, shoulders an important responsibility for producing and distributing party-state political propaganda, which means specific rules and forms of discipline are imposed on news production. As a journalist and editor at Company A, Jiang Tao characterizes these regulations as having two components: value orientation (*jiazhi daoxiang* 价值导向) and professionalism (*zhuanye zhuyi* 专业主义). By "value orientation" he means that media reports should be consistent with "mainstream values" such as patriotism, the party's leadership, and the Chinese value system. "Professionalism" denotes that news production should follow the normal procedures and professional ethics of news gathering and editing, so misinformation or paid news is unacceptable. Under these two principles, journalists like Jiang Tao can enjoy a certain amount of autonomy and be creative in their work; sometimes their leaders even encourage them to be creative to meet the "trend of new-media development." Speaking about autonomy, Jiang Tao gave me the following example:

> I once interviewed an artist. His art is very famous in China, but he always keeps a low profile. Originally, I was sent to report on his artistic contributions. After the interview I decided to move the focus to his devotion to art and his indifference to fame and wealth. But I was afraid that the moral judgment might offend others, which would also make more work for my colleagues. But my supervisor approved my request and said, "Under the premise of respecting the facts, it's necessary to offer journalists enough creative space to make their work more special." (Jiang Tao, Company A, journalist)

Arguably, since the introduction of cultural-system reform, Chinese SOCEs have developed "responsible autonomy" for their creative employees, as exemplified by the above cases. "Responsible" always refers to at least two levels of meaning: conforming to the party-state ideology and contributing to market success. If he sticks to the "bottom line" of value orientation, then Jiang Tao is allowed (and even encouraged) to be autonomous and to make his work more creative to improve propaganda. Ideally, together with the relatively generous welfare system (which will be examined in the next section), such responsible autonomy helps to make these state media organizations a desirable workplace for young creative workers.

The balance between ideology and commerce can be quite difficult to achieve in practice, however, especially because of SOCEs' bureaucratic management practices. Because the new system temporarily contracts most staff members within SOCEs, the most powerful minority still hold lifetime positions. Contrary to the hierarchy of Western creative workplaces (Holt and Lapenta 2010, 225–26), those who hold power in China's SOCEs are usually professional bureaucrats who have been appointed by the government; they have little knowledge about or respect for cultural production and creative producers. As observed by Wang Lingjie, CCTV actually has two levels of management: the "inner circle," which consists of upper and middle managers, and the "outside circle," or short-term contracted employees in production teams (Wang 2006, 74). The program producers, although they are usually the leaders of their production teams, are often situated at the middle or lower level of the hierarchy. Such a hierarchical dual-track system (*shuanggui zhi* 双轨制) can easily stifle producers' creative ideas. Simon, an experienced television producer who worked at Anhui Television, a provincial TV station in southern China, commented on the problems of the system (*tizhi* 体制) and its ongoing reforms:

> Our wages are calculated based on our rank in the company. For example, ideally the salary of producers like me should have dividends from the projects we've been involved in. But if this really happened, my salary would exceed that of our leaders. How could that be possible? Such a system is made more rigid due to the current anticorruption movement. It usually takes a month to go through all the approval procedures after submitting a proposal. When some leaders are on leave, you have to wait—sometimes for months! (Simon, Anhui Television, producer)

According to my informant Chew Fei, who worked for a local news press in Guizhou Province, most employees were contracted on a temporary basis. In terms of job promotion, those without connections to high leaders of the company had very few opportunities, regardless of their ability or work performance (Chew Fei, Guiyang Daily Corporation, journalist).

Ever since President Xi Jinping began China's anticorruption movement in 2012, conservative SOCE leaders have become more vigilant about innovation and change, as failure might put them at political risk. As a result, the regulation of companies is becoming more authoritarian and rigid, and creative autonomy seems even more unattainable than it did in the 1990s and 2000s. Simon Wong even complained that some employees were now required to write work logs every day. The new head of CCTV, Nie Chenxi, reportedly enjoys spell-checking reports and even conducting sanitation inspections of staff offices (Carl, CCTV, senior manager). When the high-level bureaucrats lack expertise as well as the courage to stand up for innovative cultural production, then ideology—as the stories about working at CCTV and Anhui TV reflect—is translated into a stringent regulative system.

The party state adds a third dimension to the "art-commerce relation" among Chinese SOCEs, making it an "art-commerce-politics" relation. Creative laborers thus are not only absorbed by capital but also must serve the party. This three-part relationship makes "responsible autonomy" more provisional than in the neoliberal scenario. Given that SOCEs are such a problematic setting for responsible autonomy, the following questions arise. Why do creative workers still choose to work for Chinese SOCEs? What does self-realization mean for them? And what does the dysfunctionality of the self-realization discourse mean for the governing of creative workers in Chinese SOCEs?

Being Creative for the State: Benefits of the System and Self-Realization

Sarah works as a commercial director for Canxing Production, a leading Chinese TV production company whose major business partners are state-owned television companies, including Shanghai Oriental Television, Zhejiang Television, and CCTV. As a commercial director, Sarah is responsible for designing advertising that meets the expectations of both the commercial sponsors and the state television companies. When asked about her motivation for work, she emphasized the sense of fulfillment that it produces:

> It's like playing a game. My job requires dealing with lots of parties: different types of work, people, and creativity. You need to surmount one challenge after another. When the expected commercial effects are finally achieved, it brings a huge sense of fulfillment, which makes me feel as though I'm self-realizing. (Sarah, Canxing Production, director)

Most of my informants in the private cultural industries shared a similar motivation, whether their job title was photographer, screenwriter, editor, or director in publishing, film, or television. This outlook largely resonates with the critiques of the "self-realization" discourse I referred to earlier: it exposes self-realization as an aspiration for creative laborers and stresses the role of self-realization as a governmental discourse that mobilizes the workforce in the creative economy (Hesmondhalgh 2010; McRobbie 2016). Given the bureaucracy and the "contingent" autonomy on offer, the question becomes how creative workers in Chinese SOCEs understand self-realization. To what extent does the discourse of self-realization succeed or fail in producing a certain subjectivity in creative workers employed by the state?

I still remember the day when Jiang Tao warmly hosted me at Company A. We toured the park in the area where the company is located. Jiang Tao invited me for dinner at their canteen, where the dishes were tasty and inexpensive. "That's one of our welfare benefits, plus a meal allowance of around 1,000 RMB (150 USD) per month." Indeed, in addition to various subsidies, reimbursements, and social insurance, staff members like Jiang Tao can also have a free single room in the staff dormitory. Central state media such as Company A and CCTV can also solve the residence permit (*hukou* 户口) problem for its formal employees. Given the exorbitant living costs and the strict *hukou* policy (Chan and Buckingham 2008) in Beijing, these benefits are very attractive for young graduates. As Lianna explained, her reason for working at another SOCE, the Chinese Film Library, was that "they can solve my *hukou* problem!" (Lianna, Chinese Film Library, curator).

Apart from the welfare system, the so-called career benefits also attract cultural workers to Chinese SOCEs. The privileged position of SOCEs in China's cultural industries provides these employees more career-building opportunities, such as networking and skills training. As in the British television industry (Lee 2011), networking plays a key role in Chinese creative workers' career development. Because of their close relationship with the government, state employees are more likely to develop a powerful social network. As tactfully suggested by Wang, even a junior employee of CCTV may be treated as a "grandpa"[5] by business partners from outside, although within CCTV the employee often must behave like a "grandson" (2006, 161–62). The same goes for local provincial SOCEs. As Robin told me, his affiliation to Anhui TV was a benefit of his work: "When my business partners learn that I'm from Anhui TV, they usually say, 'Ah! You're from Anhui TV. Good! I trust you. Let's make a deal!'" (Robin, Anhui Television, administrative assistant). Jiang Tao also emphasized that, as a journalist in Company A, he could gain access to interviewing many "big names." Even if they could not directly become his friends, he could gain much "social experience and broaden [his] horizons" from them (Jiang Tao, Company A, journalist).

The wages in SOCEs may not be as high as in large private companies such as Tencent and Alibaba, but the implicit income (*yinxin shouru* 隐性收入) generated by these career benefits is considerable. During my visit to the Shanghai Media Group (SMG), Even Yong shared with me a cameramen's moonlighting story: "The basic wage for cameramen in our SMG is just 2,000–3,000 RMB (300–450 USD) per month. Very low, right? But doing an extra project for outside companies can bring in 8,000–10,000 RMB (1,200–1,500 USD) in one go. The title of 'SMG photographer' carries great weight" (Even Yong, SMG, manager).

Most large SOCEs also have regular training programs for employees, including lectures, courses, and even study-abroad opportunities. All the respondents I interviewed confirmed that their companies organized skill-learning activities, which many of them reported as being helpful and meaningful. For example, SMG has a special annual program called "British Class," a six-week study-abroad program for about fifteen selected employees each year. By inviting experienced television workers from the BBC and ITV to give lectures and instructions, SMG expects to cultivate high-level television production teams. SMG employees appeared to welcome this project. Judie Deng, a senior producer at SMG, was one of the fifteen members of the 2016 British Class program. Speaking of her experiences, she noted that "those six weeks in London were my happiest times since I've been employed in Shanghai" (Judie Deng, SMG, TV producer).

In the cultural industries of contemporary China, these benefits often seem irresistible for young graduates, especially those who want to "realize themselves," even though the rigid hierarchy and bureaucracy of actually working inside these SOCEs can be depressing. Gloomy emotions can be offset by the privileges of working "inside the system" (*tizhi nei*

体制内). The benefits of "the system" first connote more secure working conditions. In contrast to employees of private companies, employees at SOCEs usually have a very low probability of being fired. Even for nontenured employees, contracts are extended automatically most of the time, as long as they make no serious mistakes (such as committing political gaffes or offending high-level leaders). One of the claims I often heard from these cultural workers was that it might be difficult to get a promotion, but it was also difficult to get fired. Besides, the "advantages of the system" help those who have a strong will to self-realize. That is, the system's networking and training opportunities offer these cultural workers more chances to realize themselves.

Judie Deng, discussed above, was a senior producer at SMG. Born in the late 1970s, she had worked in the television industry for more than thirteen years at the time of our correspondence. Before joining SMG in 2015, she had worked at Sichuan Television, another provincial TV station based in Sichuan Province in western China. Judie was a talented television producer and was strongly motivated to realize her creative potential. After being at SMG for just half a year, she was selected out of thousands of employees to be one of fifteen participants in the company's British Class. During the interview, she told me she wanted to create a new-media program on women's issues in contemporary China. But she also emphasized that, rather than providing criticism under the flag of feminism, she would have preferred to record Chinese women's lives and situations by means of new media. Her desire to be seen as "truly recording rather than criticizing" was actually an intentional self-censorship strategy that Judie adopted to balance her own creative pursuit with the regulatory system of Chinese cultural production: "I will do [self-censoring] spontaneously. After graduating from college, I worked in a newspaper office. From the very beginning, I've known what the 'correct value orientation' is, very clearly. I won't go off course" (Judie Deng, SMG, TV producer).

Judie's self-censorship showed great awareness and a sense of necessity. In her previous career at Sichuan TV, she had produced many programs on ethnic-minority issues, including Tibetan culture and society. Dealing with these topics, she had to carefully thematize the footage under secure and "positive" subjects, such as love, education, and social improvement. Otherwise, the social issues caused by the CCP's ethnic policies would be scarcely investigated.

To realize her creative goals, Judie chose to move from Sichuan to Shanghai. The new workplace seemed to offer her certain opportunities, such as the training program and the lenient high-level leaders. In return, she continued to obey the rules of the system, accepting and conducting self-censorship. Unfortunately, Judie could not realize her career goals in her current company. As the largest media corporation in Shanghai, SMG has more than thirteen subsidiaries. The bureaucratic problems I noted before also agitated Judie. Although she extolled the creative and open mindedness of SMG's high-level leadership, she was scathing about the working environment at the subcompany for which she worked, both regarding her leader and her employees. She scolded her direct leader as an "old Shanghai woman," a phrase that nonnative Shanghai residents often use to express their irritation at middle-aged Shanghai women whom they see as unkind, jealous, or greedy. As Judie complained, "We have different expectations. She only cares about her wallet and even worries about me replacing her" (Judie Deng, SMG, TV producer). As for her employees, she thought they were unprofessional and unmotivated after confronting the nepotism and inefficiency of the employment system. During the interview, Judie repeatedly stated her aspiration to work with like-minded people, such as those she had encountered in London. She spoke of a member of a devoted British film crew: "You can see in his eyes the deep and persistent love for his work. I really like these kinds of people. I love that atmosphere, and I really wish my colleagues could be like that. But they aren't."

Overall, Judie was upset about her current work situation, but rather surprisingly, she blamed all her problems on herself: "I often tell myself, the reason why you're always working with these kinds of people is because you're not doing well enough." Instead of complaining, Judie chose to work harder in order to improve herself and to prepare for new opportunities. Intriguingly, during the interviews, most of my informants appeared quite accepting of censorship. What bothered them was the bureaucracy involved in the practice of censorship and everyday regulations, rather than the fact that censorship existed. As Jiang Tao summarized, "All forms of mass media have their own value orientation, which is reflected in what you call censorship. Since we chose to join the company, we should adhere to its shared value" (Jiang Tao, Company A, journalist).

Among motivated employees such as Judie Deng and Jiang Tao, their working benefits make the state system an ideal workplace for creative labor. In the private industries, similar jobs are usually quite precarious. These state-employed creatives thus need to conduct self-censorship. Judie's desire to realize her career goals prompted her to resign from Sichuan TV and join SMG, as well as to censor her creativity to align with party ideology. Echoing Yiu Fai Chow's analysis of "hope" in his study of Diana Zhu, creative workers' aspiration toward self-realization in Chinese state media is also "constructed, circulated and transformed to serve the interests of the state and the capital" (Chow 2011, 787). Importantly, this aspiration to self-realization often motivates them to self-censor and thus self-govern in a way that conforms to the party state's expectation of cooperative, creative subjectivities: being creative for the state. With the introduction of the market-oriented system reform, Chinese SOCEs have developed a governance of creative workers through bio-power, exercised through the various welfare provisions that attract those aspiring to self-realize.

Loafing on the Job, Multitasking, and Resigning

Not everyone within the system is as motivated as Judie. As I will show in this section, the various bureaucracy and autonomy problems of the state-sponsored system and its discourse of self-realization can easily lose their attractiveness for creative workers.

Loafing on the Job

As an executive assistant to the CEO of a subsidiary company of Anhui Television Group, Robin's job required both administrative work and planning television production. Before being employed by Anhui TV, he had worked at another provincial state-owned media firm. When asked to compare the two companies, he asserted, "Now I think, to be honest, they're not so different. For example, if we have a hundred employees in each company, the previous one might have seventy-five members loafing on the job, while my current company has maybe seventy."

Slacking off seems to be a common problem in Chinese SOCEs. Many employees *hun rizi* (混日子), a Chinese term that literally means "dawdle the day away" and is used to describe employees who are unmotivated and lazy on the job. This phenomenon has been reported significantly more often in SOCEs than in private companies. For instance, Wang Hai, a former senior HR manager for the leading Chinese private internet company Tencent, shared that they had designed a recruiting and evaluation system. In this system, job applicants and employees were evaluated not only based on their professional skills and performance but also on their moral standards—including loyalty to work and the company (Wang Hai, Tencent, HR manager). The problem of loafing on the job in SOCEs seems to be related to workers' mindsets. As Judie also noted about her colleagues, "A very serious problem is their attitude. Because we work in a state-owned company, their favored manner of working is a nine-to-five schedule . . . they have no passion for work. None at all!" (Judie Deng, SMG, TV producer).

The unmotivated include older employees who have worked at a company for many years and have reached the "glass ceiling" of their career. Given their age and the hierarchy within the system, they can see very few opportunities for promotion. The favorable welfare system and the restrictions on autonomy also deter them from self-expression and learning new skills.

Another group of unmotivated employees is *guanxi hu* (关系户), a Chinese phrase that refers to those who have strong connections with the high-level leaders in a company or the government. They are employed for their closeness to the leadership, regardless of their personal abilities and skills. While self-realization means something to Judie, it has little attraction for these "unmotivated cultural workers." They are typically cynical about the meaning of work and don't aspire to be self-expressive or creative. Significantly, however, nobody will overtly acknowledge that they are loafing on the job. During my interviews, my respondents always described this phenomenon as "a defect of others": a misbehavior that was bad, irresponsible, and shameful within the current "work culture."

Loafing on the job thus represents a way for unmotivated cultural workers to disengage, at least mentally, from their everyday work. In doing so, they unwittingly distance themselves from the subjectivity of "being creative for the state." The presence of a large number of these "loafers" negatively affects the productivity of Chinese SOCEs; their loafing circumscribes their capacity to produce creative cultural content, further exacerbates the problem of bureaucracy, and ends up restricting the productivity of these companies as part of the state propaganda machine. As a result, Chinese state media must collaborate with private production companies and change their business model. For example, in the television industries, most state television companies have developed a "commissioning system" that outsources their content production to private companies such as Canxing Production (Sun 2011). In doing so, their previous role as the omnipotent supplier of mass culture has been transformed into being a media platform and financial investor in China's cultural industries.

The phenomenon of loafing on the job reflects the dysfunction of the self-realization discourse and reveals a contradiction inherent to the state-sponsored cultural system. From the above analyses of autonomy and self-realization, it is clear that the creativity *dispositif* in the case of Chinese SOCEs consists of both repressive, disciplinary elements (such as rigid censorship, hierarchy, and bureaucracy) and a bio-political discourse of self-realization. The demand for "double responsibility" makes the autonomy of creative labor within the system quite "contingent," while the system expects its creative workers to "be creative for the state" under the discourse of self-realization. In practice, however, as the case of loafing on the job illustrates, the system causes a marked contradiction. This contradiction disturbs the effectiveness of the self-realization discourse and furnishes creative people with opportunities to distance themselves from the expected subjectivity of "being creative for the state."

Multitasking

The second form of deviation from the expected subjectivity of "being creative for the state" in Chinese state-owned cultural enterprises is multitasking. Many researchers have acknowledged the increasing popularity of multitasking and multiskilling among young creative laborers in the West, especially young, creative freelancers (Ursell 2000; Jeffcutt and Pratt 2002; McRobbie 2011, 2016). Multitasking has become an inevitable consequence for workers in the creative industries to combat precarious working conditions such as short-term contracts, unequal pay, and unpredictable working times. For employees of Chinese state-owned cultural enterprises, multitasking is also a widespread choice that is not simply fueled by workplace precarity. Instead, I regard it as a form of struggle against the existing power relations within these companies. Apart from the jobs they are assigned by their company, some state employees also privately undertake creative activities for specific objectives. These activities are carried out not for the company or for the state but for the creative workers themselves, meaning that these activities are not publicly supported or encouraged by the companies. I divide this multitasking into two categories: commercial *zouxue* and *private production*.[6]

Zouxue is a Chinese adage that refers to moonlighting—performing in unofficial venues for extra income without approval from one's employer. This phenomenon has been popular for many years among state employees. It is not restricted to cultural workers but also occurs among other professionals including athletes, medical practitioners, and university professors. In the cultural sector, creative workers—on the strength of their fame and popularity—often engage in lucrative activities and seek extra income through endorsements and commercial performances. As Even Yong disclosed, these earnings often considerably exceed the salary they receive from their state-owned employer, making *zouxue* a favorable "hidden rule" among state-employed cultural workers (Even Yong, SMG, manager). The authorities, of course, do not support these moonlighting activities, which in some cases are prohibited; for example, according to Carl, the staff members at the News Channel of CCTV were not allowed to engage in *zouxue* (Carl, CCTV, manager).

Obviously, moonlighting outside the system will undermine the expected duty of these state cultural employees, which is to be creative for the state. Moonlighting requires a temporarily separation from both the protection and the supervision of the system. This lack of supervision brings unpredictable risks for the operation of a state company. For example, "vulgar" commercial events will tarnish the state cultural workers' reputation and thus be detrimental to the party's image. For individual workers, however, *zouxue* is a temporary escape from the system—an opportunity to enjoy the ease and freedom of work not designed to support the state, as well as abundant monetary rewards.

Working outside the system can also bring back a sense of superiority of being a "grandpa" (Wang 2006, 161–62). This emotional reward can partly compensate for the depressive feelings caused by the hierarchy and apathy within the company.

The other variant of multitasking is more personalized and implicit, sometimes even subversive. *Private production* is usually performed by cultural workers who share more idealistic or critical sentiments about work and society. By exploiting the benefits of their current positions and companies, the objective is not merely to earn more money but to also achieve personal expression and produce documentation. Private production could involve people creating diaries of intellectuals within the system, taking unpublished photographs of an official photographer, or recording a television director's nonpublic clips from a documentary. Well-known examples of private production include the secretive diary of the main character in George Orwell's *1984* (Winston Smith) and the historical writings of retired Chinese journalist Yang Jisheng (Yang 2000, 2004, 2008). As the next chapter will show, the early generation of independent Chinese documentary directors were mostly employees of state-owned television stations, which provided them with the professional equipment and networks necessary to make highly critical visual cultural productions.

Liu Kang is a renowned photographer in China. Now over sixty, he used to work as a senior press photographer for *People's Daily*, an official newspaper of the CCP. After retiring, he became a photo adviser for the Press Office of the Chinese State Council. In addition to creating propaganda for the state, he has also completed photography projects—such as the life story of his parents and of Chinese rural society—during breaks between formal work assignments. Forty years later, these unsanctioned photographs—unwanted and useless at the beginning, in the eyes of his colleagues and employers—have made Liu Kang a huge success. *My Father and My Mother*, Liu Kang's widely acclaimed magnum opus, is a sprawling photography and documentary project about the thirty-year life stories of Liu Kang's parents. This project, as shared by Liu during our interview, was originally created by Liu Kang privately during intervals in his routine work. He wished to present the lives of his parents' generation in Chinese rural society and to show their devotion to their family and children.

As a state-recognized photographer, Liu Kang receives considerable resources and support from the central and local authorities, which in return contribute to his own individual, more reflexive creation. As he told me:

> I shoot everything, inclusively. I'll cut a version that they [the government] want. But even in this version, I'll still add something I want to show, seeking a balance without touching the red line, of course. Because I'm an established director, they'll give me some personal space; otherwise they can simply ask some unknown to do this [work]. Besides, I'll make a longer and more personalized edition that includes everything. [My work] can stay in my personal collection, and I'll wait for the right time to screen it or send it to foreign film festivals. (Liu Kang, photographer)

For creative workers such as Liu Kang, this type of multitasking is an active struggle against the subjectification enforced by state-controlled cultural workplaces. Although not a complete subversion or refusal of the current regulative structure, this type of multitasking attempts to restore the political thrust of cultural work. In doing so, Liu Kang distances himself from the subjectivity of the state artist and instead identifies himself with writers and painters, who for him are the ones responsible for recording social change. Through a distancing from the subjectivity of being creative for the state, multitasking thus arguably enables a new form of subjectivity to emerge: being creative for the self and the social. Although not everyone who works inside the system can behave like Liu Kang, his case demonstrates that the creative labor of those working for China's SOCEs is not necessarily completely depoliticized or totally under the party state's ideological control.

Resigning

If loafing on the job and multitasking show the disengagement of state employees from the governance of the Chinese SOCEs, then resigning—as the examples I mentioned at the beginning of this chapter show—can also be seen as evidence of the dysfunction of the state system. For SOCEs like CCTV, labor turnover certainly entails taking a loss, especially when most of the resigning employees are experienced and skilled.

For those who have resigned, leaving seems to entail an overt rejection of the problematic working conditions at a company such as CCTV. "You should know, freedom is a sublime value," Carl told me (Carl, CCTV, manager). He worked at CCTV's chief editorial department before becoming the financial councilor of a new-media company in 2015. In terms of subjectivity, we can argue that resignation constitutes a refusal to be creative for the state.

The resignation of established employees from state companies to work at private firms also has an exemplary effect on junior staff members, who often lack the resources and opportunities and thus the nerve to resign. As Lily stressed in our interview, "Personally, it's impossible for me to stay here [at CCTV] for ten or twenty years, as my parents' generation did. Once I accumulate enough of a social network and working experience, I'll definitely get out to do something I prefer" (Lily Yang, CCTV, producer).

As a result, SOCEs have become a stepping stone for creative workers, especially those who desire self-realization. When the quitting of experienced workers becomes frequent, it will lower the company's productivity and decrease the effectiveness of its ideological propaganda. When asked to compare his current job with his previous experience at CCTV, Carl explained:

> I think they're really different. At CCTV, we have too many shackles, which refers to not just censorship but also to too much interference from the leaders. Now we have much more autonomy, though we still need to be concerned with "content appropriateness," which is not really a problem. If I think something might be too sensitive, then I'll just cut it. We don't need to behave like servants anymore.

The improved workplace autonomy on offer elsewhere often persuades CCTV employees to resign. Although the employees in question are mostly still motivated creative workers, they have been frustrated by the bureaucratic system of Chinese SOCEs. To leave for private industries is to decamp for a more autonomous workplace that will revive, at least to some degree, the joyfulness attached to creative labor.

From loafing on the job to multitasking to resignation, these empirical cases demonstrate the inherent contradictions and dysfunction of the governance system of Chinese SOCEs. These contradictions not only limit the governance and productivity of Chinese SOCEs; they also furnish creative people with possibilities to distance themselves from the expected subjectivity of "being creative for the state." In the process, these state-hired cultural workers develop their bilateral subjectivities, driven by diverse career motivations, individual interests, and their perceived cultural/social/professional ethics, while they are also constantly controlled and pulled by the state's expectation of being creative for the state.

Conclusion

This chapter has examined creative labor and worker subjectivity in Chinese state-owned cultural companies. First, I have shown that in Chinese SOCEs the governance of creativity and creative labor is conducted through neoliberal techniques, such as the discourse of "self-realization" and an autonomous managerial setting. The Chinese state's concerns about ideology and cultural control also require repressive and disciplinary regulation, as shown by how the censorship and problematic autonomy among SOCEs demand a bureaucratic management system.

Second, this managerial arrangement in return limits the functionality of the discourse of autonomy and self-realization, thus creating a contradiction within the system that can limit the efficiency of governance and cultural production in Chinese SOCEs. The governance of creative work in Chinese SOCEs constitutes a "schizophrenic" system that, as I explained in the introduction, promotes and commodifies individual creativities and autonomy while also constantly circumscribing them because they threaten the order and stability of the system. As a result, a significant number of employees of Chinese SOCEs are unmotivated and resort to loafing on the job. Others who remain motivated creative workers decide to multitask or simply choose to resign and join private creative businesses. In Chinese state-owned media companies, then, the governing system and the process of subjectivation are not always as expected by the state; the system also furnishes creative people with possibilities to distance themselves from the expected subjectivity of "being creative for the state."

Finally, echoing what I suggested in the book's introduction, the study of Chinese SOCEs reinforces the need for creative-labor studies to consider the different sociopolitical contexts worldwide. These contexts may produce diverse modes of creative-labor relations. For example, thanks to working benefits, creative labor among Chinese SOCEs may not be as precarious as it is in the Western context, where the fetishization of individual creativity has "corroded efforts to unionize and collectivize in order to offset inequalities and exploitation" (Banks 2007). But if the precarity of labor is a factor that leads to "bad cultural work" (Hesmondhalgh and Baker 2011), then we cannot simply view the not-so-precarious work within Chinese SOCEs as a form of "good work," as this would discount the limited autonomy and bureaucracy of such work. Rather, we should account for different sociopolitical specialties and perceive creative labor as a "historically and geographically situated process, or processes, that can challenge more affirmative and proselytizing industry and academic perspectives" (Banks, Gill, and Taylor 2013, 6). As the following chapters will continue to illustrate, grasping the experiences of creative labor in contemporary China and illustrating the complexities of governance and subjectivity in the cultural economies require an approach that goes beyond reductionist theorization based on a dominant Euro-American perspective.

3

From Independent to Art Film and Back Again

I wasn't very good at my subject, and I was treated like a freak. I felt at odds with the whole environment in college. But after encountering film, ah . . . suddenly I found a way of expressing myself. I knew then that I must do it.
—Jian Haodong, filmmaker

Introduction

On July 16, 2016, the documentary *The Big Screen of Nobody* was aired on CCTV. It tells the story of a young director named Jian Haodong from rural Shanxi, a province located in northern China that is famous for its rich coal resources and for the devastating environmental impact of the mining industry. What intrigues me about Jian's story is how he managed to gather money to make his film *Eyes Cheat* (2015). In 2014, after receiving a diploma in coal mining from the local college, Jian, like many of his classmates, got a job in a coal mine near his hometown. Even on his very first day, he struck the other miners as different, and he told them that he wanted to be a film director. After fifteen months of hard work, he had successfully earned 50,000 RMB (7,479 USD), money he put toward making *Eyes Cheat*. The film does not resemble today's mainstream Chinese movies. Lacking martial arts, romantic plots, or any other commercial clichés, it is about a blind old man who loses his job in the city and ends up feeling alienated again after returning to his countryside home. Based on Jian's own experiences and observations in his hometown, the film tackles serious social problems: corrupt local officials, cowardly villagers, and the fast-changing rural Chinese society. The film's low-budget production, rough filmic quality, and the critical topics it addressed characterize *Eyes Cheat* as an independent Chinese film. In 2015, it competed in several film festivals, including the Beijing

Independent Film Festival (BIFF), the South Taiwan Film Festival, and the Chinese Independent Film Festival (CIFF). Afterward, Jian moved to Beijing, rented a small, cheap apartment on the outskirts of the city, and started his filmmaking career. From being a coal miner to becoming an independent Chinese filmmaker, he achieved an astonishing transformation in terms of work, identity, and life. This story leads me to ask some basic questions concerning independent Chinese filmmaking as a special form of creative labor. Why do people like Jian choose to make independent films? What does the adjective "independent" mean for filmmaking and filmmakers in China? What insights can independent Chinese filmmaking offer to creative labor and the subjectivities it produces?

Guided by these questions, in this chapter I examine independent Chinese filmmaking as a form of creative labor. Most existing studies on the Chinese film industry and independent cinema focus on the films' aesthetics and politics. Case studies are mostly limited to influential films made by established filmmakers—earlier documentary directors such as Wu Wenguang and Duan Jinchuan, as well as "Sixth Generation" auteurs such as Jia Zhangke and Lou Ye (Dai 2000; Lu 2003; Berry and Farquhar 2006; Jiang 2012; Robinson 2013; Wang 2014). In the few valuable studies of independent Chinese filmmaking, scholars have investigated issues such as the political economy of independent Chinese film production, the implications of globalization, the micropower relations within the indie filmmaking community, and domestic and overseas distribution (Pickowicz 2006; Zhang 2007; Sniadecki 2013; Nakajima 2016). These studies have revealed that independent Chinese filmmaking, compared with "main melody" and "commercial" film production,[1] is a low-budget, politically sensitive, artistically avant-garde endeavor whose creators seek relative autonomy and critical thinking (Berry and Rofel 2010). Independent filmmaking thus scores high in cultural capital in the field of Chinese film production (Nakajima 2016). Exemplified by the early experiences of the Sixth Generation directors, independent Chinese films that use digital technology often address social issues in contemporary China (Zhang 2007). Claiming to speak "truth" by using either documentary or fiction[2] (Zhang 2007), these filmmakers sometimes violate the "propaganda and education" function assigned to film by the Chinese authorities and thus can experience difficulty avoiding censorship. Such political uncertainty makes these films difficult to get financed domestically while bringing independent Chinese filmmakers cultural capital and "cultural prestige" (Nakajima 2016, 97) among both international and Chinese audiences.

This clear-cut image of independent Chinese filmmaking has been blurred by the rapid commercialization and globalization of Chinese cinema over the past two decades. Surging box office sales have made China the world's second-largest film market after the United States, paralleling its rise as the world's second-largest economy (Yin and Sun 2017). While the thriving film industry has generally abided by the party state's thirst for a powerful and wealthy cultural industry, it has also required the authorities to deploy a more effective governing strategy to orchestrate Chinese cinema toward the state's needs for ideological propaganda and the accumulation of soft power (Rosen 2012). An ideal cinema for the postsocialist Chinese state should be, according to the newly enforced Chinese Film Industry Promotion Law, "Prosperous and healthy, with a normative and orderly market that upholds core socialist values and meets the spiritual needs of the Chinese people" (NPC 2016).

For independent Chinese film workers, this landscape brings both opportunities and challenges. On the one hand, the expanding film market engenders more space for independent films. As I will show in this chapter, domestic commercial film companies have started to invest in and support independent filmmaking, usually under the umbrella of the "art film" (*yishu dianying* 艺术电影) genre—referring to artistic, less politically sensitive films. On the other hand, those who used to be "independents" now have a more conciliatory relationship with the state and the commercial film industry (Nakajima 2016). Some established independents (for example Sixth Generation directors such as Jia Zhangke and Lou Ye) now make films with the "dragon mark" (*long biao* 龙标)—an official screening permission (*gongying xuke zheng* 公映许可证) issued by the Chinese Film Bureau—and benefit from large budgets provided by international and domestic film companies.[3]

This chapter investigates the subjectivity of independent Chinese filmmakers from a perspective of creative-labor studies. I view independent Chinese filmmaking as a form of creative work in order to study indie filmmakers' aspirations, forms of self-governance, and moments when they "become bilateral." Most current research follows the conceptual framework of Bourdieu and views independent Chinese filmmaking as a special "field" of cultural production; such commentators generalize the political economy of Chinese indie filmmaking and the "habitus" of Chinese indie directors. In doing so, they often attribute general categories or identities to these filmmakers, at the price of neglecting their distinctiveness. This scenario explains the current terminological ambiguities surrounding terms such as "independence," "independent film," and "Chinese independents," since any given definition runs the risk of overlooking the differences among the subjects indicated (Tzioumakis 2006; Berry and Rofel 2010; Jiang 2012; Sniadecki 2013). Without getting mired in these terminological debates, in this chapter I take up the notion of "independence" as a discourse that is frequently claimed and practiced by creative workers within the sphere of Chinese filmmaking. At the same time, I aim to highlight the differences between those who claim to be "independents," with the insistence that each subject has distinctive aspirations and experiences.

Unlike those who work at state-owned cultural enterprises, as explored in the previous chapter, independent Chinese filmmakers lack protection from the system (*tizhi* 体制). Their work is emblematic of the "precariat," characterized by insecure, flexible, and uncertain labor in the post-Fordist economy (Standing 2016). Inspired by Isabel Lorey's analysis of precarity and precarization (2015), this chapter illuminates three questions. First, why do Chinese people aspire to "independence" and "independent filmmaking"? Second, how is "independent filmmaking" governed in practice, and what is the impact of the governance on the filmmakers' subjectivity? Third, under this governing system, where can we locate the individual agency of these "independents," and what does this agency entail and enable in terms of "being creative"?

After a brief summary of current theoretic debates on precarity and precarization, followed by an introduction of the empirical material this chapter engages with, I will delve into the aspirations that drive filmmakers' choice to work in independent film. Based on an analysis of the stories I collected from three research informants, I suggest that their discontent with living conditions and institutions—such as education, the political culture, and commercial modes of production—is what motivated them to choose independent filmmaking. Subsequently, the chapter illustrates how independent Chinese filmmaking is precarized through forms of governmentality, and the impact that has on filmmakers' subjectivity.

Finally, based on my fieldwork, I suggest that the current process of precarization has also established an informal community of mutual caring based on difference, which combats the precarity of independent Chinese cinema. Animated by a shared aspiration to independence and freedom, such a community not only helps alleviate living and work pressures by offering opportunities for screenings, learning skills, and emotional sharing and caring but also elicits a more open understanding of "independence" and "independent filmmaking," which makes resisting the creative subjectivity promoted by the existing power relations possible. From discontented independents to art filmmakers who embrace spiritual independence, these independent Chinese filmmakers have become bilateral creative workers.

Precarity, Precarization, and Independent Chinese Filmmaking

When looking back over the last three decades of socioeconomic transformation, a similarity between the West and China becomes clear: many workers are increasingly employed on a precarious basis. With deregulation and the decline of unions, employment is becoming "uncertain, unpredictable, and risky from the point of view of the worker" (Kalleberg 2009, 2). In China, as documented in chapter 2, the transition from state socialism to the market-driven economy system has gradually changed the system of permanent employment. This transition is often referred to by media and researchers as the "smashing of the iron rice bowls" (Benson and Zhu 1999). From rural migrant workers (C. K. Lee 2016) to creative practitioners (Keane 2016; Matthews 2017), more of the Chinese workforce is confronting a fragile and insecure labor system, along with its risks and uncertainties.

This insecure state of work signifies a governmental precarization. According to Isabell Lorey, "Domination in post-Fordist societies is no longer legitimated through (social) security, and we instead experience governing through insecurity" (2015, 11). With the proliferation of neoliberal governmentality since the 1970s, "Precarious living and working conditions are currently being normalized at a structural level and have thus become a fundamental governmental instrument of governing" (Lorey 2015, 63). As Ching Kwan Lee (2016) illustrates in her study of precarious migrant workers in southern China, rural migrant workers have been precarized through authoritarian precarization and land dispossession. The implementation of labor law in China is heavily contingent on the changing priorities of the party state, while political limitations on workers' collective organization and activism circumscribe the effectiveness of labor law (C. K. Lee 2016). Rural migrant workers are made even more precarious by China's urban residence registration policy, which leads to unequal welfare distribution.

In the process of precarization, as Lorey suggests, a new form of governmentality becomes entangled with an "extreme degree of exploitation" and "a liberation from [the] traditional condition" of Fordist exploitation and social activism based on unions and representation (Lorey 2015, 10). Inspired by the political practice of Precarias a la Deriva (a group of feminist activists from Madrid), Lorey argues for the establishment of a care community, a form of political resistance based on "the relational difference, and the resultant possibility of what is common in differentness" (2015, 100). Lorey draws on Deleuze and Guattari's "lines of flight" (1987)[4] and Virno's conception of "exodus"[5] while remaining influenced by Foucault's thoughts on power and subjectivity. She underscores that the flight from power and reversal of control is always possible but never leads to an "outside" of power (2015, 102). As she states (2015, 103):

> The economization of the social, the coincidence of work and life, the demand for the whole person to be involved in performative-cognitive, affective labour, in other words, the capitalization of modes of subjectivation—these processes are not at all total, all-encompassing or wholly determined. . . . In uncertain, flexibilized and discontinuous working and living conditions, subjectivations arise that do not entirely correspond to the neoliberal logic of valorization, and which may resist and refuse it.

For Lorey, precarization thus implies not only subjugation; it is also "incalculable and potentially empowering" (Lorey 2015, 111). Such a claim of empowering precarization is problematic, however. First, if Lorey's argument about precarization correctly characterizes today's neoliberal governmentality, it is still generalized from the perspective of the developed Western world. What can it say to the workers in the global south, "for whom precariousness has always been a seemingly natural condition" (Munck 2013, 747)? Especially in the case of independent Chinese filmmaking, although these filmmakers are clearly precarious in terms of their insecure working conditions, the question of how and to what extent such precarity is constitutive of a state governmentality that can orchestrate Chinese indie film production and the subjectivity of indie filmmakers still needs to be answered.

Second, Lorey's claims about a care community based on differentness and the possibility of exodus from within precarization require empirical scrutiny. Without it, her generalization of precarity and precarization runs the risk of eliding the nuances of precarity in different sociopolitical contexts. What forms does precarization take in the context of Chinese cultural production, and what possibilities of exodus can their precarious life and work offer Chinese indie directors? As Ching Kwan Lee contends, "Chinese workers are confronting the global tendency of precarization, but with Chinese characteristics, just as Indian workers, Japanese workers, and South African workers confront theirs in specific institutional and political-economic contexts" (C. K. Lee 2016, 319).

Independent filmmakers in China can be viewed as a form of precarious labor characterized by insecure, flexible, and uncertain labor. Besides these general characteristics, filmmakers' claim to "independence" further aggravates their precarity by complicating their relationships with the state and capital. Their claim adds a political dimension to the supposed independence of their cultural production, which contradicts the Chinese party state's policy of censorship and ideological control. Their claim to independence also implies a struggle between filmmakers and this same precarious production system; they are precarized by capital and state control while still aspiring to independently produce films. To rephrase the questions I raised earlier, this chapter aims to investigate: 1) why people choose independent filmmaking as a career, despite its precarity; 2) what kind of precarity the filmmakers experience; and 3) how they respond to the precarity and governance of their life and work, and whether their precarious experiences are also empowering, as Lorey suggests is possible.

This chapter is based on fifteen semistructured interviews with independent Chinese film workers as well as my ethnographic observations of a film-production group named the New Wave Experimental Film Group (*xinchao dianying shiyan xiaozu* 新潮电影实验小组), or the New Wave Group for short. This group consists of ten young film-industry workers who converged in Beijing to realize their aspirations to produce independent cinema. My interviewees included both established film directors such as Wang Bing, Zhao Liang, and Zhu Rikun and young newcomers who had just started their filmmaking careers. I also interviewed several independent film producers. All ethnographic observations were conducted during my fieldwork in Beijing from July to October 2016, during which time I participated in several screenings and social events organized by independent Beijing film workers.

Independent Cinema as a Way to Counter Personal and Social Discontent

The first question I usually asked the filmmakers during my fieldwork was, "Why and how did you choose to go into independent filmmaking?" Although their answers varied according to the filmmakers' backgrounds, education, and circumstances, two common themes emerged: discontent with their previous lives and Chinese society, and a perception of filmmaking as a way to counter this discontent.

Jian and Chang Biao are both from Shanxi Province. Born in the late 1980s, they received bachelor's degrees from Datong University—a second- to third-tier Chinese institution of higher education. Jian majored in coal mining, while Chang Biao studied computer science. Jian came from a mining family, and his father and grandfather were both miners who helped him choose his major. At the time, coal mining was still considered a profession in which high risk was rewarded by a decent income. But Jian was not interested in mining. At college, he was interested in literature and photography and won several writing competitions. Later, inspired by the story of the renowned filmmaker Jia Zhangke (who is also from Shanxi Province), he decided to make *Youth without Regret*, a film adapted from a novel he wrote about student life. During the last year of his studies, Jian began to work in a coal mine in his hometown to earn money to make *Eyes Cheat*. After earning 50,000 RMB (7,479 USD), he made the film and moved to Beijing.

Chang Biao's parents advised him to study computer science, a major they were convinced would lead to a lucrative career. Similarly to Jian, however, Chang Biao had no interest in computers or programming. Since a very young age he had loved watching films and often borrowed Hong Kong action movies from DVD rental stores. After entering college, he encountered art films by Hou Hsiao-Hsien, Tsai Ming-liang, and Jia Zhangke online. During this period he met Jian, and they decided to make a film together called *Lao Shan* (牢山), about a retired coal miner living in a rural village. The pressures of graduation and job hunting interrupted Chang Biao's dream of filmmaking, however. He felt forced to prepare for the postgraduate entrance exam, as his parents believed a higher degree from a famous Chinese university might enhance his career prospects. As Chang Biao told me:

> At the time, I was struggling with pressure from my family. My parents worked so hard to support my studies, while I kept screwing around with my camera. My teachers and my classmates also blamed me for skipping too many classes. Frustrated, I started to wake up at six o'clock every day. I got motivated and went to the library, where I studied programming and English. (Chang Biao, filmmaker)

Soon, Chang Biao started to smoke, and he became depressed. After struggling for three months, he gave up on the postgraduate entrance exam, went to Beijing, and became an independent filmmaker like Jian. Both Jian and Chang Biao chose filmmaking primarily because of their discontent with the paths their families wanted them to take. Meanwhile, cinema—especially the independent low-budget kind exemplified by Jia Zhangke's early work—showed them how to turn self-expression into a future career. During the interview, Jian quoted a statement by Jia Zhangke: "Filmmaking is the way to freedom."

Within independent Chinese cinema, some directors were already experienced commercial or mainstream filmmakers before moving into independent filmmaking. Some early directors who are now established as filmmakers used to be employed by state-owned media agencies. Wu Wenguang was a journalist at Kunming Television, Duan

Jinchuan graduated from the Beijing Broadcast Institute and went to Lhasa Television in Tibet, and Jiang Yue worked at the Beijing Film Studio. During my fieldwork, Zhao Liang and Fan Jian—both widely recognized at international documentary and film festivals—also mentioned that they had previously worked for Chinese state-owned media. Personal histories of working within the system were very common among independent directors who started their careers in the 1990s (Johnson 2006; Berry 2006). In the past decade, with the expansion of the Chinese film industries and the rise of private production companies, several commercial film workers have also made independent films.

Jin Dixiang is the director of *Hua Shan Cross* (2015), a movie that was selected for the documentary category at the Twelfth Chinese Independent Film Festival and the 2016 Xining FIRST film festival. Before making this film, Jin had worked in the film industry for over ten years. He was employed by a video-advertising company, where he made commercial advertisements and internet-based short films. Frustrated by the stylized commercial photography the company favored, Jin decided to make an independent documentary about the social and familial issues he had observed in his hometown: "I was introduced to that video company after I graduated from the film academy. It was a good opportunity at the time for young graduates. But such commercial photography is very stylized, which means you might feel good at an early stage, while later on, after years of working, you'll get bored and frustrated" (Jin Dixiang, filmmaker).

Jin gave me three reasons why he had chosen to focus on independent documentary. First, in terms of financing, making documentaries costs less than making fiction films, and documentaries are also easier to shoot. Second, by self-funding he could remain free of the pressures of time and investors. Finally, he found making independent documentaries to be an enjoyable experience, compared with his previous tedious work in commercial production, in the sense that he could now film in a more "free" and "profound" way. *Hua Shan Cross* was made over seven years, during which time Jin struggled to leave behind his previous commercial way of filming. For him, becoming an independent filmmaker was a process of "learning a new cinematic language" (Jin Dixiang, filmmaker). To some extent, we may see this transition as a form of resistance to the alienation fostered by commercial filmmaking, which relates to the larger sociopolitical environment.

Rong Guangrong, an independent film curator and renowned director in Beijing's independent cinema circle, won the Best Asian Film award at the 2017 Rotterdam Film Festival. His film *Children Are Not Afraid of Death, Children Are Afraid of Ghosts* is based on a tragic 2015 news story of a group of "left-behind" children who committed suicide in Bijie, Guizhou Province.[6] The topic, which was very sensitive to the Chinese authorities, raised a plethora of social, economic, and political issues that haunted rural Chinese society. Not surprisingly, the shooting process was obstructed by the local government. After the award ceremony, Rong Guangrong and I talked about his work. In response to the question of why he had chosen to make independent films on such sensitive topics, Rong mentioned his early experiences. When he was a child, his father had several affairs and, as a result, had a bad relationship with his mother. They quarreled a lot and sometimes ended up in physical fights. In Rong's mind, his father was irresponsible and never helped his family. Rong's miserable childhood deeply affected him; he became irritable, righteous, and intolerant of unfairness. Living in Beijing, Rong also felt depressed and uncomfortable about the political and media atmosphere. Yet he still liked children. Perhaps due to the absence of his father during his childhood, Rong hoped to be a responsible father to his own children. After reading news about the suicide of the left-behind children, Rong felt suspicious about the official reports and decided to visit the village and make a documentary. In another interview conducted by local Chinese media, he also related his motivation for the film to his own childhood:

> The reason for my probing into the "kids' suicide case" has a lot to do with my childhood. Very often I don't consider myself a father, though I have three children. Since the birth of [my children], plus my own childhood memories, I think I can understand children better, be on their side, be as unreasonable, naughty, wild, and angry as they are. Children can directly express emotions, while adults only control and disguise theirs. I feel frustrated by the world of adults. (Xie 2017)

From the stories of these filmmakers' early life experiences, we can conclude that their motivation for making independent films largely derived from experiences of discontent, whether with the educational system, the tedium of commercial film production, or the patriarchal culture of Chinese society. Such a list, for different filmmakers, could be extended to themes such as the country's heteronormativity, gender inequality, and the existing political order. Independent filmmaking is desirable because people see it as an ideal method of self-expression and countering discontent.

In addition, as scholars such as Paul G. Pickowicz have pointed out, some independent filmmakers are also "busy chasing global fame (and in some cases global money)" (2006, 18). The chance to receive validation from overseas film festivals and the ensuing global fame and funds is clearly a factor in these young people's decision-making. The cultural capital that can be accumulated by showing one's films at international film festivals also offers independent Chinese directors the possibility of working with the domestic film industries to gain local recognition and economic returns. This possibility is exemplified by the case of Jia Zhangke.[7] Aspirations to fame and career success through indie filmmaking were quite common among the informants I interviewed, especially for young independents like the members of the New Wave Group. Arguably, however, their primary motivation for working in independent cinema was most often a sense of discontent. A sense of using independent filmmaking to make the world better can alleviate this discontent. As Zhao Liang explained to me at his studio in Beijing, "Of course, you always have a sense of heroism, a sense of justice. You have your justifications, and you think you're doing the right thing" (Zhao Liang, filmmaker). In their own perception, these independent filmmakers thus saw their creative work as a way to express their sense of justice while also paving the way for a successful career.

As I will show in the following section, this imagined balance between self-expression and success often translates into precarious politico-economic situations, leading some independent Chinese filmmakers to be coaxed into taking on the subjectivity of a depoliticized "Chinese art film worker."

Precarizing Independent Chinese Cinema

On the outskirts of southeast Beijing, just beyond the city's Fourth Ring Road, a group of people in their early twenties live together in a small village called South Bridge (*nan qiao* 南桥), with the hope of becoming global film auteurs like Jia Zhangke. Coming from Shanxi, Anhui, and northeast China, they are not from wealthy families; their parents are mostly farmers or migrant workers. Around 2015, after graduating from college, they gathered in Beijing and founded the New Wave Group. They chose their name, as one of the members explained to me, to indicate that they wished to make experimental and artistic films that were different from mainstream Chinese films. The group consists of ten formal members living together in shabby, tiny apartments. The monthly rent is cheap—around 800–1,500 RMB (120–180 USD)—because of the apartments' poor construction and inconvenient location. From my personal experience, it takes around two hours to get there from the city center. Even so, for young independent filmmakers like the members of the New Wave Group, it is an ideal area with very low living costs and a dynamic community. The area is inhabited mostly by migrant workers from all over the nation and has cheap grocery stores, barbershops, and restaurants. Most importantly, the experience of group living and working offers the young filmmakers a way of combating precarity.

Unlike earlier independent filmmakers such as Duan Jinchuan, Wu Wenguang, and Zhao Liang—who mostly started their careers working at state-owned television or film studios—the New Wave Group's members have little professional experience or knowledge and lacked a social network before they started making films. To alleviate financial pressure, the members developed their skills mostly through self-teaching enabled by the internet, and they worked to reduce production costs. In effect, most members have developed a particular expertise. For example, Chang Biao specializes in photography, Jian is an audio recorder, Mu Jing is an art director, and Wang Fa is an executive director. They are also all directors and scriptwriters of their own works, and they aspire to be Asian directors on the global stage. Their expertise allows them to make a living by working as crew members for commercial production teams. At the same time, they work together and help each other when someone is making their own independent film. For example, all the members volunteered to make Jian's film *Eyes Cheat* and Chang Biao's *Faded Time*.

Apart from financial precariousness, there is also a creative and affective precarity attached to independent filmmaking in contemporary Chinese cinema. As summarized by Chris Berry, since the 1990s, independent Chinese filmmakers under the influence of marketization and globalization have been governed under the aforementioned "three-legged" system (2006). State censorship demands that Chinese filmmakers conform to their ideology and bars politically critical or dissenting films from entering Chinese cinemas. Domestic capital and commercial corporations, often in complicity with the state (Zhang 2007, 72), provide financial opportunities for Chinese filmmakers only if they accept cooptation and engage in commercial filmmaking. Overseas film festivals and media, however, encourage film workers to identify themselves as "dissenting/artistic independents" by offering them opportunities for funding and screening.

This three-legged system makes politically sensitive productions increasingly difficult and marginal in the domestic market. The new Promotion Law on the Film Industry enacted in 2016 (NPC 2016) stipulates that any film must be censored and licensed before participating in overseas film festivals. Those violating the law will be fined and banned from filmmaking in China for a period of five years (NPC 2016). As a result, critical realist filmmaking is becoming increasingly precarious, not least for independent documentary filmmakers. For example, most of Zhao Liang's works, including *Petition* (2009), *Crime and Punishment* (2007), and *Return to the Border* (2005), remain banned in Mainland China. Despite his ostensible cooperation with the government in 2009—which was later deemed "cooptation" by some other independent Chinese filmmakers—Zhao Liang's later documentary *Behemoth* (2015) has yet to be screened within China.[8] The film focuses on the environmental issues and workers' miserable living conditions in the mining areas of northern China and captures the dehumanizing effects of economic development. Except for *Together*, Zhao Liang's films were all financed by overseas film festivals and cultural institutions. Although he is an established director, Zhao Liang still has financial problems, given the high costs of housing and living in Beijing: "Compared with the 1990s, I still face the pressure of surviving. Now everything's expensive. In the 1990s, the rent might be just three hundred [RMB] per month, while now it could be over ten thousand. Funding is usually gone once I've finished one project. If the new project doesn't come soon, it will be very difficult during the interim" (Zhao Liang, filmmaker).

On the other hand, the expanding domestic film market also provides more opportunities for independent cinema that is less "political" or "critical realist." This type of cinema, under the banner of the "art film," is reported to be gaining audiences in Chinese cinemas, both generating revenue and winning support from the state. These so-called art films are partly depoliticized and tend to present personal emotions through poetic visual symbols rather than clear story lines. In contrast, the art films produced by Fifth and Sixth Generation directors—such as *Red Sorghum* (Zhang Yimou, 1988), *The Pickpocket* (Jia Zhangke, 1997), and *Devils on the Doorstep* (Jiang Wen, 2000)—focus on grand topics such as the individual, China, and society in specific socio-spatial contexts. Examples of these new art films include the acclaimed *Kaili Blues* (Bi Gan, 2016) and *Crosscurrent* (Yang Chao, 2016),[9] both of which won awards at international film festivals and were licensed for public release in Mainland China. These art films are characterized by loose story lines, a poetic (and rather obscure) cinematic language, and depoliticized (or less political) context. Politically sensitive issues are deliberately avoided. As Shan Zuolong, the producer of *Kaili Blues*, told me, "Simply speaking, we are depoliticizing. This should not be viewed as bowing to censorship but is actually our intentional aesthetic choice" (Shan Zuolong, film producer). Depoliticization may not mean that filmmakers and their productions now have nothing at all to do with politics, or that their cinematic aesthetic has no political connotations at all. Rather, these new art films seek more abstract, aesthetical forms of creativity that will not directly challenge the mainstream political narratives and the social order. As Shan explained to me:

> Independent film is a transitional concept . . . now we've passed that era. Filmmakers of the previous generation had a heavy burden, like the Cultural Revolution and "society under transformation," all of which could be their source of creativity. Bi Gan [the director] is not interested in these topics. What he wants to explore is the language of film. Politics is not important for him; thus, his films will not offend the censors. (Shan Zuolong, producer)

In the minds of these filmmakers, such an approach of "art for art's sake" seems an ideal way to be creative under the three-legged system. The growing segmentation of the Chinese domestic film market and audience has opened space for these art films, while a less political focus has also lowered the risk of censorship. At the same time, their exploration of cinematic language and film as "pure art" also retains the possibility of success at overseas film festivals.

Based on my observations of these filmmakers, I can conclude that they imagine an "ideal" scenario for success as this: One scrapes together money to make a debut film, which should present one's emerging film genius and win international film festivals. After gaining such cultural capital, one can find more funding and continue chasing the dream of becoming a global auteur. Bi Gan's experience exemplifies this trajectory. He borrowed money from his teachers and friends to produce his first film. After winning the title of "Best New Director" at the Taiwan Golden Horse Film Festival in 2015, he quickly obtained fame as well as fortune. The film passed censorship and received a public release in Mainland China. Bi Gan was acclaimed by Chinese media and audiences as an emerging Chinese film master (Shao 2016). Afterward, he and his producer, Shan Zuolong, founded Dangmai Film, a production company that raised 30 million RMB (4.5 million USD) from the Chinese media corporation Huace Film (Shan Zuolong, film producer). Such success is hard to duplicate, however.

According to Yang Cheng, an experienced art film producer based in Beijing, funding for Chinese art films comes from three sources: self- or crowdfunding, domestic film companies, and overseas funding agencies (Yang Cheng, film producer). Apart from self-funding, access to these sources depends on the filmmaker's previous experience and social network. For young filmmakers such as those of the New Wave Group, funding remains elusive. After all, not every debut film can win big prizes at international film festivals, and art films can rarely achieve financial success in Chinese cinemas and attract financial investment from domestic capital. Given that China has yet to establish professional art film houses, the rate of art film screenings in Chinese cinemas remains very low compared to those of commercial blockbusters (Xingjue 2017). For art films that receive investment, such as *Crosscurrent* (Yang Chao, 2016), even box office revenues of several million RMB (a few hundred thousand USD) could not cover its production costs.

To seize the limited opportunities for future success, the young independent filmmakers of the New Wave Group had to learn "self-emotional management" to keep an optimistic and positive mentality when confronting their career uncertainties and precarious conditions. They first needed to persuade themselves that their current position was the most rational choice. As Jian announced:

> These problems are real. But for me, I don't have any other choices right now. I don't have a rich family. But I like cinema, and I feel delighted with my work. Most importantly, after several years of experience, I think I have the talent as a film director. I'm learning very fast, and I feel like I'm good at it. I don't know anything else that I can do. So even now if someone offered me a decent job that has no connection to film, I wouldn't accept. (Jian Haodong, filmmaker)

Members of the New Wave Group also shared a sense of optimism about their uncertain future. They liked to talk about the success of other independent directors, discussing who had gotten a new car or bought an apartment. They did not conceal their aspiration to fame and fortune, and the thriving Chinese film industry instilled them with confidence: "The Chinese film market is so active, and it's getting more open. Art film can enter cinemas, and the audience is also promoting its own aesthetic tastes. This is an opportunity . . . we all have a strong mind. It just takes a little while to get through those highly depressing moments, which after all are very rare as well" (Wang Fa, filmmaker).

Independent Chinese filmmakers are confronted with scarce and highly competitive financial opportunities offered by overseas film festivals. But independent films are largely excluded from the ostensible "golden era" of the Chinese film industry. This three-legged system corroborates Isabell Lorey's suggestion in her book *The State of Insecurity* that "precarious living and working conditions are currently being normalized at a structural level and have thus become a fundamental governmental instrument of governing" (2015, 63). In an ontological sense, all human beings are born with a certain precariousness. Following Judith Butler, their survival always depends on a "social network of hands," and one's life is always lived in relation to others (Butler 2009, 14). Such a shared ontological precariousness, because of its demand for care and protection, and because "all protection and all care maintain vulnerability" (Lorey 2015, 20), finally relates to the social and political dimension of precarity, which results in "hierarchizing precarity" (Lorey 2015, 21). This term refers to the sociopolitical classification and differentiation of bodies, as well as which decisions are to be protected and which can be left insecure, or without care.

In the field of Chinese film production, a crucial strategy of governance is thus to govern independent filmmakers by differentiating and classifying them as "underground," "dissenting," or "rebellious." "Dissenting" filmmakers are stigmatized by being described as threatening the stability and security of the nation because of their critical views toward the government and society. Their lives should remain precarious and even be made unlivable. For those art film producers who are still willing to accept the tactic of "depoliticization," their vulnerable lives are protected by the opportunities created by the complicity between the state, the market, and (to some extent) overseas film festivals. But such protection is far from sufficient because opportunities are limited and highly competitive. A contingency of precarity must remain to ensure that degradation into subversive dissent or insurrection will never happen. Managing this "threshold of precarity," using Lorey's term, is what makes up the "art of governing" (Lorey 2015) in today's independent Chinese cinema.

To summarize, independent Chinese filmmakers are governed in the current three-legged system through three forms of precarity: financial, creative, and affective. The resulting precarization moves independent Chinese cinema toward a depoliticized "art cinema," while filmmakers have to self-govern themselves through multitasking, networking, and self-emotional management in order to maintain a sense of optimism about their future. As explained in this book's introduction, this precarization and depoliticization of Chinese indie cinema constitute an active process of deterritorialization and reterritorialization of independent filmmakers. Motivated by their shared discontent with life and society, they are attracted to the cultural value of independent film, which prompts them to escape the cultural, social, and political codes they feel are entrapping them. The critical and rebellious spirit and aesthetics of their early films are meant to directly challenge the established ideological order. In response, however, the three-legged system constantly attempts to reterritorialize these "independents" into the "depoliticized art cinema" by precarizing their life and working experiences while limiting their career opportunities. If independent Chinese cinema is made governable through such precarious reterritorializing, then how do filmmakers from diverse backgrounds respond to this precarity and governance? Based on the experiences of independent filmmakers, how can we understand their embodied subjectivities, and to what extent are they becoming bilateral creatives?

A Community Based on Difference

In early February 2017, the independent Chinese film director Cong Feng was diagnosed with acute pancreatitis and sent to a hospital. After the news spread, independent filmmakers in Beijing quickly lined up to offer assistance. Famous figures such as Li Xianting and Liu Bing helped arrange his hospital stay and treatment. The news also garnered attention from fans and supporters of independent Chinese film. For example, in one of the WeChat groups I joined named the Lantern Cine-Club—an independent film-screening club in Beijing—an organizer named Guo Xiaodong successfully raised over 5,000 RMB (748 USD) for Cong Feng within three days.[10]

Besides offering mutual assistance in emergency circumstances, independent filmmakers in Beijing seem to have formed a mutual-caring community in their everyday work and life. An informal community of independent filmmakers provide each other with everything from technical assistance during filming to promotional activities after production. For young newcomers such as the members of the New Wave Group, this community provides opportunities for learning, screening films, and interacting with the audience. For instance, from August to the end of September of 2016, during my fieldwork, the Lantern Cine-Club organized ten events in which experimental films made by young graduates and filmmakers were screened. Held in small cafés and cinemas, these events created stages for newly graduated film-industry workers to share their works with audiences. These screening events and film clubs function as part of the production field, encouraging the "prosumption" of independent Chinese cinema, as suggested by Nakajima (2012). The events help promote independent Chinese film among domestic audiences while also providing occasions for networking among investors, producers, and indie directors. This informal community even has its own film festivals, such as the aforementioned Beijing Independent Film Festival and the China Independent Film Festival. These festivals, although also precarious in terms of financing and their relationship with the government, provide good opportunities for Chinese independent/art filmmakers to build their careers.

In the case of the New Wave Group, for instance, both Jian and Chao Biao have shared their films at screening events and domestic film festivals. Through these events, they met indie directors and producers who later became their friends and brought them "multitasking" (as discussed in chapter 2) and funding opportunities. During the making of his film *Faded Time*, Chang Biao was also working as a photographer for other film crews he had met in Beijing, to earn money for filming as well as his basic livelihood. Three years later, after finishing the production, he was given screening opportunities by several film clubs. With the help of established directors and indie film workers such as Hao Jie and Guo Xiaodong, he also got a contract from the leading Chinese art film production company Blackfin. Since 2015, the company has successfully produced several Chinese indie films, including *Kaili Blues* (2016) and *Free and Easy* (2016). In a WeChat conversation in 2018, Chang Biao told me that *Faded Time* would be submitted to the Locarno Festival and that he had just started a new art film project titled *Unknown Time*, financed by Blackfin and several other production companies.

The informal mutual-caring community outlined above can be primarily viewed as a spontaneous response to the precarious circumstances of Chinese indie film production, especially in terms of securing financing and good career prospects. A more complex question, however, is whether the creative and affective precarity I illustrated earlier also involves precarization as a form of reterritorializing. Are possibilities for resistance also generated from the forming of this community? How do these possibilities lead to the formation of bilateral subjectivity shared by these filmmakers?

In 2011, before the opening of the sixth Beijing Independent Film Festival, Zhu Rikun, the former CEO and artistic director of BIFF, resigned, left Beijing, and moved to the United States. One reason for his departure, as Sniadecki's (2013) ethnography shows, was his aggressive[11] and oppositional approach to operating the BIFF. According to Li Xianting, the founder and a major benefactor of the BIFF, Zhu's stance exacerbated tensions between the festival and the state, thus transforming the indie filmmaking community into a "small clique" (2013, 170). Instead, Li Xianting preferred a more conciliatory way of dealing with the state to make the BIFF and independent Chinese cinema more open and inclusive. Years later, when I asked Zhu for his current attitude toward Chinese indie film festivals and his own previous work, he replied:

> Doing these things [curating indie film festivals] will bring as much harm as good. It's hard to explain. Metaphorically, I was very much into poetry when I was at college, and I tried to help classmates who had the same interest. But now these classmates have become bureaucrats, party members. And the experience of writing poetry becomes something for them to boast about: "I like writing poetry, and I'm a literate official." (Zhu Rikun, filmmaker)

As Zhu implies, the field of independent Chinese film production has arguably allowed many film workers, especially young directors such as the members of the New Wave Group, to accrue cultural capital that benefits their future careers. If they treat independent filmmaking as a job through which they also must make a livelihood, then these filmmakers have to adopt a practical approach to their larger social, economic, and political circumstances. They must be willing to negotiate with the state, the market, and society. For Zhu, this is an unacceptable cooptation, even though for many others who remain active in the circle, being practical does not equate to a complete surrender to the state or capital; depoliticization also cannot simply be denounced as cooptation or a complete escape from being political. In the preface to the Thirteenth Chinese Independent Film Festival, Yang Cheng, the artistic director, notes:

> The "independence" of "independent film" is an absolute parameter worth pursuing. It points to "freedom" . . . but "independent film" as a term, a form of specific existence, cannot live without relativity. It needs some references to test, to determine its connotation and extension. Any simplistic either-or definition is unreliable; it's too easy to camouflage. In

> this sense, Chinese independent cinema still confronts a complicated situation, both inside and outside, but it is far from being tougher than ever. For true filmmakers, words like "hardship" and "perseverance" should be superfluous . . . "survival first" is still our motto . . . the so-called new choice does not mean choosing whether to continue being independent or not, but considering what "the new independence" is within independent film . . . "postindependence" does not exist. The perception of the world, the questioning of the self, and the exploration of film should be without bounds; therefore, each era is the "era before independence." (Yang Cheng, film producer)

For Yang Cheng, a relative understanding of independence does not call for absolute independence from the influence of capital and the state. Rather, such a relative understanding demands an independence that seeks "critical thought and independent spirit expressed in a work" (Cheung 2007). This spiritual independence points to "freedom" only in a relative sense. For reasons of survival in a precarious environment, independent filmmakers must compromise and adapt their artistic efforts and political initiatives. In this sense, absolute independence—what Yang Cheng terms "postindependence"—does not exist. Compared with mainstream filmmaking, however, the significance of independent Chinese filmmaking is embodied in its goal of seeking the freedom of choosing how to perceive the world, question the self, and explore the medium of film. Following Yang, independent Chinese film is characterized by the pursuit of relative independence and freedom, rather than its relationship with the state or to capital.

In independent Chinese cinema, precarization as governmentality largely limits filmmakers from pursuing independence and freedom in their everyday production practice. But even under conditions of precarization, the "spiritual independence" asserted by Yang Cheng is valued and adhered to by those who identify themselves as "independents." They are becoming what I have termed "bilateral creatives," in the sense that their creative labor, on the one hand, is integrated into the larger governing system of cultural production in China. The informal networks among these filmmakers are by no means completely free or equal. The hierarchy between established film workers and younger, emerging ones is obvious in this filmic *jianghu* (江湖), which literally means "rivers and lakes," referring to the world (Sniadecki 2013). Independent labor is also highly gendered, as most of the filmmakers I encountered during my fieldwork—as well as those observed by other scholars (Sniadecki 2013; Robinson 2013)—were Chinese men. Chang Biao, for example, shared with me that his girlfriend, who was a schoolteacher in his home city, provided financial support for his poor living conditions in Beijing.

In the pursuit and identification of limited and "spiritual" independence, on the other hand, independent Chinese filmmaking does open the possibility of "exodus and constituting," of "leaving and starting something new" (Lorey 2015, 104). Similarly, the practical understanding of independence and independent film signifies an agentic refusal of simplistic, fixed identifications as "dissenting artist," "underground filmmaker," and "coopted" state/commercial director.

Conclusion

As this chapter has illustrated, independent film-industry workers often choose their professional paths to balance their aspirations for career success with a desire to address discontent with their living conditions or certain aspects of Chinese society. In effect, however, their lives are often precarized by the existing "three-legged" system. The complicity between the state and capital often seduces independent filmmakers into accepting cooptation and depoliticization, while foreign film festivals encourage them to identify themselves as "dissenting/artistic independents" by offering (limited and highly competitive) funding and screening opportunities. This precarization orchestrates and reterritorializes independent Chinese cinema toward a depoliticized "art cinema," while filmmakers deploy self-governance through multitasking, networking, and self-emotional management to maintain a sense of optimism about the future.

The precarization of independent Chinese cinema has led to the emergence of an informal mutual-caring community. Animated by a shared aspiration for independence and freedom, this community not only helps alleviate living and work pressure by offering opportunities for screenings, skills learning, and the sharing of emotions but has also led to a more open understanding of what independence and independent filmmaking mean. Though this community has its own inequalities (such as being dominated by men and having a hierarchical culture), it does embrace a more inclusive and fluid conception of independence. This conception allows for the differences of its members to be preserved so they are no longer circumscribed by rigid identities such as that of "political dissenter" and "noncommercial" filmmaker. Thus, the precarious living and working conditions of independent filmmakers not only capture their labor and creativity; they also produce a condition that recognizes individual differences and challenges the existing production system. This combination of the oppressive and productive aspect of precarity and precarization has led to the formation of a bilateral subjectivity among independent Chinese filmmakers, whose work and lives both underpin and undermine the system of cultural and film production in China. This situation is not as binary as it sounds. As shown in the following chapters, we can identify this unstable and paradoxical character of creative subjectivity among creative workers in a wide range of cultural sectors.

4

(Un-)Becoming Chinese Creatives

Introduction

David Wong was born in and raised by a Chinese family in Canada. In 1949, his father left Mainland China for Taiwan, then traveled to Canada with his family when the Chinese Nationalist Party (Kuomintang, or KMT) lost the civil war. After graduating from college, David first worked in London as an architect for a few years before his passion for filmmaking led him to Denmark to study cinema. Later he spent a year in Berlin and then moved back to London, where he took up his architect job again, "just because I ran out of money." In 2011, David was introduced to Beijing by his brother, who works there in the creative field, to work as a freelance videographer. Apart from commercial video projects, he started working on an independent documentary about Beijing and the local Chinese people, simply because he was fascinated by the vibrant and diverse city life of Chinese society. Compared to London, he saw the creative field in Beijing as more relaxed and less hierarchical. He also found it easier to find jobs in Beijing, thanks to his European educational and professional background and the network he was able to build with assistance from his brother.

After six years in Beijing, however, he regularly considered leaving China and returning to Canada. With his father getting older, David felt obliged to return home to care for his parents. He also was not fluent in Mandarin, which limited how far he could go in his creative career in Beijing. Since he was working as a freelancer—which in China did not entitle him to a long-term work permit—David also had to leave Mainland China every ninety days to renew his visa. But leaving was a difficult decision for him. Apart from the fact that he had established a social network in Beijing, which was crucial for his creative work, he felt he would miss the vibrancy of Chinese society. As David explained:

> Maybe [I'll leave] next year or in a year and a half, but I'm not sure yet. I do want to keep on filming things in China, even though I feel Beijing is kind of slowing down, becoming less interesting, or just because I'm used to it now. I've also been to other places, like Chongqing, which reminded me of Beijing five or ten years ago, full of energy. And in general I think China is such a chaotic place, which . . . I like! It's interesting for us. Europe and Canada are very quiet. America is a little chaotic, but compared to China it's still settled. I'm interested in the contradiction between its fast-paced development, the depth of history, and your people living in different social layers, reacting to such contradiction . . . there are really interesting things happening in China all the time. (David Wong, filmmaker)

This vignette reveals the aspirations and anxiety of international professionals working in Beijing who wish to build a career in the Chinese creative industries. The social dynamics of contemporary China and the career opportunities engendered by its booming creative economy compelled David Wong to move from Europe to Beijing. His aging family and his visa issues discourage him from staying, however, and will thus potentially lead him to renewed transnational mobility.

David's story demonstrates why we should study the experiences of international creative workers in China. In comparison to the extensive scholarship on overseas migration from Mainland China and the Chinese diaspora (e.g., Choi 1975; Sun 2005; Martin 2017), a growing number of researchers acknowledge that "the rise of China" is now reversing the direction of migration and is affecting the transnational mobility of labor. The economic opportunities engendered by "the rise of China/Asia" lead people from overseas to regard China as an aspirational place for work and life (Yeoh and Willis 2005; Selmer 2006; Bodomo 2012; Castillo 2014; Lan 2017). In his study of African diasporas in Guangzhou, Castillo (2014) finds that although China's immigration policy and precarious work and living conditions discourage Africans from becoming permanent immigrants, they should not be seen as only dispossessed. Precarious living and work conditions, according to Castillo, produce a precarious residency that is "paralyzing" but also produces a network community that facilitates "individual and collective attempts to 'feel at home' while on the move in China" (Castillo 2016, 11). Comparing the different experiences of British and Singaporean professionals in China, Yeoh and Willis (2005, 270) note that contemporary transnational subjects are not just mobile careerists "circulating in an intensely fluid world"; they are also "embodied bearers of culture, ethnicity, class or gender" that give rise to differentiated transnational experiences. These subjects not only belong to the "space of flows" (Castells 2005) but also to the "space of place." In other words, their transnational experience is situated, and they become copresent with others, including locals (Yeoh and Willis 2005).

Building on this research, in this chapter I focus on the transnational mobility of creative labor in China. As I will show, the specific politico-economic conditions of cultural production in China complicate the work and life experiences of transnational creative workers in China, opening up a set of new questions concerning transnational mobility and subjectivity.

Previous chapters have shown that the "state question" (Wang 2001) significantly complicates the governance of creative labor in China. Creative workers must balance their own creative career aspirations with the party state's ideological control and expectation of a politically conforming and cooperative creative subjectivity. At the same time, economic globalization also connects China to the international cultural market. The emerging Chinese market continues to attract foreign capital, while the Chinese party state also wishes to perform its creativity on the global stage for national branding purposes, to wield soft power through Chinese international cultural companies (Keane 2013). Against this background of the rise of China and the specific political economy of cultural production in China, this chapter examines the transnational mobility of creative labor in Beijing by responding to three questions:

1) What motivates international creative workers to choose China/Beijing as a place to work and live?
2) What are the working and living conditions of these transnational subjects in Beijing?
3) What kind of transnational subjectivity is produced by the mobile but also situated lives of these international creative professionals in Beijing?

To address these questions, I will move the focus from local Chinese creatives to international creative professionals in China and will examine the life and work of foreign expatriates working in China's creative industries. As part of a study on the governance and subjectification of creative labor in contemporary China, the chapter not only adds to our understanding of Chinese governance of creativity and creative labor but also broadens our conception of creative labor and its relationship to the nation-state in a globalizing age. Specifically, this chapter will first demonstrate that the globalization of the Chinese cultural economy has propelled the transnational mobility of creative laborers into China. Although attracted by China's career opportunities, international creative professionals do not form a privileged "elite class," but rather they encounter precarity in their everyday lives and in the workplace.

By underscoring precarity as a form of productive governance, I continue the discussion from chapter 3 about precarious creative labor, but I shift the focus from local Chinese creative workers to international creative professionals in Beijing and their transnational labor mobility. My main argument is that the life experiences of foreign creative professionals in Beijing fuel interaction and mutual understanding between them and Beijing locals, creating conditions for the emergence of a cosmopolitan subjectivity. This cosmopolitan subjectivity aligns with the bilateral creative subjectivity examined in other chapters of this book: it goes beyond the Chinese authorities' expectation of a conforming and economically productive creative workforce, thus creating the potential for mutual understanding and care among people from diverse cultural backgrounds.

Creative Labor, Mobility, and Precarity

As I have shown in the introduction and chapter 1, business scholars and Western policy makers have celebrated the policy discourse of the "creative class" as the driving force behind the construction of the "creative city" and the prosperity of the creative industries (Florida 2002). The vibrancy and tolerant attitudes of the city are crucial factors for attracting creative talent (Hansen and Niedomysl 2009). Empirical studies suggest that factors such as employment opportunities, education facilities, and a low cost of living, which motivate "noncreative" migrants, also foster creative professionals' mobility (Murphy and Redmond 2009; Hansen and Niedomysl 2009). Lily Kong points out that, along with the mobility of the creative class, the transnational mobility of ideas, technology, finance, and images contribute to the making of the "creative city" (2014).

Over the last decade, the discourses of the creative city and cultural/creative industries, particularly their emphasis on labor mobility, have been reproduced within the Chinese policy context. Since 2000, the Chinese Communist Party has reluctantly incorporated the cultural industries into its national agenda and has authorized the central government to establish new institutions and formulate a host of policies such as five-year plans, special funds, and policy reforms to boost the domestic cultural economy (see chapter 1). At the local level, Chinese metropoles such as Beijing (2014), Shanghai (2017), and Shenzhen (2016) have lined up to promote their own creative-city planning, in which attracting international creative talents is a primary strategy. Emphatic about the contribution of labor mobility to economic growth, the major motivation for these policies is to attract creative talents, namely established, highly skilled creative practitioners. As one policy asserts, "The key is to cultivate and attract international leading talents for high-end cultural management, capital operation, cultural technology, and international cultural trade" (Beijing 2014, n.p.).

What these policies tend to overlook is the impact of mobility on the work and lives of cultural workers, who come from far more diverse social backgrounds than the category of "creative talent" suggests. Behind the global flows of creativity lies a creative workforce characterized by substantial inequalities and differences engendered by race, class, relationship status, age, skill level, job title, gender, and salary (Banks 2017). Professionals in the cultural sectors, especially the less established ones, have become a "creative precariat" who suffer precarious working conditions and face problems such as short-term contracts, unequal earnings, and a lack of unions (Curtin and Sanson 2016; Hesmondhalgh and Baker 2011). In his study of Hong Kong cultural workers in China, Chow Yiu Fai (2017) suggests that the mobility of creative labor from Hong Kong to Mainland China is quite often contingent on these workers being able to move quickly and respond to the precarious conditions in the cultural sector. Consequently, creative-labor mobility is often a circuitous process among various places, rather than a simple push-pull model between two locations (Chow 2017). McRobbie also points out that the highly mobile creative workplace engenders a "time-space stretch mechanism" that disavows motherhood and family (2016, 2). These critiques remind us that the mobility that characterizes creative labor is not always a choice, and precarious labor conditions may also force cultural workers to move between multiple locations. Mobility, then, has increasingly become an intrinsic characteristic of creative labor.

To study creative-labor mobility thus entails examining the factors that have driven the labor movement and how the diverse creative workforce has been shaped and governed, producing a kind of subjectivity. As Tim Cresswell notes (2006, 9), mobility as a research topic is never just a simple fact of movement from one place to another; rather, mobility is "meaningful and laden with power." In contemporary society, some scholars believe the prevalent mobility, triggered by economic globalization, is "restructuring the 'social as society' into the 'social as mobility'" (Urry 2012, 2).

With the globalization of creative industries, creative workers now also live what Elliott and Urry describe as a "mobile life" (2010). Then how exactly is this mobile life lived by transnational creative workers in Beijing? As Conradson and Latham stress, the study of transnational mobility needs to focus on the everyday texture of such mobility and transnationalism by attending to "how inevitably emplaced forms of sociality, such as kinship, friendship and national identity, are being reworked and re-imagined through such movement and mobility" (2005, 228). Kevin Dunn also reminds us that "transnationals are unevenly empowered within emergent transnational fields" (2010, 4). The access to and the experience of transnational mobility thus can be radically different, given transnationals' "embodied differences"—such as their race, disability, and gender—as well as their job title and religion and the social context of their destination country (Dunn 2010). As McRobbie's (2016) and Yiu Fai Chow's (2017) research shows, the unfolding of creative-labor mobility can vary across different localities such as western Europe and China. To study international creative workers in Beijing thus entails not only illuminating their lives, but also unpacking such mobility in the local power relations in the places they work and live.

The intention of this chapter is not simply to repeat the argument that creative labor is precarious. As I have argued in previous chapters, my aim is to illuminate experiences of precarity in different social contexts. This chapter, for example, investigates the precarious experiences of international creative professionals in Beijing (and in the wider context of the Chinese state's governance of cultural production and labor mobility) and the consequences of these experiences for their subjectivity.

Precarious circumstances require subjects to constantly adjust their living strategies. This self-governance causes their lives and work to be highly demanding, but following Lorey (2015), their self-governance is also quite productive and incalculable, as became clear from my discussion of independent Chinese filmmakers in chapter 3. As Lorey (2015, 103–4) puts it:

> The processes of precarization are a contested social terrain, in which the struggles of workers and their desires for different forms of living and working are articulated. The processes of precarization are not only productive in the sense of contributing to capitalist exploitation. In the post-Fordist conditions of precarious production, new forms of living and new social relationships are continually being developed and invented. In this sense, processes of precarization are also productive.

What Lorey reminds us of here is that precarious living conditions, rather than being singularly repressive, can also be productive in terms of subjectivation. According to Elliott and Urry, the globalization of mobility has produced a "portable personalhood" that is "inscribed in the scripts of mobile life" (2010, 3). What is possibly shared by those "globals," a term used by Elliott and Urry to refer to today's elite class living a transnationally mobile life, is the "language of cosmopolitanism" that respects and hopes to learn from the differences of others and believes in shared humanity (Appiah 2010). As the final section of this chapter will show, while their transnational labor mobility incurs certain forms of precarity, this precarity also leads international cultural professionals in Beijing to foster a situated cosmopolitan subjectivity that fuels interaction and mutual understanding between local and global subjects—constituting the bilateral and similarly paradoxical creatives in contemporary China.

After a brief account of the research method used in this chapter's main exploration, the following sections will successively examine the different motivations behind transnational creative-labor mobility, the precarious working conditions with which international creative workers are confronted in Beijing, and how these conditions lead to the production of a cosmopolitan, bilateral subjectivity.

Methods

The empirical data used for this chapter is based on field research conducted from July to September 2017 in Beijing. I chose Beijing as the fieldwork site for its status as the political and cultural center of China, hosting one of the largest international communities in the country. During my fieldwork I conducted ethnographic observations in places such as galleries, *hutong* pubs, and creative districts, where creative international workers habitually spend time. By using the snowball sampling method, I conducted fifteen in-depth interviews (see Appendix I) in places where transnational creative professionals were working in a diverse range of sectors, including design, film, photography, advertising, video game development, contemporary art, journalism, and state-run television. Participants from Western countries[1] and Asia (Hong Kong and Taiwan) were included. At their request, some informants' names have been pseudonymized for security and privacy reasons. Most of the participants (eleven) had been in China for more than four years and were able to communicate in Chinese. Apart from one participant who was over sixty years old, all interviewees were between twenty-five and forty-five. Apart from conducting interviews, I also analyzed Chinese policy documents on cultural industries and used secondary sources, including media reports and nonacademic writings.

Why Come to Beijing?

In 2015, Lance Crayon had been working in Beijing for five years, mostly as a videographer for Chinese state-run international media, including Chinese Radio International (CRI) and *China Daily*. His job was to make videos for cultural programs on food, landscape, customs, and history—all the "charming aspects" of China that the state media were

Name	Gender	Job	Interview Date	Nationality
David Wong	Male	Videographer	7/13/2017	Canada
Sarah Lau	Female	Freelancer	7/15/2017	Hong Kong
Simon	Male	Entrepreneur	7/18/2017	Malaysia
Laurent	Male	Photographer	7/24/2017	France
Pedro Baker	Male	Artist	7/24/2017	Netherlands
Jolene	Female	Journalist	8/1/2017	Taiwan
Mike	Male	Video game producer	8/3/2017	Netherlands
Lance Crayon	Male	Videographer	8/6/2017	USA
Elsa	Female	Graphic designer	8/7/2017	Belgium
Nancy	Female	Television editor	8/12/2017	France
Dahlia	Female	Freelance designer	8/12/2017	Netherlands
Amy	Female	Newspaper editor	8/12/2017	Taiwan
Anna	Female	Art space director	8/16/2017	Germany
Denis	Male	Commercial translator	8/17/2017	Great Britain
Ruben	Male	Photographer	8/21/2017	Netherlands

Figure 4.1. List of participants.Given the lack of statistics on the number of foreign professionals working in the Chinese cultural sectors, this research sample is not representative. For this reason, I do not claim to present a comprehensive image of international cultural workers in China in this chapter. Instead, I highlight some of the more common situations faced by the research participants.

eager to promote overseas. With full awareness of the limitations caused by censorship and bureaucracy, Lance was generally happy about his experience in Beijing, which he described as "overwhelming" in the sense that it provided plenty of good opportunities for him to perfect his filming and editing skills. According to him, these skills "never seemed to develop in America." More importantly, this job also gave him the opportunity to experience Beijing and China and explore intriguing subjects for his independent creative work. That is how he came to make *Spray Paint Beijing* (2016), an independent documentary on graffiti artists in Beijing. Lance's jobs at state media companies allowed him to practice his creative skills, while the cultural vibrancy of Beijing inspired his creativity. Together, these aspects helped him to create his own films, which benefited his future career.

Lance's career path was familiar to my interviewees. Compared to the developed cultural economies, the emerging Chinese market has generated abundant career opportunities for creative overseas professionals. These careers are also interesting to junior cultural workers still in the early stages of their career, many of whom are also desperately looking for opportunities to gain work experience and improve their skills. As I will show, foreigners are wanted in China for their "creative know-how," language/cultural skills, and even simply their "foreignness." There are several ways that Chinese contemporary society provides a seemingly diverse sociocultural environment for international cultural workers to creatively experiment with their craft.

First, international creative professionals are generally believed to be equipped with the creative know-how that the ambitious Chinese creative companies and the local authorities long for. As Michael Keane points out, an important goal for China to catch up and learn from the "advanced soft-power nations" (mostly developed Western economies as well as Japan and South Korea) is the acquisition of foreign creative "know-that" and "know-how" (2016, 217). The former stands for the propositional knowledge of what we know about the world, while the latter refers to the abilities, propensities, capacities, and habits (2016, 217) about how to be creative. Employing these international creative workers is an ideal way to enable the flow of creative expertise from the West to China. David Wong shared with me that a Chinese film producer once asserted that the best people to hire in the film industry are Westerners who live in China or Chinese nationals who were educated in the West. Both groups are often believed to be more professional and devoted to work than local Chinese people, who are frequently perceived to be working only for money.

Such belief in the "creative know-how" of foreigners on some occasions also creates opportunities for junior creative workers, due to their foreignness, Westerness, or whiteness. For instance, Elsa is a Belgian designer who works in a Chinese design company. She was educated in the Netherlands, and after working for one year in a Dutch design company, she moved to Beijing and was employed by a Chinese design company as a senior designer. Elsa did not expect that she would be a senior designer prior to getting the job, since she had less than two years of working experience in Europe. "They just assume I'm [senior] because I'm foreign." This recognition benefits Elsa's career but also brings her more responsibilities and expectations. The company has many government clients who, according to Elsa, sometimes value the designers' race more than their design skills. Elsa's boss also frequently takes her to meetings with clients to show that they are an international company.

Second, the internationalization of the Chinese creative industries and market also creates increasing demand for employees with a bi- or multilingual/cultural background. As Keane illustrates, "There is a lack of understanding within China of how to make content that might be successful overseas" (2016, 227). Managers believe that an understanding of the secret to success overseas often starts with hiring creative foreigners who speak the language and understand the audience overseas. For instance, Chinese state-run international media—CRI, *China Daily*, and CCTV—all have foreign employees working on their international programs. Meanwhile, foreign companies are also lining up to profit from China's enormous cultural market, creating job positions for those who can speak Chinese and understand international creative business.

Mike is a Dutch game producer who works in China for an international game company. After graduating in 2013 from Leiden University with a degree in Chinese studies, he came to China to explore the country and to practice the Chinese language and cultural knowledge he had gained in Leiden. Unexpectedly, his friend introduced him to his current company, an international game company that was looking for a Chinese-Dutch translator. He accepted the job and later became a game producer vetting local independent Chinese game developers for international production companies. His knowledge of Mandarin and his previous experience with video games in the Netherlands also qualified him to be a game producer who could introduce the local Chinese game developers to international audiences and game culture. In addition, foreign companies eager to access China's enormous market generated job positions for those who could speak Chinese while also understanding the international cultural sector.

Finally, Beijing—the capital city of China, with ancient, colonial, and communist history—is an attractive place for creative workers from outside China looking for "marketable" inspiration. Just as Lance was intrigued by the graffiti artists in Beijing and decided to make a documentary about them, the Dutch painter Pedro Bakker was inspired to make a series of paintings about Chinese communist history and the story of Chairman Mao and his wife, Jiang Qing. In August 2017, when I was visiting Beijing, Pedro was working in an art space called the Institute of Provocation on a new painting about the homosexual scenes in the Chinese classic novel *Dream of the Red Chamber* (*Cao Xueqin* 曹雪芹). Both of Pedro's projects were supported by art residencies funded by European art foundations and Chinese art spaces during the time of China's growing economic and political power on the global stage. The difference between Lance and Pedro is that Lance is a junior creative worker building a career at Chinese companies, while Pedro is an established artist who only stays in China for short-term art residencies. Still, they were mutually motivated by their fascination with Chinese society and the potential market opportunities of working in China.

The convenient city life and the international atmosphere of Beijing attract international creative workers. The city is enriched by local elements, exemplified by the colorful spaces in the hutongs, the most prominent and popular neighborhoods of Beijing. Although Beijing's traditional hutong alleys have increasingly come into conflict with the local authorities, as discussed below, they have the attractions that these transnational workers desire. Behind the traditional appearance of the hutong lie live music pubs, local breweries, underground indie cinemas, art galleries, street food vendors, and local restaurants (Figure 4.1). The international cultural atmosphere in Beijing also creates opportunities for international cultural workers to exhibit and promote their work in the city, as demonstrated by their active presence in creative districts such as the 798 Art Zone and Caochangdi, as well as at various hutong venues and galleries. For example, the I:Project space (an independent art space) at Banqiao Hutong and the Institute of Provocation[2] at Heizhima Hutong—two art spaces I visited during my fieldwork—both collaborate with European art foundations and have established residency and exhibition projects for international artists whose work is related to China.

Arguably, the global proliferation of the cultural industries and their uneven prosperity around the globe have propelled the global mobility of creative labor. The emerging Chinese cultural market and the existing gap between China's cultural economy and its Western competitors has led to a thirst on the part of the Chinese authorities and companies

Figure 4.2. Jianchang No. 9, a local pub at Jianchang Hutong (photo by author 2017, Beijing).

for creative know-how, which has fostered job opportunities for international cultural workers. Equipped with the necessary expertise, these international professionals are often thought to enable the future success of China's cultural industries. Such labor mobility is highly racialized and gendered. As I will illustrate in the following section, it is not a career path open to everyone; as white Europeans who speak Chinese, Mike and Elsa are widely considered excellent candidates for their jobs. It is less likely for someone coming from non-Western societies such as the global south, which has less developed regional creative economies, to be regarded as being equipped with sufficient creative know-how to be such professionals. Just as Elsa's remarks show, one's race and bilingual language proficiency (Chinese and English) matter for international creative workers in the Chinese creative fields. Many scholars (e.g., McIntosh 1988, 2018; Pulido 2000; Leonardo 2004) have noted and studied such white privilege, yet as this chapter shows in the following, the actual situations these international creative workers face in China are more ambiguous and complicated than the term "white privilege" implies.

The presence of international creative personnel in Beijing as part of the Chinese creative workforce has broadened the geopolitical conception of "Chinese creative labor" and "Chinese creativity." Their expertise and their presence in Beijing both contribute to the city's image as a global creative city, to the thriving of the Chinese/global cultural industries, and to China's aspiration for an economic transformation "from made in China to created in China" (State Council 2016). Nevertheless, overseas people's potential importance and contribution to China's cultural economy—despite their white privilege—does not necessarily guarantee a comfortable life without precarity. As I will examine in the next sections, China's restrictions on immigration and the working conditions found in the cultural sectors discourage these international creative workers from settling down in Beijing permanently, and instead push them to embrace a mobile, adventurous way of life that does not easily accommodate family, care, and stability.

Precarity: Unbecoming Chinese Creatives

Sarah Lau is a freelance film and literary critic from Hong Kong. After working in Beijing for over nine years, she finally chose to leave in November 2017. Her decision, according to Sarah, was partly prompted by the government's increasingly strict control of the city. As a film critic, Sarah was previously a regular customer of the pirated DVD shops at Sanlitun Houjie, a street commonly known as Zangjie (脏街), or "Dirty Road." It was one of the most vibrant nightlife streets in Beijing and famous for its cheap bars and restaurants, opened mostly by migrant workers from other parts of China. In 2017, however, a government-led clearance campaign led to the demolition of Zangjie and the shutting down of many shops and street vendors where Sarah used to be a regular customer.

Later that same year, the city government launched a similar operation named "Bricking Up the Holes in the Wall" in Beijing's traditional hutong alleys (Myers 2017). The operation targeted "illegal buildings" that opened their doors or windows into alleyways without prior permission from the city authorities. As a result, most of these "illegal doors

Figure 4.3. "Demolishing illegal buildings!" (photo by author 2017, Beijing).

or windows" were bricked up, impeding business at many shops, bars, and restaurants (Figures 4.2 and 4.3).

Though some shops still secretly do business, uniform cement walls have replaced the colorful alleys in hutongs such as Jianchang and Fangjia. Throughout Beijing, rapid urban development and reconstruction have led to modern skyscrapers replacing many of the traditional alleys, transforming them into central business districts. The remaining hutongs, with their increasing popularity among tourists and foreigners, merely serve as places for "fetishized tourist novelty; cramped and often dilapidated homes for communities of families; or as romanticized and renovated digs for foreigners, who like to stay within walking distance of their favorite *hutong* bar or restaurant" (Mouna 2017, 63).

These hutongs have been transformed from partly residential areas into homogenous spaces for consumption. Often without legal permission from the government, the remaining residents seek to reconstruct and enlarge their houses for commercial use. They rent them to tourists or foreigners fascinated by the hutong, or to migrant entrepreneurs to open souvenir shops, restaurants, and beer bars. For the city government, the diversity found within the hutongs makes them chaotic spaces that require effective governance. Bricking up the "illegal buildings" can directly reduce such "chaos" and meet its goal for the city, which is to renovate the hutong environment and bring back the vintage look of Beijing as an ancient capital (Yu 2017).

What happened at Zangjie and the traditional hutongs accords with what Zhang Li (2001) found in her study of migrant communities in Beijing: the presence of unauthorized reconstruction and community in the city creates complex tensions between migrant workers, the state, and urban society. The "informal privatization of power and space" within these areas causes anxiety among the city authorities about their ability to effectively regulate urban society and the emerging private economy (Zhang 2001, 4). The migrants' reconstructing practices also run counter to the party state's urban aesthetics, which is, according to Zhang (2001, 4), "promoted by the state to attract foreign investment and international and domestic tourism."

For international cultural workers, however, these informal economies and lively neighborhoods are the most attractive elements of the city. They serve as spaces to consume local culture and as social spaces to connect with local and international communities. Consequently, as the story of Sarah Lau shows, the authorities' deliberate reconstruction of these areas reduces the charm of the city and discourages international creative professionals. Compared to Hong Kong, Beijing for Sarah was a more inclusive city that accommodated people from diverse backgrounds. She was attracted to stay by the city's cultural diversity and inclusiveness, which the authorities were now attempting to destroy. Although international creative workers are not the direct targets of the city authorities in these campaigns, the destruction contributes to the growing tension between "creative foreigners" and city governance. International creatives are welcomed for their creative expertise, but their search for a "hipster lifestyle" and "cultural diversity" clashes with the authorities' demand for social stability and homogeneity.

The second source of tension is the result of China's complex regulations on entry visas and cultural production. According to the official requirements, foreigners need at least three documents to legally work in China: an employment permit, a work visa, and a work-residence

Figure 4.4. The "Bricking Up the Holes in the Wall" operation (photo by author 2017, Beijing).

permit. Qualified employers first need to apply for the employment permit for their foreign employees, who later will apply for a work visa to gain entry to China. Within thirty days of entry, the employees need to apply for a longer-term work-residence permit through the city government (Travel China Guide 2018). Creative freelancers, however, are not entitled to this Z-type work visa because they are self-employed and thus do not have a legal employer. Instead, they can only apply for a short-term ninety-day tourist visa. Although there are certain agencies that provide visa services for self-employed foreigners, the process can still be quite complicated, and applicants have to exit China every ninety days to renew their visa, as David Wong does.

China has issued its own "permanent residence permits" program, yet the high threshold for approval has barred most foreign expatriates; only a small number of them who have special skills, a business, or local family qualify (Liu 2009). As Bork-Hüffer and Yuan-Ihle (2014, 571) note, despite the changes in the migration law made over the past decade, the Chinese government has no intention of substantially easing restrictions on immigration; only those whom the authorities regard as "highly skilled talent" benefit from the current immigration law. As far as cultural workers are concerned, the current entry regulation system provides convenience for those who are established and designated "creative talent" while posing an obstacle for freelance and junior creative workers from overseas.

In terms of everyday work, employees of Chinese companies are often thought to be more skillful and creative, and thus are expected to shoulder more responsibilities. Sometimes these responsibilities require them to work longer hours because they make a higher salary than their Chinese colleagues. In the meantime, they cannot enjoy the same social welfare as Chinese employees do, such as social insurance and housing funding. Even at CCTV, the largest Chinese media company, foreign employees are not entitled to the full welfare system. According to Nancy, who has worked there for over four years, the benefits they miss out on include social insurance, housing funding, and an annual bonus. The opacity of the Chinese legal system and the dysfunction of work unions also make it difficult for foreign employees to have legal recourse against unfair treatment.

The increasingly competitive job market not only demands higher levels of creative skills but also requires these foreigners to remain adaptable to local creative production. Chinese regulations on cultural production applies to every company that produces and distributes its cultural content in the Chinese market. According to the regulation on "foreign investment in Chinese cultural sectors" enacted by the Chinese government in 2005, foreign businesses are permitted to participate in reproduction and distribution businesses such as printing, disc reproduction, audio-visual product (excepting film) retail, cinemas, and museums. Yet they are not allowed to run a media-production business in China, as the policy document asserts:

> It is prohibited for foreign businesses to invest in and operate news agencies, radio and television stations, film production, internet culture businesses, and internet surfing services (except for Hong Kong and Macau),

> culture and art performance, film import and distribution, and video screening. They are not permitted to invest or engage in book and periodical publishing (including wholesale and import business), audio-visual products and digital publishing (including wholesale and import business), or to use digital networks to launch audio-visual programs, news websites, and online publishing. (Ministry of Culture 2005)

In practice, such restrictions on running a media and cultural-production business mean that these international creative professionals are prohibited from starting their own businesses in the listed cultural sectors, so they at least have to seek assistance or collaboration with local production teams or companies. Transnational creative workers in Beijing thus must adapt their individual creativity to the local/global creative-production system, in which creative skill is demanded while the product must be acceptable to the Chinese authorities. Of course, this situation does not mean that international creative workers in Beijing have completely lost their individuality and criticality, but only that they require meticulous self-governance. As Anna, the cofounder of the aforementioned I:Project space, noted of sensitive topics:

> I mean, if you become very political and criticize the [authorities'] political decisions, it will probably have consequences. Even though we work with lots of political artists, but for residency [reasons], most of them are not Chinese, so they won't necessarily criticize China. For exhibition projects, which are mostly for Chinese artists, if it's political work and we think it's relevant, we'll definitely show it, one hundred percent. But we'll still think about how to promote it. I mean, you don't try to self-censor yourself, but for promotion, you'll be more careful and do things more properly.

Once again, echoing the findings in the previous chapters, working in China's creative sectors requires meticulous self-governance. These international creative workers must calculate their creativity and business strategies to eliminate any political risk that their work might bring. Finally, the international creative workers' highly mobile work and life in Beijing, coupled with different cultural norms, discourages them from getting married and having families. As Nancy explained to me:

> For foreign [Western] women, it's difficult to find a Chinese partner. It's rare to see a couple consisting of a Chinese man and a Western woman. The relationship between a Chinese mother-in-law and daughter-in-law is way too complicated for Western women. As a foreigner, having children in Beijing [in international hospitals] is also very expensive, let alone Chinese environmental pollution, education, and health care. So if we start thinking about settling down and having a stable family life, we'll probably leave China.

The desire to start a family and to have a stable home conflicts with the mobility and flexibility required of foreigners doing cultural work in China. As in other parts of the world, the bohemian work environment is marked by significant inequalities in terms of gender, race, class, age, and disability (Conor, Gill, and Taylor 2015). The idea of "coolness" attached to creative work also presupposes a young, single, and passionate-to-work subjectivity, which goes against the ethos of collectivity, motherhood, and family (McRobbie 2016). Specific Chinese institutional predicaments, such as restrictions on visas and immigration, environmental issues, and obstacles to accessing education and the medical system, aggravate this situation for international creative workers in Beijing.

Besides the gendered form of precarity shown by Nancy, other forms confront those who are from different racial backgrounds or who lack Chinese language proficiency. For example, during my fieldwork, I tried to (but never succeeded in) finding creative professionals from Africa or Latin America. The international community in the Chinese cultural sectors seems to be dominated by white Westerners, East Asians, and people from the Chinese diaspora. The relatively monolingual environment in Beijing brings more obstacles for those seeking employment security who cannot speak fluent Chinese.

China's limitations on migration, the precarious working conditions and political restrictions in the cultural sector, and various social-environmental problems have discouraged transnational creative workers from becoming permanent residents or Chinese citizens. It seems, then, that the career opportunities brought by the emerging Chinese creative economy are accompanied by risks and precarity, as well as a requirement of effective self-governance.

The Production of Cosmopolitan Subjects in Beijing

Until now, this chapter has shown how career opportunities have motivated international creative workers to move to China, where they often find themselves confronted with precarious conditions. This precarious living in Beijing calls for self-governance—workers adapting their creativity and subjectivity to the local production and social systems. To obtain a network that might bring new career opportunities, they need to socialize with local Chinese people. To do this, they must understand and speak the local (cultural) language. The bars, art galleries, and music spaces in Beijing's hutong alleys are crucial sites for such network-building interactions between local and international cultural workers.

These socializing activities, which are part of their self-governance, are an immediate response to the precarious living and working conditions of international creative workers in Beijing. This behavior corresponds to the neoliberal mode of flexible work and subjectivity, which, as researchers of creative labor in the Western context have argued, intensify gender and racial inequalities as well as precarity (Conor, Gill, and Taylor 2015; McRobbie 2016). As this section will show, however, this behavior also creates something extra, even when it is unwanted by the Chinese state's capitalist system. My fieldwork for chapter 3 on independent Chinese filmmaking, for instance, showed that underground film screenings in hutong bars are important occasions for independent Chinese filmmakers to encounter and network with international creative workers. For local filmmakers, these events bring potential opportunities to connect with the international market—such as through overseas film festivals and agencies—that can provide alternative distribution channels, allowing Chinese indie filmmakers to dodge the stringent censorship and regulation of the Chinese market.

For international creative subjects, these social events provide opportunities to encounter similarly precarious local producers, and by interacting with them, they develop a more comprehensive understanding of their self and the (Chinese) "other." Denis, a British man who has studied and worked in China since 2013, explained to me how he viewed his identity and the question of "integration":

> I am British, born in London, with parents from a European background. I have to say that my four-year experience in China has also become a big part of my identity. . . . In China, I am definitely a foreigner, and I definitely belong to the international community in Beijing. I know many people say that they don't like China and don't want to stay because that they can't integrate into Chinese society, which I understand but don't believe. I don't believe in that kind of monolithic Chinese society. In a country as big as China, there are lots of different societies, different economic or social groups with different backgrounds. I think it can be possible for foreigners to become well integrated into certain subcultural groups.

Denis speaks fluent Chinese, and he lives in a hutong community with his Chinese girlfriend. Apart from doing translation work for advertising companies, he likes to photograph street life in Beijing's traditional hutongs, and he is a devoted viewer of local independent Chinese documentaries. In terms of his perspective on Chinese identity, Denis questions any monolithic interpretation of Chinese-ness. In August 2017, he participated in a hutong photography contest organized by local Chinese people. Through such interaction with the local society and communities, transnational creative practitioners such as Denis develop a more holistic understanding of the complexity of China and of being Chinese. Based on his living experiences in a hutong, Denis acknowledges that there are certain good reasons behind the ongoing rebuilding project in hutong spaces led by the city government; the previous government neglect of hutongs has brought inconveniences for its inhabitants, including poor transportation, ventilation, and sanitation. The problem with the government, Denis stresses, is its way of doing this (referring to the "Bricking Up the Holes in the Wall" operation). In terms of identity, Denis questions any monolithic interpretation of Chinese-ness by emphasizing the very differences among Chinese societies.

Similarly, working as a video game producer for an international game company in China, Mike sometimes volunteers as a subtitle translator for an indie filmmaker. His daily communications and interactions with local Chinese people, enabled by his job and language ability, seem to have helped him integrate into the local society:

> Maybe because of my language and because of the people I know, somehow my best Chinese friends forget I'm not Chinese, and I forget they're not "foreigners." You'll realize this at one point if you have some sort of communication and relationship, and then this stuff [of identity] just matters less. Like, I'm never gonna think of my friends in the way like, "You're typically Chinese or not-so-typically Chinese." That simply doesn't make sense to me.

The cultural differences do exist, but they do not necessarily preclude active communication, which calls for more studying and mutual understanding.

> I often tell my Chinese friends that if you want to make me angry, you can simply say, "You don't understand." Sometimes, indeed, I do not understand. That's actually the point! There are some basic differences in terms of education and life experience between those with a Chinese passport and people like me with a Dutch passport, but a simple judgment like "You don't understand" is not relevant. For some foreigners, similarly, these differences and such words as "You don't understand" can lead them to very simplistic conclusions about China and Chinese people. "Oh, Chinese people are like this!" That really annoys me because you can't have these opinions without any further study on [the subject]. As I see it, both two sides are blind.

Claims such as "You don't understand" and "Chinese people are like this" annoy Mike and have helped him realize that such judgment is simplistic and largely overlooks the actual heterogeneity among people, whether they are labeled "Chinese" or "foreigners." He acknowledges cultural differences, but according to Mike, they do not necessarily preclude active communication leading to mutual learning and understanding.

International creative workers' precarious living conditions also prompt them to take advantage of technology for their own purposes. To avoid the inconvenience of China's censored internet, they use virtual private network (VPN) technology to remain connected with the outside world. Discounted airfares and the flexibility of their creative work also give them the freedom to temporarily escape Beijing's environmental pollution and hot summers. Finally, the growing and globalizing Chinese economy ensures that their Chinese expertise will continually bring them new career opportunities even after they leave China. These conditions give them considerable leeway to combat their everyday precarity in Beijing, while also allowing some of them to embrace the mobile, more improvisatory lifestyle required of them.

Dahlia is a Dutch freelancer who has been in China for over eleven years. After getting her degree in fashion studies from a college in the Netherlands, she came to Beijing to visit her parents, who were staying there at the time, and the city fascinated her. Because she was looking to temporarily escape from the subject she had studied, she decided to move to China, without expecting to stay long. Over the years, she has taken on jobs ranging from foreign language teacher, graphic designer, consultant, and program manager to cultural officer at the Dutch embassy. According to Dahlia, change itself really attracts her, regardless of the risks it may entail:

> Of course, I don't know where that change is going, [toward] good or bad. There's some energy here behind the change. I've never worried about the negative impact that such mobility might bring. . . . I did have some difficult moments when I was in London, but inherently I don't have such fear. . . . People need risks in life. It's good for them. I think more people should take more risks.

The above stories illustrate how the precarious life and need for self-governance in the transnational creative workplace in Beijing can yield a subjectivity that is incalculable and potentially empowering. Over the years, these transnationals have developed a certain modality of cosmopolitanism. Denis's understanding of identity and Chinese-ness, Mike's remarks on cultural difference and mutual understanding, and Dahlia's embrace of a changeable and mobile life all suggest that they share a common positive stance toward the diversity and coexistence of cultures. This fearless and empathetic mentality fits into the classic configuration of cosmopolitan as "someone who crosses borders and is ready to [be exposed] to new people, to appreciate their cultures, and to respect them independently of their national, ethnic or religious affiliations" (Nowicka and Kaweh 2016, 51).

Figure 4.5. A Dutch singer and his friends from a local Chinese band (photo by author 2017, Beijing).

According to Nowicka and Rovisco (2016, 2), cosmopolitanism is both a moral ideal and an everyday practice "apparent in things that people do and say to positively engage with the 'the otherness of the other' and the oneness of the world." My fieldwork shows that many transnational creatives are active participants in Chinese society and local culture. For instance, Laurent's previous research and work experiences encouraged him to volunteer to assist locals in Beichuan, a county in Sichuan Province that had been rebuilding ever since a catastrophic earthquake in 2008. In August 2017, Laurent hosted a special exhibition and sale of his photographic works in Beijing, then donated all the money to his friends in Beichuan. Meanwhile, as I have already mentioned, many international creatives are supportive audiences for (and sometimes coproducers of) Chinese local independent cultural productions. In this sense, the work and life possibilities in China enable these transnational creative professionals to actively participate in Chinese society and, therefore, to become cosmopolitans.

This is not to suggest that every international creative worker in Beijing has embraced cosmopolitanism in this way. I do not assume that international cultural workers in China are a homogeneous group. Notably, this cosmopolitanism comes about on a highly gendered and racialized basis; diversities of gender, race, and linguistic ability can create different experiences of precarity and cosmopolitanism among transnational creative workers in Beijing. Mike, Denis, and Dahlia all come from a white European background, while an adventurous spirit embracing change and mobility very much goes against the idea of "marriage and care," as aspired to by Nancy. Those who openly embrace a cosmopolitan outlook often have obtained fluency in Chinese, which makes it easier for them to meaningfully interact and communicate with local Chinese people.

The experiences of transnational creative workers in Beijing, although characterized by a degree of precarity and a need for self-governance, nonetheless provide a foundation for a cosmopolitan subjectivity. Following Beck (2006), it should be noted that this process of "cosmopolitanization" can be unconscious—a side effect of the everyday experience of working and living in a transnational context. It is also important to emphasize that the type of cosmopolitanism fostered among this specific group in Beijing is not what Elliott and Urry (2010, 78) call the cosmopolitan "global elite" who keep a "distance from locality." As I have shown, life in Beijing for these transnational creative workers is rendered precarious by their socioeconomic circumstances. Echoing David Ley (2004, 162), their cosmopolitan experience in Beijing is situated and "imbued with partiality and vulnerability." These cosmopolitan workers also differ from what Pheng Cheah (2006, 492) critiques as "a new technocratic professional class whose primary aims in life are making a profit and conspicuous consumption." It is the global capitalization of creativity that brings these international creative workers to China, but their goals are not restricted to making money and consuming local goods, as the above cases of these international workers' active participation in the local cultural scene underscore.

Their actual experience in China is also as precarious as it is financially productive. The cosmopolitanization of these international cultural workers is the result of the precarity produced by global/Chinese capitalism but is also incalculable and transcends the subsumption of capital. The process of these transnationals (un-)becoming Chinese creatives—that is, their becoming part of the Chinese creative workforce without being able to fully embrace a Chinese identity—helps to envision "Chinese creative labor" as a fluid assemblage that allows for the coexistence of heterogeneous elements and the continuous unfolding of the difference that they embody. Arguably, these international creative workers in Beijing shared with the creative workers analyzed in the previous chapters in becoming bilateral creatives. It is the heterogeneity embodied in their labor and subjectivity that, echoing those cultural workers studied in previous chapters, might bring change and disruption to the existing system of creative-labor governance both in China and internationally. To govern creative labor in China thus also entails the governance of the "border," which, according to Mezzadra and Neilson (2013, xi), "plays a key role in the production of the heterogeneous time and space of contemporary global and postcolonial capitalism." In its complex relation to the nation-state in the globalizing era, the border functions as a social institution that helps manage the global flow of people, capital, and things while transforming sovereign power and the nexus of politics and violence (2013, 3–4). The cross-border movement of the transnational creative workforce can potentially destabilize the previous imagination and governance of cultural production and creative labor in China and can result in the adaptation of the Chinese nation-state's expectation of creativity and labor from the global creative capitalism system (and vice versa).

Conclusion

This chapter has investigated the experiences of a specific group of cultural workers in China: international creative professionals in Beijing. Their expertise and everyday practices have built the image of Beijing as a "global creative city," the thriving Chinese/global creative industries, and China's aspiration to achieve an economic transformation by moving from "made in China to created in China" (State Council 2016). As suggested, these people often come to Beijing seeking emerging career opportunities, while in their everyday work and lives they confront precarious situations that discourage them from becoming Chinese and may incite them to leave when they reach the stage of wanting to lead a more stable life and start a family.

At the same time, the precarious life produced by the mobility and flexibility demanded of international creative workers in Beijing also fuels interaction and mutual understanding between local and global workers, which provides the conditions for a cosmopolitan subjectivity. This subjectivation of international cultural workers may transcend the Chinese authorities' expectation of a conforming and profitable creative workforce.

As such, the experiences of these international creative workers in Beijing can be seen as another example of bilateral subjectification in China's cultural industries. Once again, the transnational mobility of creative labor in Beijing epitomizes the process of deterritorialization and reterritorialization analyzed in the previous chapters. International creative workers' experiences in Beijing have engendered conditions conducive to a similar paradoxical and bilateral subjectivity as independent Chinese filmmakers and those employed by the state media companies. Finances and career demands drive this international mobility of creative labor while also engendering conditions for a situated cosmopolitanism. Such subjectivity not only surpasses the conforming culture that Chinese governance of the cultural economies desires but also connects with diverse forms of identification espoused by both local and international workers. At the same time, processes of reterritorialization also incorporate their labor and life into the larger Chinese and global creative economies, causing a form of precariousness and inequality (i.e., in terms of gender and race) that turns them into Chinese creative workers.

This chapter, like chapter 3, has underscored that it may be too hasty to see the precarity caused by the economic globalization of creative labor as exclusively negative. We need to pay more attention to the notion of "productive precarity"—the unexpected effects that precarious lives, forms of creative work, and economies can have. As the following chapter will demonstrate, in China this precarious yet also productive system not only incorporates talented, educated, and professionalized cultural workers but also mobilizes a massive group of people with more grassroots backgrounds and vernacular creativities to become an "unlikely" creative class.

5

The Unlikely Creative Class

Lonely, I feel alive,
I just wanna touch the sky.
And you, girl, please don't cry,
You know I'm your Mr. Right!
Boy, playing guitar,
Girl, loving her star,
And together we sing a song that will take me to your heart!
—"Lonely Hero" (一人我饮酒醉), translated by
Jiu Xing, 2016

Introduction

The above words are uttered by a young man in a black sleeveless T-shirt sitting in front of a computer screen. Tian You is his name, and he calls himself an MC.[1] In a recorded video of a livestream, he expresses his anger at the prevalence of discrimination, the unequal distribution of wealth, and China's social inequality in the form of *hanmai*[2] (喊麦), a Chinese rap-like performance that has been popular on the internet since 2014. Thanks to livestreaming platforms such as YY and Kuaishou, the style's fusion of coarse narration and rhythmical music is now celebrated by millions of Chinese youth. Not long ago, Li Tianyou—Tian You's real name—was a scrawny high school dropout struggling to make a living in a small, dreary industrial city in northeastern China. Since 2014, he has been one of the best-known *wanghong* (internet celebrities 网红) on the Chinese internet, commanding a fan base of over 35 million people for his livestreaming shows on Kuaishou and earning more than 1.9 million USD a year in payments from his fans and advertisers. And Tian You is not alone. Enabled by emerging Chinese digital platforms, thousands of Chinese youths like him are posting images and short videos and making livestreaming shows to flaunt their creative talents while also hoping to get rich. Most of them are uneducated Chinese youths from small cities and rural areas. They earn an average monthly income ranging from 2,000 to 4,000 RMB (300–600 USD), but successful performers can earn as much as 1 million RMB (150,000 USD) per month (Arcbering 2017; Hernández 2017).

But this new form of creative business is not without risks. *Hanmai*'s ranting style and its enormous popularity, with massive online fan bases, have also troubled the Chinese authorities. In early 2018, Tian You was accused by China Central Television, the central television network controlled by the state, of talking about pornography and drugs during his livestreaming. Shortly after, Tian You and other top-ranked livestreamers were banned by all Chinese platforms, and their performance careers seem to have come to an end (Chen 2018).

When thinking about the "creative class" (Florida 2002), one tends to imagine an urban elite—a predominantly young, educated group of people who work in the cultural industries and gather in hipster bars with their MacBooks, dressed in the latest local and cosmopolitan designer brands. But, as the story of Tian You shows, the emerging platform economy and the *wanghong* industry—a term widely used to refer to the social media entertainment industry in China (Craig, Lin, and Cunningham 2021)—also offer opportunities for less educated, marginalized people to be producers in the Chinese creative economies. According to the "Forty-Fourth Survey Report—Statistical Report on Internet Development" (CINIC 2019, 75), by 2019 the Chinese digital economy had created 191 million jobs. Platforms and apps such as Taobao (e-commerce), WeChat (social media), Didi (transportation), Eleme (food delivery), and Kuaishou (short video and livestreaming) created over 60 million jobs (*People's Daily* 2019). Geographically, this thriving digital economy is not necessarily limited to the urbanized east coast and other developed regions. As disclosed by the "White Paper on the Chinese Digital Economy and Employment 2019" (CAICT 2019, 37), in 2018 there were over 9.8 million e-commerce companies located in China's rural areas, creating 28 million employment opportunities for local farmers.

As early as 2018, the Chinese platform economy had also contributed to 55.5 percent of total economic growth in the broadcast, television, film, and recording industries (CAICT 2019, 34). Such convergence is blurring the boundary between traditional media and the rapid growth of user-generated content production, which is the foundation of the Chinese wanghong industry. The short video platforms Douyin and Kuaishou combined, for example, boast a user base of over 648 million, with an average usage rate of 78.2 percent (CAICT 2019, 35). When the Chinese and global economies were severely disrupted by the COVID-19 outbreak in 2020, the wanghong industry and platform economy might have been one of the very few sectors that still managed to thrive and grow. According to media reports, the daily average online time per user of leading Chinese social media platforms such as Douyin, Kuaishou, Taobao Live, Douyu, and Huya increased by seventy minutes in the first quarter of 2020 (Youwenyouda 2020). In the same period, the total revenue of Douyu and Huya—the two most popular livestreaming platforms in China—reportedly increased by 50 percent (Duan 2020; Xu 2020). While the pandemic has inhibited physical immobility, the Chinese platform and wanghong economy are positioned to benefit, since production and consumption are not necessarily constrained by creators' and consumers' geographic location.

According to Nieborg and Poell (2018, 2), such platformization marks "the penetration of economic, governmental, and infrastructural extensions of digital platforms into the web and app ecosystems, fundamentally affecting the operations of the cultural industries." Data-intensive digital/internet technologies afford platforms such as Kuaishou fast connectivity, which allows them to mediate between content producers, end users, and advertisers, to ultimately incorporate them into the platform-dominated network system of "multisided markets" (McIntyre and Srinivasan 2017; Nieborg and Poell 2018). The platformization of cultural production blurs the boundaries between traditional media forms and leads to the exponential growth of user-generated content production. The multisided network system not only enables traditional media companies to expand their content business but also, as Tian You's story shows, produces opportunities for marginalized people to become self-employed "creative workers"—wanghong creators.

This chapter investigates this emerging yet "unlikely" creative class in China, which is part of the rapid platformization of China's cultural production and engages with the aesthetics of their work. How are these diverse and sometimes marginalized groups of people and their creativities mobilized and incorporated into the wanghong industry and platform economy? What kinds of aesthetics and culture are produced by these online creators? How does the platformization and emergence of the wanghong industry relate to the Chinese state's governance of culture, economy, and society? And what does the emergence of the "unlikely creative class" say about the subjectivity of Chinese social media creators, especially in comparison to international social media creators and the other Chinese creative workers explored in the previous chapters? To address these questions, this chapter focuses on one particular platform: Kuaishou. Labeled by the Chinese mainstream media as "revitalizing rural Chinese culture" (Liu 2017), the app has attracted hundreds of millions of Chinese people from the countryside and from China's second- and third-tier cities. Since 2012, it has become one of the most popular video-sharing platforms in China, allowing its users to watch, make, and distribute various genres of short videos. They can also also become "complementors" of the platform (Nieborg and Poell 2018)—professional content producers who contribute to the platformization of cultural production in China.

In the following section, I will introduce Kuaishou and the "unlikely creative class" it enables from three conceptual angles: the political economy, the digital system, and individual practice. Throughout, my focus is on the production of creator subjectivities in China's wanghong industry. By considering the vibrant interaction among the state, the platform, and individual creators, this chapter illuminates the specificities of platformization and influencer culture in the context of contemporary China.

Wanghong and the Platform Economy

As a popular term, "wanghong" in Chinese refers to *wangluo hongren* (literally, "internet red" 网络红人), which is sometimes translated as "online celebrities" or "microcelebrities" (Tse et al. 2018; Han 2021). The widespread use of the term began in the early 2000s, when the internet had just reached the Chinese public (Han 2021). The rise of wanghong as an emerging industry, however, is reported to have started in the mid-2010s, when Papi Jiang received a 12 million RMB (1.79 million USD) investment from venture investors (Zhang and Su 2016). According to ByteDance China CEO Kelly Zhang, on Douyin (China's version of TikTok), 22 million wanghong creators made over $6 billion USD in 2019, with revenue expected to double in 2020 (Choudhury 2020). This estimate, however, was limited to those revenue streams for creators across a single platform in an environment populated by hundreds of platforms. While most wanghong creators are not rich, and many struggle to generate sustainable income, in 2019, the top wanghong creators earned $67 million USD (Youmshajekian 2019). Behind the commercialization and industrialization of wanghong lies the participation of Chinese people with a vast demographic diversity. Just like Tian You, they have rarely received sufficient professional training and appear to be merely amateurish content creators. At the same time, according to Craig, Lin, and Cunningham (2021, 2), though they often start as hobbyists, wanghong creators are "social media entrepreneurs and platform and intermediary media professionals working within a highly competitive platform landscape." They are "incubated through regulatory protection" and motivated by "lucrative monetary opportunities" (Craig, Lin, and Cunningham 2021, 2).

In terms of labor, wanghong is organized by a highly networked platform economy. Critical scholars have offered detailed accounts of how these platforms convert users into "prosumers," thus contributing to the exploitation of free, creative labor (Ritzer and Jurgenson 2010; Fuchs 2010). Van Doorn, for example, notes that in the platform economy, contracted labor has been replaced by "platform labor" that adopts "a more austere and zero-liability peer-to-peer model that leverages software to optimize labor's flexibility, scalability, tractability, and its fragmentation" (van Doorn 2017, 901). In this sense, workers are regarded as complementors or subcontractors (instead of employees) of the platform companies, which are therefore exempt from providing labor protections. Paying less attention to the actual practices of creators across digital and social media platforms, these critical scholars focus mostly on theorizing how inequality and precarity are produced in the online economy. By operating entrepreneurially and independently within a flexible work regime (Gregg 2013; Gill 2014), creators are representative of aspirational labor (Duffy 2016) and visibility labor (Abidin 2016). As Brooke Duffy notes, "While a select few may realize their professional goals—namely to get paid doing what they love—this labor ideology obscures problematic constructions of gender and intersectionalities with class" (2016, 3).

Although these arguments provide valuable insights into the new labor conditions in the global platform economy, in this chapter I have chosen to zoom in on the active practices of these wanghong creators. The multisided markets of platform businesses suggest a more complicated relationship among different actors in the operation of platformization than terms such as "prosumption" and "exploitation" can capture. The networked mode of production indicates that "the costs of the production and consumption of goods and services" will affect other complementors of the platform such as content producers and advertisers, and vice versa (Nieborg and Poell 2018, 4). As the word "complementor" implies, the commercial relationship between platform companies and complementors is not only exploitative; it is also collaborative and symbiotic. The long-term financial success of digital platforms is thus not only based on the exploitation of platform labor but is also contingent upon commercial collaboration between platform companies, content creators, and other complementors.

In the case of Kuaishou, as I will show in the following sections, by actively utilizing the digital system afforded by the platform, grassroots wanghong producers are enabled to hone their digital entrepreneurship. Diverse content creators actively develop and monetize their creativity and individuality to establish a new form of lifestyle/career—a creative digital business that can not only bring financial benefits but can also allow for social mobility (e.g., from migrant worker to the creative class). The critiques of prosumption cited above may lose sight of the active interactions and the symbiotic relations between the platform companies and their complementors. To achieve a more grounded and balanced understanding of wanghong labor and subjectivity on Chinese platforms such as Kuaishou, we need to look at the everyday experiences of various individual creators—their motivations, struggles, and strategies—and locate their experiences in relation to the networked system of the Chinese platform economy and the wanghong industry.

Meanwhile, the Chinese state is a crucial agent in this networked system and in the development of the platform economy. As Yu Hong (2017a, 10–13) illustrates, the Chinese government has pledged to place information and communication at the center of its national economic restructuring plan, using information and communications technology (ICT) as industries and infrastructures to transform traditional industrial sectors. As Tian You's experience shows, however, the state not only wants to "profit" from information and culture; it also wishes to control and shape them.

As reiterated in this book, the Chinese state always expects that the commercialization of culture and creativity will conform to its ideological control and thereby maintain social and political stability. In their study of the wanghong industry, Craig, Lin, and Cunningham (2021, 19) point out that the industry in China is governed by multiple policy agendas: the "cultural industries" aim to revive cultural heritage and legacy state media, the "creative industries" focus on individual creativity and the private creative economy, and the "social industries" exploit the potentials of the wanghong industry for boosting employment and reducing income gaps. As a result, the state governance of the wanghong industry appears to be schizophrenic: both protective (in the sense that the state aspires to an internationally competitive domestic creative and platform economy) and restrictive (in terms of censorship and cultural nationalism). When regarding creators on Kuaishou, we therefore need to begin by questioning the relationship between the Chinese state and the platform. How is the Kuaishou platform regulated by the state, and how does the state governance affect the practices of Kuaishou creators? To address these questions, in this chapter I will explore the role of the state in the governance of Kuaishou's wanghong economy, as well as the vibrant interactions between the state, the Kuaishou platform, and the vast number of individual creators on it.

Finally, the digital economy is also based on a sociotechnical infrastructure of digital hardware, software, algorithms, data centers, and the labor regime (Rossiter 2017). Following Brian Larkin (2013, 329), infrastructures are not only a group of things that move and support other things; infrastructures also involve the relations between things and the system that these things operate on to create the possibility for other objects. Infrastructures "encode the dreams of individuals and societies and are the vehicles whereby those fantasies are transmitted and made emotionally real" (Larkin 2013, 333).

In this sense, in order to study Kuaishou and its wanghong creators, we also need to probe how a digital system as an infrastructure becomes entangled with other political and economic factors in the governance of the diverse people acting on its platforms. The software system of online content platforms, as Ned Rossiter shows in his study of logistical media, might also set up "new protocols and standards that can shape social, economic, and cross-institutional relations within and beyond" (2016, 4) the media and cultural industries. Algorithms, for example, through the computational calculation of massive amounts of data collected from the public, are becoming crucial engines of the platform economy and the wanghong industry. Their use generates a "new knowledge logic" that replaces the traditional "editorial logic" and promises to offer information and knowledge that is "free from human error, bias, or manipulation" and solutions that "we cannot merely rely on, but must believe in" (Gillespie 2014, 192). Approaching these digital technologies as nonhuman agents, how does the algorithmic system affect the production of culture and subjectivity within the wanghong industry? In the context of China, how does such an autonomous algorithmic system interact with other actors such as capital and state power, which always seek to profit from and shape culture and creativity?

Using this conceptual framework, in this chapter I study Kuaishou and its content creators by engaging with the larger political economy of the Kuaishou platform, its digital system, and the individual creator labor that produces the online content. The chapter starts with an introduction to the political economy of the Chinese platform economy and the specific position of Kuaishou in this system. As this introduction shows, the Chinese platform economy is distinguishable from its Western counterparts through its special state-platform relations, which simultaneously promote and limit platformization. The close link with the state constitutes a third dimension of contingency, in addition to the "platform dependence" and "contingent commodities" identified by Nieborg and Poell (2018) as the forms of contingency characterizing the Western cultural/platform economy, which I will elaborate on below. The following section analyzes the workings of the Kuaishou platform.

Using Light, Burgess, and Duguay's (2018, 882) walk-through method—"a way of engaging directly with an app's interface to examine its technological mechanisms and embedded cultural references to understand how it guides users and shapes their experiences"—in this chapter I examine how the "contingent" platform business that is manifested by the complicated state-commerce relationship is encoded in Kuaishou's algorithms. Finally, to probe the characteristics of this unlikely creative class and the specific aesthetics they produce on the platform, I analyzed two hundred trending videos and the everyday online activities of twenty popular Kuaishou accounts. My selection of videos and accounts followed three methods. First, to minimize any personal preference, a newly registered account was set up to download the first twenty videos listed under the "Trending" tab for seven days. The second collection of videos was selected from the first twenty accounts on the ranking list of the "most popular livestreamers on Kuaishou" provided by xiaohulu.com, a third-party start-up company that offers data-analysis and operation services for content producers on major Chinese content platforms. The final selection of videos consists of the ten most viewed videos on Kuaishou in August 2018, based on data provided by Short Video Factory (2018), another third-party company that publishes business reports on short-video platforms in China.

Besides the visual analysis of the videos, this study is also based on fourteen in-depth interviews conducted in 2017 and 2018 with managers from the Kuaishou company, content producers on Kuaishou and other Chinese social media platforms, algorithm engineers, and other professionals whose work is related to Kuaishou and the Chinese wanghong industry. I argue that the platformization of cultural production in China accommodates the state's "entrepreneurial solutionism" while also producing a digital creative entrepreneurship among grassroots Chinese people and a dynamic digital culture permeated with contingency and negotiation.

Kuaishou and the Chinese Internet Economy

In 2015, in his annual speech at the National People's Congress, the then Premier, Li Keqiang, announced China's "internet+" agenda, a new national development strategy to boost and restructure the national economy by upgrading digital infrastructure and pursuing technological innovation (State Council 2015b). Internet+ was the continuation of the state's economic restructuring plan, which sought to replace the unsustainable export-driven, investment-dependent model with a consumption-based and innovation-driven economy. The new policy agenda put the internet at the center, attempting to bring network connectivity into the disruptive business model of decentralized, private, post-Fordist corporate management in traditional sectors ranging from manufacturing, agriculture, energy, finance, and transportation to public services and education (State Council 2015b; Hong 2017b). Those behind the internet+ strategy also pledged to propel a new digital economy that could foster and benefit small start-ups, entrepreneurship, and innovation. As such, it dovetails with another policy agenda championed by the state government under the name "Instructions on Constructing Platforms to Promote Mass Entrepreneurship" (*dazhong chuangxin, wanzhong chuangye* 大众创业万众创新) (State Council 2015a). The latter policy sought to mobilize the creativity and innovative power of "grassroots individuals" for national economic growth. Internet+ complements the mass-entrepreneurship strategy, in the sense that a prosperous digital economy provides opportunities for "grassroots individuals" to find employment and become entrepreneurs. According to Premier Li Keqiang,

> Internet+ not only produces new economic driving power but will also create the largest platform for the sharing economy, which stages the "Mass Entrepreneurship and Innovation" program and will deeply affect our economy, society, and everyday life. It provides opportunities for not only techno elites and entrepreneurs but also millions of grassroots individuals (*caogen* 草根) to exploit their talent and to realize their special value. (Li 2018)

In practice, as the official statistics cited earlier indicate, the state agenda of internet+ and mass entrepreneurship has greatly contributed to the surging platform and wanghong economy in China. Kuaishou, together with its competitors Toutiao and Douyin,[3] enable both traditional media companies and grassroots Chinese people to establish and expand their content businesses.[4]

Launched in 2012, Kuaishou is an algorithm-based video and livestreaming platform that allows registered users to create and post short videos online. These videos show activities ranging from cooking, bodybuilding, skills training, makeup applying, and short fiction films. The remarkably diverse content made by millions of online users is analyzed and pushed to targeted viewers by Kuaishou's algorithmic recommendation system. The algorithm system, as Gillespie (2014) suggests, replaces the role of traditional editors in the selection and distribution of content, providing a seemingly more objective model based on the AI computation of user data rather than on editors' subjective preferences. The most important distinguishing characteristic of Kuaishou is that most of its users are uneducated Chinese youths who are rural or based in second- and third-tier cities (Huo 2016). As shown in the following, Kuaishou enabled this group to become an "unlikely creative class." On this platform, they could actively perform their vernacular creativity (Burgess 2006) through self-taught skills, using cheap makeup and amateur cameras. In addition, they use the digital system of Kuaishou to monetize their creative production through advertising and e-commerce. At first sight, Kuaishou's digital entertainment business and its "unlikely creative class" thus seem to fit comfortably with the state's expectation of "mass entrepreneurship."

The challenge for Kuaishou, however, is that its user-generated content must be in line with the Chinese authorities' expectations of what kind of stories should be told. This expectation is especially challenging because the stakes are high; internet+ is not just about restructuring the economy but also about restructuring culture and society. The Chinese authorities have been eager to promote a carefully curated national imagery to wield soft power on the global stage while expecting a conforming culture that ensures social stability and national unity. As Sun Wanning (2009, 66) highlights, this means that they have a double agenda—to "globally present [China] as a player whose values, ethics, and sensibilities are compatible with . . . its international counterparts" while domestically "avoid[ing] 'chaos' at all cost, including heavy-handed censorship, in order to ensure social stability and national unity." This double agenda also applies to Chinese digital platforms.

The platformization of cultural production (Nieborg and Poell 2018) puts users at the center of production, endowing content creators with more autonomy. Yet, as long as these platforms operate domestically, they are not immune to censorship or the state's demand for a compliant culture. According to the Cyberspace Administration of China (CAC), all types of content providers should "abide by the law, adhere to proper values, and help disseminate core socialist values and cultivate a positive and healthy online culture" (CAC 2017). As the central supervisory entity for the Chinese internet communication sectors, the CAC is a powerful government agency. It is under the leadership of the Central Cyberspace Affairs Commission, headed by the Communist Party's general secretary, Chinese president Xi Jinping. Founded in 2014, the CAC has released fifteen policy documents on the regulation of a variety of online content production services, from social media, including WeChat and Weibo, to search engines, mobile applications, and online news production. Apart from the requirement that all content production and distribution adhere to the law and official ideology, these documents also specify regulations on employee management and user registration, as well as punitive measures for any breaches of these regulations. According to these requirements, platform companies are fully responsible for all content circulated and will be "interviewed" (*yuetan* 约谈)—the codeword for this in China is "being invited for tea"—when any of them violate the law or regulations. For example, in April 2018 Kuaishou and Toutiao were both "invited for tea" by the CAC for "ignorance of the law and disseminating programs that are against social moral values" (Liu 2018). The CAC required the two companies to implement a "comprehensive rectification." As a result, they shut down thousands of user accounts (including Tian You's) for posting "unhealthy content" and set up special official accounts for disseminating "positive and healthy values."

Thus, under the policy agenda of internet+ and mass entrepreneurship and innovation, the state's aspiration toward economic restructuring drives the Chinese platform economy and also shapes the wanghong industry. The state-corporate relationship is complicated, largely due to the state's dual concern with economic restructuring and with cultural regulation and social stability. This state-commerce relationship renders content production on the Kuaishou platform acutely "contingent" and distinguishes the platformization of cultural production in contemporary China from that in the West. The relationship thus adds a third dimension to what Nieborg and Poell (2018, 2) summarize as the two aspects of the "contingency" of platform cultural production: *platform dependency* and *contingent commodities*. The former refers to the dominant power of only a few platforms, such as Google, Apple, Facebook, Amazon, and Microsoft (GAFAM) in the West and Baidu, Alibaba, and Tencent (BAT) in China, which "allow[s] content developers to systematically track and profile the activities and preferences of billions of users" (Nieborg and Poell 2018, 2). The latter refers to how cultural commodities on digital platforms are "contingent," in the sense that "they are malleable, modular in design, and informed by datafied user feedback, open to constant revision and recirculation" (Nieborg and Poell 2018, 2). The power of the state, at least in the case of China, engenders a third dimension of contingency that constantly shapes the practice of wanghong production on Chinese digital platforms. But how is this contingency further translated in the digital setting and governance of Kuaishou and its wanghong creators? How does Kuaishou's digital system also affect the networked relations between the state, corporations, and individual users, and what kind of subjectivity and culture are produced within this intricate network? The following two sections will address these questions.

Walking through Kuaishou: Algorithmic and Digital Governance

According to the three algorithm engineers and computer scientists I interviewed, the algorithmic recommendation system of Chinese platforms has four basic components: content analysis, user analysis, evaluation, and security auditing. The first two components use computational models to analyze and classify content and user data. Based on this datafication, diverse content is tagged and distributed automatically among users who are predicted by the algorithm to be target groups. The evaluation component fixes and optimizes the recommendation system based on the feedback from its operation. Finally, the security-auditing component checks, filters, and censors all kinds of online content, including that provided by content producers and interactive content such as end user comments. Through AI machine learning, the auditing system will become increasingly accurate. This is only a basic overview of the algorithmic recommendation system, as the technical components are very complicated. For security-auditing systems in particular, AI is not yet safe enough, meaning that Chinese platform companies often hire manual teams for online censorship. The state's requirement of a positive and healthy internet culture thus increases the operational costs for these platforms. For instance, one of Kuaishou's HR managers

Figure 5.1. Kuaishou's vision (screenshot from Kuaishou's official website, August 2021).

told me in 2017 that the company had recently recruited three thousand new employees in its branches in Harbin, Chengdu, Yancheng, Tianjin, and Wuhan to conduct manual censorship and online surveillance.

Under such algorithmic logic, Kuaishou has forged an ostensibly decentralizing and democratic system for content production and selection. In principle, everyone is treated equally by the algorithmic machine, whether they are movie stars or migrant workers. The key for content production is to obtain as much online traffic through the creative content as possible. According to the online archives of the Kuaishou website[5] and its update records in Apple's App Store, Kuaishou has described itself through slogans such as "Something interesting" (2015), "Record the world, record you" (2016–18), and "Embrace all lifestyles" (2021). On its website, Kuaishou defines its online culture and values as "Authentic, Diverse, Beautiful and Beneficial." It claims to foster a vibrant ecosystem to help users "discover a vast world of content that will expand their interests and horizons and will resonate well with them."

Such phrases conjure up ideas of worlding, the self, and locality, thus grounding the platform's contents in the everyday realities of China. The images shared on the website and in the App Store further strengthen that sense of everydayness; ordinary Chinese youths are captured traveling, staying at home, or working. Keywords such as "authentic," "beautiful," "diverse," and "beneficial," together with the photos, indicate

Kuaishou's vision—to invite "grassroots individuals" to discover and share the interesting and beautiful moments in their own and others' everyday lives (Figure 5.1). By promising a diverse, authentic, and beneficial community, Kuaishou absorbs users' creativity and everyday lives into its own wanghong and platform-economy ecosystem.

Kuaishou is a free app, and its revenue sources consist mainly of in-app advertising and a gifting economy through livestreaming. As a typical content platform that connects multisided markets, Kuaishou offers two methods of in-app advertising. The first is called "fans headlines" (*fensi toutiao* 粉丝头条), which allows wanghong creators to promote their video content on the platform. According to the app's description,[6] after users pay 37.9 RMB (5.67 USD), their posted videos can gain ten thousand views from end users. Producers can simply click on the "fans headlines" button under the "Settings" menu of the app interface. Another form of advertising is offered to third-party companies or brands that buy advertising space on the interface. Commercials are mixed with user-generated videos and fed to targeted viewers by the algorithm. Kuaishou has not publicly specified the cost of its advertising space, but a new-media agency has disclosed (Qirui 2017) that, apart from the one-off service fee of 5,600 RMB (837 USD), advertisers pay 0.2 RMB (0.03 USD) for each click.[7]

Another important revenue source comes from the gifting economy in Kuaishou's livestreaming service. Only a select group of users are authorized to livestream on the platform. Fans interacting with streamers use *kuaibi* (快币)—a virtual currency unique to Kuaishou—to buy virtual gifts and send them to their favorite streamers. One RMB (0.15 USD) can buy ten *kuaibi*, with the price of each virtual gift varying from one to 188 *kuaibi*. According to the platform's regulations, after deducting 20 percent for tax, half the remaining income from gifting goes to the platform company, while streamers usually get less than 40 percent. Clearly, Kuaishou's business model is largely dependent on how much data and data traffic the platform can collect from users. The more popular its content, the higher financial returns the platform reaps and the more money its complementors can obtain.

Kuaishou has a very simple interface. Users can use email or an account from WeChat, Weibo, Facebook, or Google to register.[8] There are three tabs on the main interface: "Following" (*Guanzhu* 关注),

"Trending" (*Faxian* 发现), and "Nearby"[9] (*Tongcheng* 同城); see Figure 5.2. The default tab is "Trending," which lists all the videos selected and pushed by the recommendation algorithm. There is no category-selection button under the tab, and videos that appear here seem to be randomly selected. After using the app for a while, the streaming list will be updated and filled with new content that is further calculated by the algorithm. Most of these videos are indeed "trending." The majority have obtained at least hundreds of likes, and most have been posted that day. Every fifth video is usually a product advertisement. The number of videos and their genres will increase as the app is used over time. Under the "Following" tab, content based on the accounts the user follows is listed in chronological order. The recommendation algorithm does not apply here, since it is based on the user's preferences. For content producers, this tab provides a window to interact directly and continuously with their target audience. The "Nearby" tab arranges videos based on the physical distance between video makers and end users. The platform gives priority in this tab to accounts that have bought "fans headlines" services and accounts that are livestreaming. By adding a geo-locational feature to the streaming system, the platform exploits users' offline social networks, which might create more user engagement.

To post content on Kuaishou, users do not need to change to a different account. By simply clicking on the camera icon above the interface (Figure 5.2), they can upload and post a short video up to fifty-seven seconds long. Users can use smartphones to capture real-time activities and edit them with background music or animation effects provided by the app. They can also use the app to publicize premade, more professional content. As with other Chinese internet service providers (ISPs), a mobile phone number is necessary for verification. Before users can stream a video, it must be uploaded to the database and analyzed by the algorithmic system. Verified "legal" content will then be pushed to a small group of end users for the first round of promotion with geographically nearby users, subscribers, and those predicted by the AI system to be "potentially interested users." After the first twenty-four hours, the system will evaluate the content based on the feedback of users' interactive data and decide whether the content is worthy of a second- or third-round push. If users buy the "fans headlines" service, the posted videos will receive the purchased amount of data traffic. The

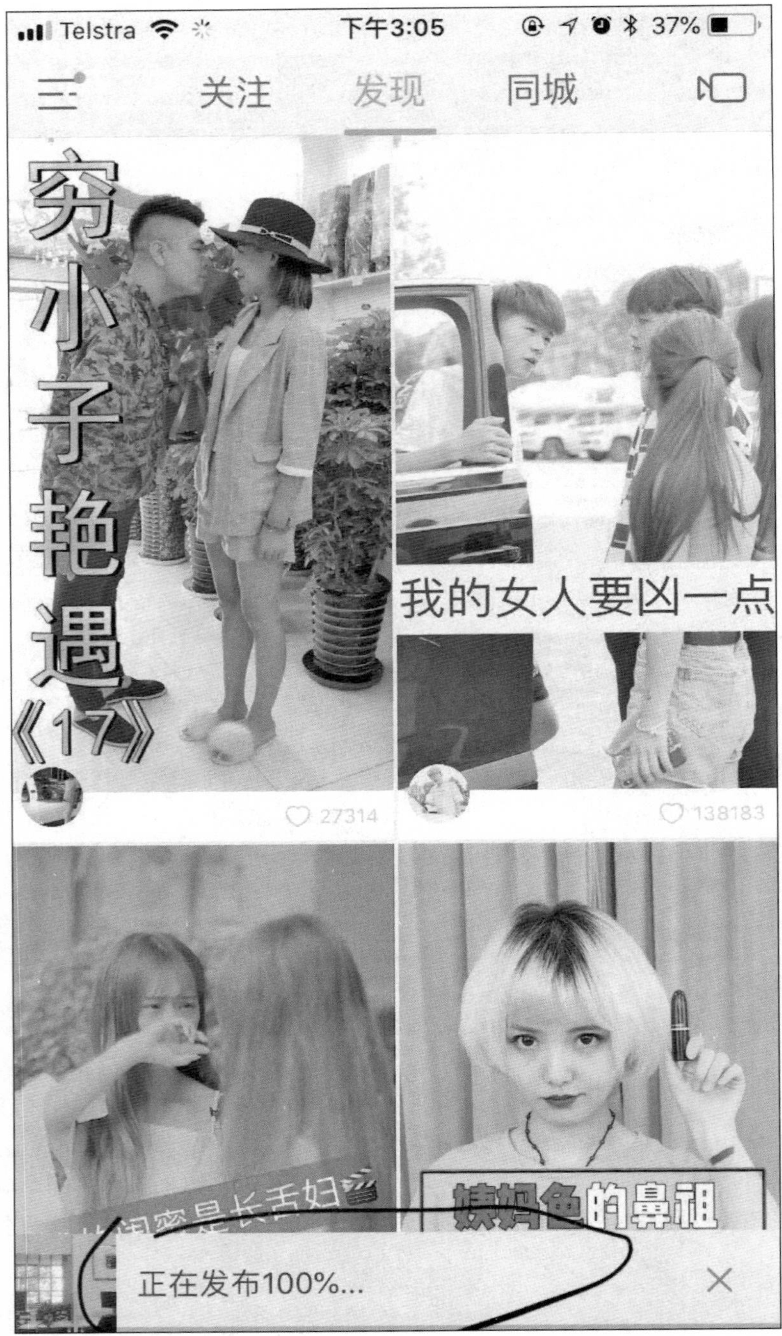

Figure 5.2. The Kuaishou interface (screenshot, August 2018).

data traffic generated by the content is the platform's most valuable asset; it will bring subscriptions, interactivity, and subsequent advertising opportunities for the account holder. If their account remains highly active for weeks, obtains a large number of subscriptions, and has no history of violating the user regulations of the platform, then content producers can contact customer service for authorization of a livestreaming function.

According to the platform's regulations, there are three standards for evaluating an account: 1) It should have a high level of interactivity—users should continuously upload original content and have a large number of followers and online interactions; 2) the account should add to the positive image of the platform and should not have any record of violating the regulations; and 3) users should link their accounts to mobile phone numbers using two-factor authentication to reduce the risk of being hacked.

In 2017 and early 2018, Kuaishou stirred discussion among the public and was "interviewed" by the CAC due to some online hosts' "vulgar" and "unhealthy" behaviors during livestreaming. As a result, the platform has more cautiously regulated the livestreaming service. The ambiguous rhetoric of the regulations gives it the flexibility and power to control and manage the livestreaming service in accordance with its own interests and those of the state.

The algorithmic system and its immense database remain largely invisible to content producers. Kuaishou holds a powerful position in its platform system, in a similar way as Instagram. The company never discloses to users any technical details of its algorithms. In addition, content producers only have very limited access to interactive data—such as the number of followers, comments, and likes—through the app's user interface. They can check their followers' public homepages, but detailed user data such as demographic and behavioral information is not available. In addition to restrictions on illegal or malicious content that violates Chinese law, the Kuaishou user agreement also prohibits users from engaging in unauthorized commercial activities such as selling products or posting private advertisements. By posting content on the platform, users automatically grant the Kuaishou company "a world-wide, royalty-free, nonexclusive, sublicensable, and perpetual (unless withdrawn expressly by you) license, to use the content uploaded (including but not limited to copy, publish, release, as well as adapt, reproduce, translate, transmit, perform, and display in original form or other forms)."[10] This user agreement abides by the company's commercial interests and the Chinese state's requirement of a conforming and "positive" culture. Any violation of the agreement could lead to punishments such as changing and deleting posted content, or even suspending or terminating the user's account.

At a time when the state government is tightening its control over the cultural and media sectors, Kuaishou and other platforms are also strengthening their management of online content, as the case of Tian You shows. More aggressive enforcement underlines the unequal relationship between content producers and the company that runs the platform. Content producers must meticulously manage their creative production to ensure the accumulation of online data traffic without breaching the platform's regulations. The governance of digital platforms thus creates a pervasive sense of uncertainty and insecurity among content producers. In the face of this uncertainty, many content producers feel obliged to post words on their homepages expressing their appreciation of Kuaishou, such as "Thank you, Kuaishou, for providing such a wonderful platform" or "I support Kuaishou for transmitting positive values" (Figure 5.3).

The analysis so far has shown that Kuaishou's algorithm-based system epitomizes the platform contingency caused by the special state-platform relationship, which distinguishes the Chinese platformization of cultural production from Western models. As a result, platform governance is subject to state regulatory power, which both promotes and circumscribes wanghong production. The algorithmic machine allows the Kuaishou platform to absorb the most creativity from "grassroots individuals," but state-platform contingency also limits the automation of platform governance, for example by requiring manual censorship.

For individual creators on Kuaishou, the algorithmic system and its immense database remain largely invisible. The question I engage with in the following section concerns the creators and the content they produce. How do they address state-platform contingency and the need to walk the tightrope between censorship and creativity, between production and commodification, and between subjectivity and being subjected?

Figure 5.3. One Kuaishou user's homepage (screenshot, August 2018).

Unlikely Creative Class, Unlikely Aesthetics?

Wang Qian grew up in the countryside of Dazhou in western China's Sichuan Province. At the age of fifteen, after graduating from middle school, he followed his relatives to Shenzhen, where he became a factory worker. In 2016, inspired by the stories of people making money through Kuaishou, he quit his job at the factory and decided to make videos. Using the name "Brother Qian" (*qiange* 谦哥), he performs and teaches magic tricks in his videos and livestreams on Kuaishou. Wearing a stylish hat and facial makeup, Wang Qian looks and performs like a professional magician in his videos. Yet he never received any training—he learned all his skills from the internet. After two years, his account had over 1 million subscriptions. This large fan base allows him to sell and advertise magic props through the platform. As Wang Qian disclosed in our interview, the wanghong business enabled by Kuaishou generated average sales of 70,000 RMB (10,466 USD) per month. Deducting production costs and salaries for his assistants, Wang's monthly income can reach 50,000 RMB (7,476 USD). Compared to his job at the factory, his new job had multiplied his earnings and changed his appearance and identity. He had jettisoned the stigmatizing label of "migrant worker" to become part of the affluent, fashionable, and popular wanghong scene. Through Kuaishou, Wang had jumped from a sweatshop in Shenzhen into the urban creative class.

Wang Qian's experience is not uncommon on Kuaishou. In Li et al.'s (2020, 13) study of the use of Kuaishou among a group of rural students, the video-sharing app allowed low-income rural youths to "express their resistance against education" through the circulation and production of the "society man" (*shehui ren* 社会人) subculture. Kuaishou promised these rural youths an upward socioeconomic mobility by capitalizing on their memories and creativity in the production of the *shehui ren* subculture.

Kuaishou's massive rural popularity, culture, and aesthetics distinguish it from other Chinese and Western social media platforms. At first, Kuaishou was best known for targeting users from the urban lower social class and rural society, enabling them to "record the world and themselves." According to a manager from Kuaishou, the company has never tried to sign or promote any particular type of "online celebrity."

Instead, Kuaishou embraces an aesthetic of the vernacular, which can be described as foregrounding "the un-hip, the un-cool, and possibly the downright square, [it] embraces those marginal and non-glamorous creative practices excluded from arts- and culture-based regeneration. Vernacular forms of creativity are neither extraordinary not spectacular . . . but are part of a range of mundane, intensely social practices" (Edensor 2009, 10; see also Burgess 2006).

To further examine the vernacular aesthetics circulated on Kuaishou, this section analyzes two hundred trending videos and the everyday user activities of twenty popular Kuaishou accounts. These selected short videos constitute what Lauren Berlant has termed a "silly archive"; these everyday experiences of ordinary citizens may be "the silliest, most banal, and . . . of erratic logic" (Berlant 1997, 12). It is precisely the improvisatory ephemerality, popularity, and effects on everyday life, according to Berlant (1997, 12), that make such a "silly archive" worthy of serious reading.

In the selection of videos, five recurring genres of content were observed:

1. Everyday life, such as cooking, cosmetics, pets, and family life
2. Country life, including fishing, hunting, crafts, and vernacular landscapes
3. Creative skills, such as singing, magic, dancing, fitness, and professional skills
4. Fictional short films
5. "Positive value content," mostly produced by official sponsored accounts

For the first four genres, the idea of "grassrootsness" is crucial; it is performed to add "authenticity" to the videos by making them look more real and more similar to the audience's own life. For Wang Qian, behind his polished appearance in the videos, such grassrootsness is demonstrated by his accent and his way of performing magic. Unlike professional magicians, he shows only forms of magic that he learned from the internet, and he teaches magic to his fans by revealing how tricks work. In one of his videos, he remarks at the end, "Come on, brothers. With this trick you'll find a girlfriend!"

Figure 5.4. Before and after using makeup (screenshot of one selected video, August 2018).

Other wanghong creators on Kuaishou also choose to deliberately display their underclass identity through their accent, dress, skin color, or behavior. For instance, in a series of videos on cosmetic skills, a female model has dark skin and chubby cheeks that do not meet the current standard in China for a "beautiful girl." Thanks to her skillful use of cosmetic techniques, the model drastically changes her appearance to give herself fairer skin and thinner cheeks. Her new look (Figure 5.4) is still not comparable to that of professional models in television advertisements, yet videos like these are quite popular on Kuaishou; within a few hours a cosmetics video like this one can easily gain hundreds of thousands of likes from users. The secret to the popularity of these videos is precisely the "grassrootsness" and "authenticity" they represent; not every ordinary person is born with the beauty of a movie star, yet, by virtue of the "right" makeup and application techniques, Kuaishou wanghong creators convince their viewers that they can change their physical appearance.

On the homepage of another account named "Zhang Deshuai," a creator who identifies himself as a "country boy" (*nongcun xiaohuo* 农村小伙) posts homemade short films. These films usually use shabby villages as a background and tell amusing stories about relationships, family life, and friendship. In contrast to their rural landscapes, however, the cast members in these videos always dress in trendy fashion with a stylish haircut, while the hilarious story lines are not necessarily about "country life." The characters in the films, for example, talk about watching movies, shopping, drinking milk tea, and buying a car. Thus, while these films choose rurality as their background, the characters they show and the stories they tell push the limits of rurality by parodying the trendy life of Chinese urban youth.

From Wang Qian's magic demonstrations and the popular cosmetic videos to these self-made fiction films, the aesthetics of the videos on Kuaishou articulate the imagination of Chinese "grassroots individuals" who are marginalized in mainstream popular culture. It is this imagination from the margins that fascinates many Kuaishou users, who experience grassrootsness and marginalization in their own everyday lives. In that sense, Kuaishou's wanghong culture does not necessarily fall into the existing scholarly categories of youth culture, urban culture, or even subculture. Kuaishou has expanded beyond the urban imagery of popular culture and invites often marginalized Chinese populations to become wanghong creators, forming what I term the "unlikely creative class."

This formation of a new creative class is also driven by their "unlikely" aesthetic, which sharply contrasts with the solemn, delicate screen culture of Chinese television and cinema. "Shougong Geng" ("Handcraft Geng"), for example, is a popular wanghong channel on Kuaishou that posts videos of handcraft inventions made by Geng Shuai, a local farmer from Baoding, Hebei Province. Praised by his fans as "the useless Thomas Edison," Geng designs inventions that are all ingeniously designed and crafted yet are unnecessary in everyday life. For instance, he creates a "Handstand Hair-Washer" to wash his hair while doing a handstand. "Smile Assistant" is a device that can help those who do not like to smile, and "Robotic Washing Machine" is made of a discarded gas cylinder that can automatically wash clothes with its electric mechanical arms. These sophisticated yet "useless" machines, together with his amusing facial expressions, create a sense of absurd humor that has won Geng widespread popularity on Kuaishou and elsewhere on the Chinese internet.

The unlikely aesthetics of Kuaishou become even more bizarre when they collide with state-sponsored content usually dubbed as representing "positive values" (*zheng nengliang* 正能量). Since the Kuaishou company was interviewed by the CAC in April 2018, these "positive and healthy values" have guided content regulation on the platform. The once very popular "crazy videos" depicting adolescent pregnancy and self-abuse have been deleted and their accounts banned. In their place, the platform has established a new genre of "positive value" content. Apart from its own official account "Kuaishou positive value" (*Kuaishou zheng nengliang* 快手正能量), the platform invites government institutions such as public-security bureaus to open accounts and post videos on "everyday ethical models," "Chinese economic achievements," "the positive image of soldiers and the police," and "official policy and ideology." The algorithmic system has been configured to support the videos uploaded by these accounts. This is why, in August 2018, "positive value" videos made up seven of the ten most-viewed videos on Kuaishou (Short Video Factory 2018).

In this regard, the "unlikely creative class" on Kuaishou has to meticulously calculate their creativity to align with the platform's value orientation while also making their content attractive to an online audience. For these creative people, the platform and its digital affordances not only denote a way of performing creatively but are also an effective tool for making money and building a career. Data traffic becomes a crucial asset that every creative producer aspires to accumulate. To do so, they first need to understand and utilize the various digital affordances of the platforms. For example, they should update their accounts on a daily basis. From their profile photo to their username, everything that can give end users a sense of what the account is about needs to be deliberately designed and optimized. To be creative through the digital, one must know what, how, and when to create media, and for whom. Constant posting and streaming also requires time-management skills. On Kuaishou, producers normally choose to post their videos in the evening around 8:00 p.m., a time when most high school students (one of the largest demographics on Kuaishou) are at home and have just finished their homework. What Melissa Gregg (2013, 2) calls the "presence bleed"—how digital and communication technologies enable "work to invade places and times that were once less susceptible to its presence"—becomes imperative for platform-based creative labor. The goal of this intensified and extensified[11] (Jarvis and Pratt 2006) work for content producers is to generate profits, which leads to users appropriating digital technologies for their own business purposes. Although Kuaishou prohibits unauthorized advertising and commercial activities, wanghong creators can still find their own ways to avoid the platform's supervision. Some streamers integrate contextual advertisements for third-party merchants in their short videos and livestreams. For example, someone might post videos of their pets on Kuaishou and list their WeChat account number on the homepage to sell pet food, using acronyms such as "WX" or icons like "V❤" as a substitute for WeChat (*weixin* 微信) to dodge the platform's AI monitoring (Figure 5.3).

At the same time, the interactivity of the digital platform requires content producers to orient their creativity toward business purposes while managing their affect and personality to cultivate intimacy with their target users and audience. On Kuaishou, a phrase that appears frequently in short videos is "Come on, bro! Double tap 666! Follow me." The action of double tapping on a video equals a "like" from a viewer, and "666" in Mandarin sounds similar to *liu* (溜)—meaning "cool" or "awesome." These words are often spoken in a euphoric tone with local accents. The goal of this performance is to add a sense of authenticity to the videos and develop intimacy with the audience. To gain more popularity and subscriptions, another strategy used by content producers is to create a special character (*renshe* 人设)—to perform a certain personality—through creative practices that will forge intimacy with viewers, who will later become their followers, or fans. As exemplified by the above videos, a personality on Kuaishou is carefully nurtured and maintained through performing "grassroots authenticity." A frequent discourse that emerges from these diverse stylizations is that of being real and down to earth (*jiediqi* 接地气), thus underscoring how the personalities that producers create should be relevant and similar to those of the platform's users.

In comparison to the creative workers studied in other chapters, the bilateral nature of Kuaishou creators lies exactly in the formation of the "unlikely creative class" and their "unlikely" aesthetics. Kuaishou creators are partly empowered by the various digital affordances of Kuaishou to negotiate their marginal position in Chinese society, thereby developing their online communities and creative entrepreneurship and becoming the "unlikely creative class." Data and datafication matter not only for giant corporations and institutions (van Dijck 2014), but they also become crucial production tools and assets for these new, "unlikely" creative subjects on Kuaishou. Though confronted with an extremely precarious working environment—strict platform regulations, fierce competition, and exploitation from multichannel networks (MCNs)—they also see considerable career and financial potential as well as social mobilities that promise to uplift their social position and identity. To creators, wanghong creativity and subjectivity become desirable alternatives to working as cooks, farmers, high school teachers, or college graduates waiting to be hired by companies. The banality of the everyday has been converted into the productive footage of their online creativity, signifying a moment when mundane life, creativity, and career converge.

The "grotesque," "useless," and "meaningless" but creative and entertaining content on Kuaishou not only represents the vast diversity, energy, and creativity shared by these unlikely creators but also offers a sharp and valuable contrast to the always "delicate," "professional," and "serious" screen culture produced by the established Chinese media. The beauty tutorials, fictional microfilms, and Handcraft Geng's amusing inventions only become meaningful and creative when they are shown in the context constructed by Kuanshou and catch the attention of millions of followers who may live similar lives as these creators as farmers, migrant workers, and ordinary, voiceless people. They create a cordial resonance with their viewers' similarly mundane lives and fill their empty, forgotten time that is both unavoidable and intolerable. Wanghong culture thus lightheartedly reframes mundane everyday life and legacy screen culture, both of which can be experienced as "boring" and "meaningless" within the Chinese hierarchical social, cultural, and economic order. The scale, diversity, and sheer energy of wanghong culture makes the guardians of this order nervous, as all the punishing efforts mentioned in this chapter can demonstrate. Without posing a direct challenge to that social and cultural order, Kuaishou creators and wanghong industry in general absorb them into their own productions.

Conclusion

This chapter has looked at a special group of creative workers—online video creators on the Chinese social media platform Kuaishou, which has been enabled by the emerging Chinese platform economy and wanghong industry. I first examined the state-platform contingency caused by the complicated relationship between Kuaishou and the state governance of culture and economy, and how such contingency is embedded in the digital algorithmic system of the platform. A third dimension of platform contingency distinguishes the functioning ecology of Chinese media platforms from those in the West. This contingency maximizes the subsumption of individual vernacular creativity in China's platform creative economy while also enabling marginalized grassroots Chinese people to become an "unlikely creative class."

To some extent, Kuaishou creators resemble the independent filmmakers examined in chapter 3, in the sense that Kuaishou and its platform economy provide a channel for these "grassroots individuals" to deterritorialize from their previous "unsatisfactory" lives. These diverse Kuaishou creators move from being migrant workers, rural residents, or uneducated members of the lower social classes to forming this "unlikely creative class." The platform economy and the wanghong industry accommodate the Chinese state's "entrepreneurial solutionism" (Keane and Chen 2017) exemplified by the state's policy on internet+ and mass entrepreneurship. These policies presume digital technology and entrepreneurship to be the solution to China's social, economic, and cultural problems. This emerging industry thus provides opportunities for grassroots people from diverse backgrounds to become creative workers, thus abiding by the state's goal of restructuring the economy.

Importantly, this unlikely creative class has transcended the passive "digital labor" and "prosumer" models that political economists have criticized (Ritzer and Jurgenson 2010; Fuchs 2010). Despite the institutional regulation and censorship of the internet, these Kuaishou creators actively participate in the Chinese wanghong industry and digital economy, appropriating the algorithmic system and negotiating with the state/platform governance to achieve their own creative and financial goals. Inherent in this formation of the unlikely creative class and its unlikely aesthetics, the bilateral subjectivity of Kuaishou creators constitutes a mixed process of becoming that transcends the simple identity of either their "authentic," everyday job or the professionalized creative worker. It is from these online, vernacular creativities that we can find moments of play and resistance—moments in which the official "Chinese Dream" narrative is juxtaposed with other dreams from people who hardly ever get a face or a voice in mainstream Chinese media.

6

The Future of Bilateral Creatives

Introduction

The ongoing COVID-19 pandemic has challenged the Chinese creative industries and cultural governance. In 2020, from production to consumption, the entire cultural industries were severely hit with financial losses predicted to be over 1 trillion RMB (150 billion USD) (Cheng 2021). Museums, performing arts venues, the film industry, and tourism were all suspended in the early months of the outbreak. For example, on January 22, the authorities demanded that all Chinese cinemas shut down for 180 days. As a result, the total box office sales in 2020 contracted 68.23 percent, with only 650 new films produced: a 37.3 percent decrease from 2019 (Hu and Wang 2021). In a survey conducted by a local research institute (BICIC 2020), among 2,136 cultural companies in Beijing, 78.9 percent had suspended their operations, especially small enterprises, over 90 percent of which reported being in complete lockdown. For creative workers, the situation might become even worse; almost 50 percent of these surveyed companies were reportedly planning to fire workers, which mirrors what Comunian and England (2020) found in their study of the response of the British creative industries during COVID-19. The pandemic has further intensified the labor precarity experienced by those working in China's media and cultural industries.

As I will illustrate in this final chapter, the Chinese state and China's creative media companies have recognized digitalization, artificial intelligence, and globalization as new directions for the future of the Chinese creative industries. In the Fourteenth Five-Year Plan, published in March 2021, the state announced that it would promote digitalization as the central developmental strategy of China's cultural industries. In the future, the Fourteenth Five-Year Plan states, China wants to "accelerate the development of new cultural enterprises, businesses, and consumption and enlarge the industries for digital creativity, internet audio-visual, digital publishing, digital entertainment, and online performance" (NDRC 2021, n.p.). Importantly, digitalization and new technologies also renew the long-standing strategy of the Chinese state's "going-out policy" (中国文化走出去). According to the state, one of the central goals of cultural going-out is "to cultivate the global competitiveness of the digital cultural industries and to push their digital cultural products and services to go global" (MCT 2021, n.p.). In practice, as shown below, internet and tech companies have become increasingly active and powerful in the Chinese and global media and cultural sectors, with new AI-based smart and automation technologies promising to transform and advance cultural and media production in China and beyond.

In this chapter, I consider the future of the creative industries and of Chinese creative labor in light of the recent application of AI and automation technologies in the Chinese creative economy, and the globalization of Chinese social media platforms. Built on earlier investigations of the bilateral subjectification of creative workers in China, this book concludes by highlighting the schizophrenic nature of the Chinese creative economy as both an industrial organization and a governing system. It is still too early to lament or celebrate these new developments and the surrounding discourse of "the rise of China"; if there is a post-pandemic future to come, it may bring similar dilemmas, frustrations, and aspirations.

Digitalization, Automation, and the State

As some Chinese scholars have noted, COVID-19 has forced Chinese cultural companies to implement the state's digitalization strategy for content production and distribution. In May 2021, two months after the state publicized its renewed "National Five-Year Plan," the Chinese Ministry of Culture and Tourism released the Fourteenth Five-Year Plan for the Cultural Industries, which followed the national plan's definition of the digitalization strategy as "developing new cultural businesses," "upgrading traditional cultural industries," "advancing innovation and application of cultural technologies," and "constructing [an] innovative ecology for cultural development" (MCT 2021). The plan recognized "cloud computing," "big data," and "artificial intelligence" as key technologies for infrastructure, production, distribution, and consumption in the cultural sectors.

Digitalization has been part of China's cultural-industries policy throughout the past two decades. As I have shown in chapter 5, the platform economy and the wanghong industry have been integrated into the state agenda for restructuring the national economy, which has experienced a significant boost since 2015. This is the first time that digitalization and smart technologies such as AI and automation have been at the center of cultural-industries policy and placed as the primary strategy for the future of China's creative economy. The goal, according to the plan (MCT 2021, n.p.), is "to stimulate cultural innovation and creativity, to comprehensively upgrade content production and distribution and the business model of the cultural industries, to adapt to the direction of high-tech development, and to facilitate a deep integration of culture and technology."

If the wanghong industry (see chapter 5) signals the emergence of a new entertainment industry in China, the country's new digitalization strategy is a more ambitious move to integrate technological innovation into the whole cultural sector. In effect, the strategy incorporates an "industrialization of the digital" and the "digitalization of the industries," both of which refer to the digital information and communication industries, and the convergence between digital and communicative infrastructure and the established cultural sectors.

Tencent, for instance, developed the AI-based journalist robot Dreamwriter in 2015. According to Tencent's official statement, this system primarily focuses on producing fact-based news in fields such as finance, sports, real estate, and the automobile industry, because the news production in these fields usually requires less analytical input from human editors (Gan 2019). By January 2019, Dreamwriter had published over five hundred thousand pieces of news. According to the robot's developer, their technology significantly boosted the efficiency of news production "that has struggled to meet demand" (Gan 2019). In general, the Chinese financial industry generates over nineteen hundred announcements per day, which would require at least one hundred hours for one professional editor to read and analyze (Gan 2019).

Dreamwriter promises to alleviate the pressure on editors and journalists. As Liu Kang, the director of the Tencent Artificial Intelligence Lab, states, "I hope it always serves as an assistant to, instead of replacing [journalists and editors]. It helps collecting and analyzing information, and then we [editors and journalists] bring them to life—it takes only 0.46 second to produce a news item" (Gan 2019, n.p.).

Tencent is not alone in developing such AI-based news-production systems. ByteDance and Alibaba, as well as the Xinhua Agency (the largest Chinese news agency), have all invested in their own news robots based on similar technologies of machine learning, big data, and automation. In graphic design, Alibaba developed a similar automation system named Luban in 2017 (Alitech 2017). By virtue of the massive user data accumulated in Alibaba's e-commerce ecosystem, Luban allows shop owners to easily design banners and pictures for the goods listed in their online shops on Alibaba and Taobao. The system takes an estimated one second to design over eight thousand posters, and in one day it can create up to 600 million. On November 11, 2019, on the Chinese Singles' Day Festival—a major Chinese online shopping event launched by Alibaba—Luban was reported to have produced over 1 billion banners, and "almost every banner and product picture shown on Taobao and Tmall was designed by the system" (Huang 2020). This system also incorporates real-time user feedback and continuously optimizes its algorithm, which successfully boosts the click rate of online products shown online (Huang 2020).

These examples show that the imaginaries of AI and automation technologies in China's cultural industries now echo what Holford (2019, 145) critiques as "the neo-liberal socioeconomic quest for profit maximization and organizational efficiency." That is, the aim of digitalization is to enhance the global competitiveness of the Chinese creative economy and Chinese cultural enterprises. The future of China's cultural industries continues to lie in the exploitation of culture and creativity, but new smart technologies are the main driving force to "upgrade the industrial structure and turn China into a socialist cultural powerhouse" (MCT 2021, n.p.). Despite a shared popular belief that the creative occupations will maintain their "bright outlooks and are strongly complemented by digital technology" (Bakhshi et al. 2017, 14), the above cases of AI-based journalism and design hint at a possible future of automation in creative production that has the potential to replace (or at least reduce) certain forms of creative work from symbol-based production to sign-based production (Holford 2019). In the traditional sense, artistic creativity deals with symbols, which in linguistics are multivocal and polysemic, expressing meanings that are vague and contextualized (Ricoeur 1976; Womack 2005). Mathematical technologies, however, can only process language based on signs, which explicitly have only one meaning (Tillich 1987). As a result, the application of AI and machine learning in creative fields could lead to "efficient enactment of truncated knowledge" (Holford 2019, 149). If human artistic production negotiates meanings, then the sign-based automated representations can easily induce symbolic violence, which reduces complex human experiences into algorithms and unequivocal signs (Berrio-Zapata et al. 2015).

The creative labor that undergirds the celebratory discourses of liberation and efficiency is also forgotten in policy for and practices of digitalization. In commercial sectors such as graphic design, we might witness the advent of "digital Taylorism" (Brown, Lauder, and Ashton 2010; Scott et al. 2013; Moorkens 2020). AI-based machine learning and automation will significantly lower the requirement for creative skills, replacing some forms of skilled work with unskilled labor, since tasks will be decomposed into smaller and smaller units. As in the case of Luban, professionally trained designers may still be wanted. For online shop owners, however, the system will complete most of the basic design jobs, leaving the rest of the tasks to be outsourced to nonskilled employees. The prevalence of a more sophisticated surveillance system also offers higher efficiency to monitor creative labor and to ensure standardized and calculated content production with the potential to generate a profit. In the Chinese context, such a system also ensures the production of "safe creativities" deprived of politically sensitive content. The algorithmic culture found on short video platforms such as Kuaishou, Douyin, and its international counterpart TikTok, for example, demonstrates how cultural production and management is "now increasingly organised by a logic of surveillance, data aggregation and monetisation," through a wide integration of "carefully engineered and commercially oriented algorithms" (Collie and Wilson-Barnao 2020, 182). The automation of content circulation ensures a continuous production of short videos that are "playful, meme-based, visually engaging, reproducible and apolitical" (Collie and Wilson-Barnao 2020, 183). These algorithms are thus by no means neutral, as shown by Kuaishou's and TikTok's deliberate promotion of positive value content domestically (see chapter 5), yet they suspiciously limit the visibility of content that is critical of the Chinese state when operating globally.

Since late 2020, when Jack Ma's Ant Group was suspended from public listing in Shanghai and Hong Kong, the Chinese authorities have started a series of antitrust campaigns targeting Chinese internet giants. Companies such as Alibaba, Tencent, ByteDance, and DiDi were interviewed and fined (Niewenhuis 2021). In August 2021, amid the new round of "Operation Qinglang" (清朗行动) led by the Cyberspace Administration of China (CAC) to clamp down on "misbehaving celebrities" and fan culture, the CAC enacted a new regulation on platforms using recommendation algorithms. The CAC stipulated that all platforms must provide buttons for users to deactivate recommendation algorithms. Platform companies, according to the regulation, should "adhere to the mainstream values and optimize the recommendation algorithms to promote the dissemination of positive values" (CAC 2021, n.p.). These moves appear similar because the same concerns of internet monopolies and their dominance in public societies have also motivated the European Union and the United States to take similar actions (Chorzempa 2021). But the efficiency of the Chinese regulatory model is distinct.

In July 2021, the biggest Chinese tech companies—including Huawei, Alibaba, Tencent, Baidu, and ByteDance—gathered in Beijing and signed a convention on fair competition, consumer protection, and strengthening innovation (Borak 2021). Shortly after, Tencent and Alibaba respectively pledged over 100 billion RMB (15 billion USD) in "common prosperity" initiatives (Kharpal 2021). "Common prosperity" had recently been declared by the Chinese state to be a national goal for economic development. These moves show that the state discursive formation (analyzed in chapter 1) still dominates China's cultural-industries policy and digitalization strategy. This realm is also where China's approach to AI and digitalization is distinguishable from the neoliberal logics found in Anglo-American societies. This book reiterates that the party state envisions the cultural industries and new technologies as crucial instruments for both restructuring the Chinese economy and sociocultural governance: "To coordinate all activities in the nation as in a chess game" (*quanguo yipanqi* 全国一盘棋), as the state always emphasizes. Organizational efficiency and profit maximization thus refer to the efficiency of national coordination and governance. Creative workers in this sense may anticipate renewed precarities and opportunities brought about by these new technologies, but their subjectivities will remain bilateral and paradoxical, dragged by multiple and sometimes contradictory forces from the market and the state.

Platformization from China

Chapter 5 has shown how the emerging Chinese platform and wanghong economy, exemplified by the case of Kuaishou, accommodates the state's agenda of using the "internet+" agenda and "mass entrepreneurship" for economic restructuring. As I argue, the strict state surveillance and regulation in order to maintain social and political stability also make the wanghong business and platform economy "contingent" and vulnerable. Creators on Kuaishou are confronted with as much career uncertainty as opportunity as they become an unlikely creative class.

The thriving wanghong and platform economy in the domestic market has also pushed Chinese tech and media companies to go global. As a local researcher predicted in early 2020, "The severe pandemic overseas has created opportunities for China's digital cultural industries to actively expand their global market" (Cheng 2021, n.p.). In practice, national champions such as Tencent and Alibaba, along with emerging social media giants such as ByteDance and Kuaishou, are ambitiously expanding their overseas empires. With Tencent and Alibaba mainly targeting overseas Chinese people, second-generation platforms such as TikTok and Kwai aspire to expand their user bases beyond the Chinese-speaking communities.

Indeed, TikTok has overtaken Facebook as the most downloaded app in the world (Nakafuji 2021). The platform had an average of 689 million active users per month in 2020—with 200 million in the United States or Europe—and had generated over 1 billion USD (6.67 billion RMB) in revenue (Iqbal 2021). And TikTok is not alone. In the same list of the top ten most downloaded apps in 2020, at the eighth spot was Likee—a much less visible social video app developed by Joyy, a NASDAQ-listed

Chinese tech company that owns the popular Chinese livestreaming platforms YY and Huya. Snack Video, an app from ByteDance's main domestic competitor, developed by Kuaishou, was the sixth most downloaded app in the Asia-Pacific region (Nakafuji 2021). Bigo Live, a leading livestreaming platform in Southeast Asia, was originally a start-up company based in Singapore. In 2019, the platform merged with Joyy. In April 2021, Kuaishou's international parallel, Kwai, has opened operations in Argentina, Colombia, and Mexico, while in Brazil the app has an average of twenty-six million active monthly users (Bulhões 2021). Before India shut them down in late 2020, six of the top ten most downloaded apps in that country were Chinese-owned apps (*Business Insider* 2019). The large populations, underdeveloped digital economy, and reduced international competition in these regions seem to provide great opportunities for Chinese social media platforms to expand.

Just as most Western media and platform companies failed to enter China, the state-sponsored Chinese media and cultural products—viewed as carriers of Chinese soft power—haven't managed to reach globally beyond Chinese-speaking communities in the past decade (Sun 2009; Keane 2013). But the worldwide popularity of Chinese short video platforms appear to have gained more credibility and communication capacity (Sun 2009) than the traditional media organizations such as CCTV and *People's Daily* during the process of cultural "going out." Their success signals a new phase of globalization and platformization (Helmond 2015) and actualizes the idea of "platformization from China" (Craig, Lin, and Cunningham 2021); the technological innovations, business ecologies, and creator cultures developed within the Chinese internet now are infiltrating and disrupting the global internet and platform society.

Social media platforms developed in the American-centric ecosystem can easily define themselves as global and claim the shared values of an open internet and free speech (Cunningham and Craig 2019). The challenge for Chinese platforms going global, however, lies in their figurative "Chinese-ness." This term refers to the platform logics embedded in companies' operational mechanisms, creator practices, online culture, and platform governance. For example, the domestic business ecology of Chinese social media platforms such as WeChat, Douyin, and Bilibili is largely defined by the "social industry model" (Craig, Lin, and

Cunningham 2021). This model incorporates innovative and interactive features including short video, livestreaming, and live commerce in a highly commercial online system. The model creates abundant opportunities for monetization and collaboration among platforms, creators, brands, MCNs, and end users. As illustrated in chapter 5, this platform ecology fits into the state's agenda for a digital economy and increased innovation (Keane and Chen 2017) but also echoes the state's call for social stability and cultural control, achieved through a pervasive regime of censorship and state supervision. Such an ecology propels a platform logic that maximizes the exploitation of labor and creativity from diverse backgrounds while also situating the platform as being financially profitable and politically secure (Zhang 2020; Chen, Kaye, and Zeng 2021).

In liberal societies, however, a call for an open internet has contradicted Chinese platform logics, which has led to a surge of disputes about these Chinese apps' platform governance. For example, TikTok has been criticized for causing social media addiction, especially among its teenage users (Stokel-Walker 2020). In countries such as Indonesia, Pakistan, and India that have large religious communities, some of the popular content on TikTok is seen as immoral, vulgar, and encouraging of pornography (*Nation* 2020; Su 2020). In Western liberal societies, the app has been attacked for its lack of transparency in content moderation and censorship (Biddle, Ribeiro, and Dias 2021). According to Kaye et al.'s research (2021), such contradictions in platform governance have forced companies such as ByteDance and Kuaishou to adopt a parallel platformization strategy to establish their business in two distinctive markets. For example, TikTok has inherited most of the technical and commercial features from its Chinese counterpart app, Douyin, but TikTok remains a separate and independent platform with its own servers and managerial teams. The same strategy is evident in the operations of Kuaishou and its international counterpart, Kwai.

In their global operations, Chinese platforms deliberately distance themselves from their Chinese origins (Kaye et al. 2021; Craig, Lin, and Cunningham 2021) and localize and diversify their platform governance (Jia and Liang 2021). These strategies of parallel platformization and localization contribute to a further expansion of the market and incorporation of individual labor and creativities from around the world. For international creators, the social industry model has promised a more profitable and "spreadable" (Jenkins, Ford, and Green 2013) media ecology, as demonstrated by Kaye et al.'s forthcoming study of "socially creative features" on TikTok. Interactive features such as "duet," "stitch," and "video reply" to comments on TikTok facilitate the production of creativities based not merely on the idea of originality but on imitation, memeification, and sociality.

As a result, platformization from China creates an ironic dilemma: the globalization of technological innovation from China contrasts with its discursive decoupling from China worldwide. In terms of bilateral creatives, we can now also speak of bilateral platforms—the more globalized they become, the less "Chinese" they must be. As a previous business development manager of TikTok told me, TikTok has succeeded thanks to its localized creative design and business management (Andy, April 2021):

> My experience is that Chinese colleagues have better analytical skills, but local [American] staff is better in "small innovations"—how to get down to the nitty-gritty. . . . For example, on Douyin we usually have beauty cameras and filters to make people's chins look sharper and their skin whiter, but none of these are acceptable in American culture. Therefore, from the beginning TikTok has built a large local creative team in the US and left all the creative designing jobs to American colleagues.

The "Chinese" character of TikTok and other globalizing platforms thus is derived more from their technical infrastructure—algorithms, programming, and finance—while the creative design, community building, and business operation are highly reliant on localization. It is thus questionable to what extent the globalization of Chinese social media platforms can really represent Chinese soft power, which, according to the Chinese authorities, refers to the international influence of Chinese culture, values, governance, and economic models (Zhao and Li 2009).

The Bilateral Future

Importantly, alongside platformization from China, global platforms are seeing increasing numbers of Chinese social media creators and content, along with more international creators on Chinese platforms and media. On YouTube, we can see the viral popularity of Li Ziqi's romanticized documentary of her life in the Chinese countryside and Yeshi Xiaoge's "authentic" show on Chinese food and cooking. Conversely, international social media creators are becoming wanghong on Chinese platforms. Jerry Kowal (or Guo Jierui 郭杰瑞) is an American vlogger active on Bilibili, a Chinese video platform. His channel introduces American culture and shows his intercultural experiences in both China and the United States. These videos have attracted almost seven million subscribers to his channel on Bilibili and 670,000 on YouTube, which is also featured in Chinese. In my interview with Dutch TikTok MCN manager Fabian, he shared that he always pushed his signed TikTok influencers in Europe to use and explore the Chinese parallel, Douyin. Because Douyin has a much larger user base, and its creators have more sophisticated creative skills, according to Fabian, TikTok's international creators can learn from Chinese creators' inspirations and monetization strategies.

These individual practices and anecdotes suggest that new developments in technology and globalization can have cultural implications. Once again, they demonstrate what I argue in this book about self-governance being incalculable. Although the state never stops appropriating these individual practices into its own narratives and agenda, we can also detect more organic flows of creativity. For example, the Chinese state media apprised the nostalgic depiction of rural China in Li Ziqi's videos as "opening a new window to let the world see the beauty of China," and their success was believed to serve as "a valuable model to study Chinese international communication" (Li 2020, n.p.). CCTV invited Jerry Kowal to broadcast live in a temporary hospital in New York, where he talked about inadequate measures taken by the United States to fight COVID-19. Both Li Ziqi and Jerry Kowal have been suspected of being sponsored by the Chinese state to produce "international propaganda" (*waixuan* 外宣), although the aesthetics they rely on and the stories they tell significantly distinguish their content from state-sponsored propaganda.

Li Ziqi's videos resonate with the disillusion of younger generations—whether in Shanghai or New York—with urban life. Her performed personality and lifestyle are an impossible but appealing alternative to those who struggle in contemporary cities (Matei 2020). In Kowal's vlogging series *Diary of Fighting the Pandemic Overseas* (*haiwai kangyi riji* 海外抗疫日记), he took to the streets of New York and Washington, DC, to document contrasting views about lockdowns, wearing masks, and racism in response to the George Floyd protests and the riots in the US Capitol after the 2020 election. Given that the majority of his viewers are in China, his videos are distinctive compared to the often-biased international news broadcast by state media such as CCTV.

To echo the analyses in previous chapters, China's governance of cultural and media industries is not always successful but is full of contradictions and negotiations. If digitalization and platformization from China are solutions for the future, then that future may share the schizophrenic nature we have seen in the past. The state actualizes its imagination of the future through an endless reterritorialization of new technologies and new economies, as well as the appropriation of individual creativities. But just as the above examples indicate, this process also generates rifts that can undermine or deviate from the original goals, plans, and intentions defined by the state.

Conclusion

This book so far has illustrated several dilemmas confronting the Chinese creative economies, the foremost of which is the dilemma of governance. The party state recognizes culture and creativity as engines for economic restructuring and instruments for social governance. In the postsocialist era, the party state has renewed its ruling legitimacy through marketization reform, which encourages cultural diversity and incorporates people's creativity into economic development and restructuring. But the vast diversity and differences that the cultural industries have mobilized can also undermine or threaten the social order and the political stability that China's one-party system relies on. Driven by this dual concern with economic prosperity and political stability, the Chinese authorities have set up policies, apparatuses, and institutions to promote and circumscribe the creative economies. Within this dynamic system, the state and capital constantly collaborate and struggle against each other. Together, these forces induce job and life insecurities for creative workers in China, but they also produce an unstable governing system permeated with contradictions that contribute to the formation of a bilateral creative subjectivity.

The fragmented administrative system, the decentralized authoritarian regime, and the complicated state-commerce relationship all profoundly affect the process of making and implementing policies for the contemporary Chinese cultural sectors. Together, they create abundant space for agency, deviation from official policies, and flexibility for diverse actors in the cultural and media sphere. There is thus a complex, dynamic relationship between administrative power and various production subjects. The crucial task for cultural producers in China is to negotiate and find ways to "play" with state power, which is contested, nonunitary, and multivariate. More specifically, the commercialization reform among China's state-owned cultural enterprises has resulted in an entanglement of neoliberal techniques (the discourse of "self-realization") and repressive and disciplinary regulation (strict censorship and rigid bureaucracy) in their everyday management. This entanglement has acutely reduced the efficiency of management, leading to a significant number of employees loafing on the job or resigning. The thriving film industry and strict censorship have precarized independent Chinese filmmakers, reterritorializing independent Chinese cinema toward a depoliticized "art cinema."

In terms of international creative professionals, their presence in Beijing is generally believed to bring the creative know-how that ambitious Chinese companies and local authorities long for and thus contributes to the thriving of global Chinese creative industries. Yet in their everyday work and life, these professionals also confront the precarious situations depicted in chapter 4. These problems discourage them from becoming Chinese and may incite them to leave when they reach the stage of wanting to lead a more stable life and start a family.

In the emerging platform and wanghong economy, Kuaishou accommodates the Chinese state's agenda of "internet+" and "mass entrepreneurship" for economic restructuring, while the strict state surveillance and regulation in order to maintain social and political stability also make the platform's business "contingent" and vulnerable.

Finally, these dual and sometimes contradictory logics of governance also characterize the Chinese state's vision of smart technologies and platformization from China. The imaginaries of organizational efficiency and profit maximization should always fall under the state's coordination of economy and culture. The globalization of social media platforms provides an alternative approach to Chinese cultural "going out," yet the surging controversies in global society also force these Chinese companies to distance themselves from and deviate from their inherent "Chinese-ness."

Within this dilemma of governance lies a dilemma of aspiration. The promised benefits of creative work—autonomy, cultural value, and playfulness—are not necessarily illusory. Such merits and the perceived value of cultural work capture diverse individual creators' hopes for a better alternative. Becoming part of the "Chinese creative workforce" deterritorializes them from their unsatisfying previous lives as coal miners, unmotivated college students, migrant workers, and international cultural workers. Upon entering the cultural field, however, these aspiring creatives soon find out that their hopes for an alternative become compromised by the often-precarious living and working conditions—a process of reterritorialization that I clarified in the introduction to this book. As a result, their creative aspirations end up at odds with their career and life aspirations.

A motivated creative worker often must sacrifice other important aspects of well-being such as family, friendship, financial security, and community. In addition, the imagined creative autonomy or "independence" of art is also undermined by the rule of the market economy and, in China, by the party state's tight regulation of cultural production. Many Chinese creatives, like the independent filmmakers described in chapter 3, must choose between hunger and cooptation, or depoliticization. Transnational creative workers in Beijing, too, experience their work as both compelling and perilous, both rewarding and precarious. In the Chinese context, then, various types of cultural workers need to learn the art of balancing. They are forced to balance creativity and financial reward, and between expressing their discontent and catering to the image of China the authorities want to present domestically and internationally.

Precarious life is not just perilous but is also productive. When viewed at different angles, the empirical studies in this book demonstrate the incalculable nature of self-governance. For example, the commercialization reform within Chinese state-owned cultural enterprises has brought contradictions and caused dysfunction in governance. Such reforms not only limit the governance and productivity of Chinese SOCEs but also furnish creative people with possibilities to escape the expected subjectivity of "being creative for the state." In independent Chinese cinema, the precarious life of independent filmmakers leads to a depoliticized "art cinema" and forces filmmakers to multitask and network to maintain a sense of optimism about the future, but the incalculable self is also produced in the form of an inclusive mutual-caring community. Similarly, transnational creative workers in Beijing also manage to find spaces for interaction and mutual understanding between the transnational creatives and the local population, which generates the conditions for a cosmopolitan subjectivity. The presence of these situated cosmopolitans not only enriches and diversifies the Chinese creative economy but may also disturb the Chinese authorities' expectation of a conforming and profitable creative workforce. The emergence of the wanghong economy and culture, exemplified by the case of Kuaishou, not only gives voice to those marginal social classes who are often ignored or misrepresented by the mainstream Chinese media but also creates channels for social class mobility and transformation.

Arguably, cultural production and creative workers in contemporary China are governed through an unstable collusion between the party state and capital that both ignites and delimits individual aspirations to being creative. While navigating the tensions between governance and aspiration, Chinese creative workers are confronted with precarious yet productive working conditions. They are encouraged to experiment with their creativity and to adjust their expectations and aspirations to the party state's agenda. But by fusing technologies, capital, the state, and individuals, the governing system, too, must continually adjust its techniques to subsume individual creativity and labor. The process of governance has become a never-ending game of capture and escape, in which individuals and organizations aspire, become frustrated, and then hope for a better, more creative future again. In this sense, I claim in this book that Chinese creative workers are becoming bilateral. Deterritorialization and reterritorialization continually mingle in the process of these people becoming "Chinese creative workers." Their aspirational work and lives both serve and challenge the governance and operation of China's contemporary cultural economies.

During the production of a bilateral subjectivity, the Chinese cultural economy has itself also become schizophrenic. The cultural economy's financial prosperity, which subsidizes the ruling legitimacy of the party state, is premised on the incorporation of a vast diversity of individual people and organizations. To sustain this economy's operation, China's cultural industries therefore also require an effective management and the regulation of heterogeneous individual and organizational forces. Much like creative people are pushed to master the art of balancing, the Chinese authorities also need to maintain an equilibrium between promotion and regulation, reward and punishment. Despite all the struggles and frustrations that this schizophrenic state of governance causes, it may constantly generate and maintain hope for the future of those who live and work within China's cultural economies.

ACKNOWLEDGMENTS

The completion of this book marks the end of an incredible journey in which I have received assistance from numerous people and institutions. The European Research Council, the Amsterdam School for Cultural Analysis (UvA), the Groningen Centre for Media and Journalism Studies (RUG), the Institute for Culture and Society (WSU), and the USC-SJTU Institute of Cultural and Creative Industry have all offered generous funding support for my research.

My deepest gratitude goes to Jeroen de Kloet and Esther Peeren for their amazing supervision and friendship during my seven years of study, work, and stay in the Netherlands. Chow Yiu Fai has been a wonderful mentor and caring friend. His pioneering work on creative labor in Asia inspired my research. I heartily thank all my informants in China who helped me during my fieldwork and kindly shared their experiences. I thank Hu Yang, Ling Xianjing, Wu Yuwen, Cheng Yaobin, Yang Yiwen, Anouchka van Driel, and He Yang for their generous help during my field research.

I am privileged to have received support and advice from scholars including José van Dijck, David Craig, Stuart Cunningham, Anthony Fung, David Hesmondhalgh, Mark Deuze, Michael Keane, Terry Flew, Thomas Poell, Marcel Broersma, Ned Rossiter, Deborah Stevenson, Stefan Landsberger, Lan Shanshan, Ben Lee, and Joke Hermes. The research and writing greatly benefited from discussions with several colleagues, including Robert Prey, Joëlle Swart, Bharath Ganesh, He Kun, Penn Tsz Ting Ip, Rowan Parry, Laura Vermeeren, Wang Shuaishuai, Chen Siyu, Zoénie Deng Liwen, Arjen Nauta, Anoud Arps, Jori Snels, Zheng Jiyu, Guan Zexu, Evelyn Wan, Henry Chow, Vincent So, and Zeng Guohua.

The Department of Media Studies and Journalism at the University of Groningen and the incredible colleagues there provided a warm and stimulating environment. Special thanks to the College of Media and

International Culture at Zhejiang University for offering a new job and the opportunity to come home.

Sincere gratitude to New York University Press and its editorial team, especially editors Furqan Sayeed and Eric Zinner, and series editors Jonathan Gray and Aswin Punathambekar, for their patience, expertise, and zealous endorsement. Andrew Schrock has provided marvelous editorial services for the preparation of the manuscript. I thank all the anonymous reviewers for their constructive and insightful critiques and suggestions.

Last but not least, I'm deeply indebted to my friends and family for their care and love. My parents have always encouraged me to be a better person with independence, integrity, and dignity. I was especially lucky to have my sister, who has cared for me since I was very young.

APPENDIX I

Interviewee List

No.	Name	Organization or type of work	Job	Interview date	Gender	Case study	Interview place	Notes
1	Liana Cui	Chinese Film Library	Film festival curator	7/27/16	Female	SOCEs	Beijing	
2	Jiang Tao	Company A	Journalist and editor	8/4/16	Male	SOCEs	Beijing	
3	Lily Yang	CCTV	Producer/ director	8/5/16	Female	SOCEs	Beijing	
4	Chew Fei	Guiyang News Group	Journalist	9/1/16	Male	SOCEs	Beijing	
5	Carl	CCTV	Senior manager	9/2/16	Male	SOCEs	Beijing	
6	Simon Wong	Anhui Media Group	Producer	9/4/16	Male	SOCEs	Phone	
7	Judie Deng	Shanghai Media Group	Director/ producer	9/20/16	Female	SOCEs	Shanghai	
8	Robin Chen	Anhui Media Group	Administrative manager	9/26/16	Male	SOCEs	Hefei	
9	Even Yang	SMG	Business manager	10/25/16	Female	SOCEs	Shanghai	
10	Liu Kang	State Council; *People's Daily*	Photographer and filmmaker	11/25/16	Male	SOCEs	Amsterdam	
11	David Wong	Freelance	Filmmaker	7/13/17	Male	International	Beijing	Canada (nationality)
12	Sarah Lau	Freelance	Journalist	7/15/17	Female	International	Beijing	Hong Kong
13	Simon	Unknown	Entrepreneur (digital media)	7/18/17	Male	International	Beijing	Malaysia

No.	Name	Organization or type of work	Job	Interview date	Gender	Case study	Interview place	Notes
14	Laurent	Freelance	Photographer	7/24/17	Male	International	Beijing	France
15	Marc	Freelance	Artist	7/24/17	Male	International	Beijing	Netherlands
16	Pedro	Freelance	Artist	7/24/17	Male	International	Beijing	Netherlands; non-recorded
17	Jolene	Freelance	Journalist	7/25/17	Female	International	Beijing	Taiwan
18	Mike	Game company	Creative producer	8/3/17	Male	International	Beijing	Netherlands
19	Lance	Freelance	Filmmaker	8/6/17	Male	International	Beijing	USA
20	Elsa	Unknown	Graphic designer	8/7/17	Female	International	Beijing	Belgium
21	Dahlia	Embassy, designer	Freelancer	8/12/17	Female	International	Beijing	Netherlands
22	Nancy	CCTV	TV editor	8/12/17	Female	International	Beijing	France
23	Amy	*New York Times*	News editor	8/14/17	Female	International	Beijing	Taiwan
24	Anna	I:Project space	Art curator	8/16/17	Female	International	Beijing	Germany
25	Denis	Unknown	Interpreter, freelancer	8/17/17	Male	International	Beijing	UK
26	Ruben	Unknown	Journalist, photographer	8/21/17	Male	International	Beijing	Netherlands
27	Liu Huanhuan	Freelance	Scriptwriter	9/25/16	Female	Indie film; general	Phone	
28	Jian Haodong	Freelance	Filmmaker	7/18/16	Male	Indie film	Beijing	
29	Shan Zuolong	Dangmai Pictures	CEO, film producer	7/21/16	Male	Indie film	Beijing	
30	Bai Xiaohong	Freelance	Screenwriter, director	7/30/16	Female	Indie film	Beijing	
31	Jin Dixiang	Unknown	Filmmaker, photographer	8/21/16	Male	Indie film	Beijing	
32	Chang Biao	Freelance	Filmmaker	8/26/16	Male	Indie film	Beijing	

No.	Name	Organization or type of work	Job	Interview date	Gender	Case study	Interview place	Notes
33	Zhao Liang	Freelance	Filmmaker	8/31/16	Male	Indie film	Beijing	
34	Yang Cheng	Unknown	CEO, film producer	9/10/16	Male	Indie film	Beijing	
35	Guo Xiaodong	Freelance	Film editor; producer	9/11/16	Male	Indie film	Beijing	
36	Xie Shuchang	Freelance	Filmmaker	11/22/16	Male	Indie film	Amsterdam	With Rowan Parry
37	Fan Jian	Freelance	Filmmaker	11/25/16	Male	Indie film	Amsterdam	With Rowan Parry
38	Lola	Freelance	Filmmaker	11/25/16	Female	Indie film	Amsterdam	
39	Zhu Rikun	Freelance	Filmmaker	11/25/16	Male	Indie film	Amsterdam	With Rowan Parry
40	Wang Fa	Freelance	Filmmaker	2/28/17	Male	Indie film	Phone	
41	Chang Biao	Independent	Filmmaker	7/11/17	Male	Indie film	Beijing	Second interview
42	Jenny	Women's issues	Filmmaker	7/23/17	Female	Indie film	Beijing	
43	Wang Lu	Alibaba, digital entertainment	Marketing and operations	7/17/16	Female	General	Beijing	
44	Hu Yang	Alibaba, digital entertainment	Marketing and operation	7/17/16	Male	General	Beijing	
45	Chen Yuxuan	Miwei Media	Director	7/19/16	Female	General	Beijing	
46	Yan Di	Chun Feng De Yi Media	Film marketing manager	7/26/16	Female	General	Beijing	
47	An Ruyi	*Asura* cast	Assistant producer	8/1/16	Male	General	Beijing	
48	Sun Xu	Enlight Media	Producer	8/2/16	Female	General	Beijing	
49	Cao Jun	Miwei Media	Director	8/3/16	Male	General	Beijing	
50	Xu Zhiyuan	One-Way Space (OWS)	Writer, founder of OWS	8/19/16	Male	General	Beijing	

No.	Name	Organization or type of work	Job	Interview date	Gender	Case study	Interview place	Notes
51	Eddy	Video, OWS	Photographer, video editor	8/19/16	Male	General	Beijing	
52	Qiao	Reading, OWS	Editor	8/19/16	Female	General	Beijing	
53	Weina	Salon, OWS	Chief director	8/24/16	Female	General	Beijing	
54	Xiao Wei	Wezeit, OWS	Deputy chief editor	8/24/16	Male	General	Beijing	
55	Li Shihong	Drum Tower West Theatre	Marketing manager	8/26/16	Male	General	Beijing	
56	Wu Qi	Reading, OWS	Chief editor	8/29/16	Male	General	Beijing	
57	Wang Hai	Tencent	HR manager	9/1/16	Male	General	Beijing; phone	
58	Xian Jing	*Entertainment Capital*	Entertainment reporter	9/1/16	Male	General	Beijing	
59	Jing Yu	*Entertainment Capital*	Entertainment reporter	9/2/16	Female	General	Beijing	
60	Xiao Yue	Unknown	TV (web) show director	9/11/16	Female	General	Beijing	
61	Song Jiaxin	Douyu Media	Live show hostess	9/11/16	Female	General	Beijing	
62	Xu Yajing	Tencent	Advertising editor	9/25/16	Female	General	Shanghai	
63	Sarah	Can Xing Production	Commercial director	10/23/16	Female	General	Shanghai; phone	
64	Li Qin	Women's issues	Curator	8/4/17	Male	General	Beijing	
65	Xian Jing	WeChat; Weibo; Sina	Content creator	4/2/18	Male	Digital	Beijing	
66	Silvie	WeChat	Developer; content creator	4/4/18	Female	Digital	Beijing	
67	Xie Fei	Youdao	Product manager	4/7/18	Female	Digital	Beijing	
68	Xiao	University researcher	Computer scientist	4/15/18	Male	Digital	Phone	

No.	Name	Organization or type of work	Job	Interview date	Gender	Case study	Interview place	Notes
69	Ellen	Unknown	Software engineer	4/17/18	Female	Digital	Beijing	
70	Jackie	Unknown	Content creator	4/18/18	Male	Digital	Shanghai	
71	He Yang	WeChat; Taobao	Content creator; intermediary	4/23/18	Male	Digital	Shanghai	
72	He Xin	Toutiao	Content creator	4/24/18	Male	Digital	Phone	
73	Derek	Kuaishou; Tencent	Algorithm engineer	4/24/18	Male	Digital	Phone	
74	Xie Mei	Douyin; Toutiao	Content creator	4/25/18	Female	Digital	Phone	
75	Mou Ming	WeChat	Content creator	4/25/18	Female	Digital	Phone	
76	Bai Chao	Tencent	Media worker	4/27/18	Female	Digital	Phone	
77	Lei Lei	WeChat	Content creator; intermediary	4/27/18	Male	Digital	Phone	
78	Qian Ge	Kuaishou	Content creator	9/6/18	Male	Digital	Phone	
79	Wang Hai	Kuaishou	HR manager	9/9/18	Male	Digital	Phone	Second interview
80	Fabian	TikTok multichannel network (MCN)		9/22/20	Male	Digital	Skype	
81	Andy	TikTok; Hago		4/8/21	Male	Digital	Skype	
82	A. Chen & A. Wu	MCN	Entrepreneurs	4/7/21	Male, female	Digital	Skype	

APPENDIX II

A list of Chinese cultural industries policy (1987–2017 selected)

Date	Policy Title	Government Bodies
02/02/1987	Interim Provisions on the Administration of Cultural Institutions Conducting Commercial Service and Activities	MoC; MoF; SAIC
16/03/1988	Interim Provisions on the Administration of News, Journal and Publishing Presses Conducting Commercial Service and Activities	SAPP, and SACI
10/06/1991	Several Economic Policies on the Cultural Undertakings	The State Council; MoC
30/12/1992	Procedures of Financial Management in Cultural Sectors	MoC
22/03/1993	Notice about further supporting Cultural Propaganda Undertakings	STA (State Taxation Administration)
25/04/1995	Provisions on Special Funds for Propaganda and Cultural Development	MoF
05/09/1996	Regulations on further Improving Cultural Economic Policies	The State Council
07/07/1997	Interim Regulations on the construction fee for the Cultural Undertakings	The State Council; MoF; STA
06/06/2000	Instructions on Deepening Reform in the Film Industry	SARFT; MoC
18/12/2000	Policies on Supporting the Development of the Cultural Undertakings	The State Council
18/10/2001	The Tenth Five-year Plan for the Development of the Cultural Industries	MoC
22/12/2001	Instructions on Deepening Reform in the News, Publishing, Broadcasting, Film and Television Industries	The Central Committee of the CCP; The Publicity Department of the CCP; SARFT; SAPP
03/06/2002	Instructions on the Conglomeration of Press and Publishing Industries	SAPP
17/06/2002	Instructions on the Cross-region Operation of the Press and Publishing Industries	SAPP
20/04/2003	Instructions on the Development of the Animation Film and Television Industries	SARFT
04/09/2003	Instructions on Supporting the Development of the Cultural Industries	MoC

Date	Policy Title	Government Bodies
30/12/2003	Instructions on Promoting the Development of the Broadcast, Film and Television Industries	SARFT
31/12/2003	Regulations on Supporting the Development of the Cultural Industries and the Enterprise Reform of Cultural Units	The State Council
18/10/2004	Instructions on Encouraging, Supporting and Guiding Non-public Economy in the Development of the Cultural Industries	MoC
10/11/2004	Decisions on Naming the Exemplary Bases of the Cultural Industries	MoC
29/03/2005	Tax Policies for Supporting the Cultural Industries	MoF; GAC (General Administration of Customs); SAT
29/03/2005	Tax Policies For the Enterprise Reform of Cultural Units	MoF; GAC; SAT
13/04/2005	Decisions on the Entry of Non-public Capital into the Cultural Industries	The State Council
10/07/2005	Instructions on Promoting and Improving the Export of Cultural Products and Services	The State Council
04/11/2005	Instructions on Promoting Private Art Performing Groups	MoC; MoF; MoH (Ministry of Human Resources and Social Security); SAT
18/08/2006	Regulations on the Special Funds of National Film Industry Development	MoF; SAT
13/09/2006	National Plan for the Cultural Development in the Eleventh Five-year Era	The Central Committee of the CCP; The State Council
14/09/2006	The Eleventh Plan for Cultural Development	MoC
05/11/2006	Policies for Promoting the Export of Cultural Products and Services	The State Council; MoF
07/12/2006	Notice about the Naming of in the Cultural Industries National Research Centres	
11/04/2007	Catalogue of Industries for Cultural Export	MoC (Ministry of Commerce); MoC; SARFT
25/06/2007	Notice about the Naming of the Selected First Round of National Cultural Industrial Parks	MoC
13/08/2008	Instructions on the Promotion of the Animation Industry	MoC
12/10/2008	Regulations on Supporting the Development of the Cultural Industries and the Enterprise Reform of Cultural Units	The State Council
26/03/2009	Tax Policies For the Enterprise Reform of Cultural Units	MoF; SAT
27/03/2009	Tax Policies For Supporting Cultural Enterprises	MoF; SAT
17/07/2009	Tax Policies For Supporting the Animation Industry	MoF; SAT
20/07/2009	Instructions on Promoting the Healthy Development of the Audio-Visual Industries	SAPP

Date	Policy Title	Government Bodies
08/09/2009	Investment Catalogue of the Cultural Industries for	MoC
29/09/2009	Instruction on Speeding up the Development of the Cultural Industries	MoC
28/10/2009	Scheme of Reform of the Audio-Visual and Publishing Industries	SARFT
01/01/2010	Instructions on Further Promoting Press and Publishing Industries	SARFT
21/01/2010	Instructions on Promoting the Development of the Film Industry	The State Council
09/03/2010	Instructions on Using Financial Tools to Promote the Cultural Industries	Publicity Department of the CCP; PBC (People's Bank of China); MoF
09/06/2010	Notice about Strengthening the Administration of the Cultural Industrial Parks	MoC
10/10/2010	Instructions on Developing E-book Industry	SARFT
29/12/2010	Notice about the Insurance Industry Supporting the Cultural Industries	IRC (Insurance Regulatory Commission); MoC
23/02/2012	Planning of Multiplying the Growth of the Cultural Industries during the Twelfth Five-year Era	MoC
24/02/2012	Instructions on Speeding up Conglomeration Reform in the Media Industry	SARFT
07/05/2012	Interim Regulations on the Special Funds for the Cultural Industries	MoF; MoC
08/06/2012	Instructions on Promoting and Guiding Private Capital in Investing the Cultural Sectors	MoC
06/07/2012	Notice about Further Strengthening Regulation on Internet Audio-Visual Programmes such as Web Series and Micro Film	SARFT; CAC (Cyberspace Administration of China)
26/02/2014	Instructions on Promoting the Integration of Cultural Creativity, Design and related industries	The State Council
17/03/2014	Instructions on Promoting the Intergration of Cultural and Financial services	MoC
19/06/2014	Several Economic Policies on Supporting Film Industry	MoF; SARFT
08/08/2014	Instructions on Promoting the Characteristic Cultural Industries	MoC; MoF
09/08/2014	Instructions on Promoting the Development and Reform of Tourism Industries	The State Council
20/08/2014	Instructions on Supporting Small and Micro Cultural Companies	MoC; MoIIT (Ministry of Industry and Information Technology); MoF
29/08/2014	Instruction on Strengthening the Administration of Internet Security in Telecommunication and Internet Sectors	MoIIT

Date	Policy Title	Government Bodies
15/01/2015	Instructions on Speeding up the Construction of Modern Service System for Public Culture	The Central Committee of the CCP; The State Council
08/05/2015	Made In China 2025	The State Council
16/06/2015	Policies on Promoting Mass Entrepreneurship and Innovation	The State Council
04/07/2015	Instructions on Promoting the 'Internet +'	The State Council
04/09/2015	Scheme for the Promotion of Triple Play in Telecommunication Industry	The State Council
05/09/2015	Scheme for the Promotion of 'Big Data' Initiatives	The State Council
14/09/2015	Instructions on Promoting the State-owned Cultural Enterprises to put social benefits first, while Uniting the Social Benefits with Economic Benefits	The State Council
03/10/2015	Instructions on the Development and Prosperity of Socialist Culture and Arts	The Central Committee of the CCP
26/06/2016	Notice about Further Strengthening the Regulation of Broadcasting Hosts and Guests	SARFT
07/11/2016	The Film Promotion Law of the People's Republic of China	NPC (National People's Congress)
29/12/2016	Action Plan of Cultural Development for the 'One Belt One Road' (2016-2020)	MoC
07/05/2017	Scheme of Planning for Cultural Development and Reform in the Thirteenth Five-year Era	The State Council

NOTES

INTRODUCTION: THE BILATERAL CREATIVES

1 Quotations in this book taken from Chinese policy documents, media reports, and Chinese informants were originally in Chinese and have been translated by the author.

2 English translations of Chinese terms or names will be followed by the pinyin and Chinese rendering in parentheses in this book.

3 As I will illustrate in chapter 1, conservative officials and cultural traditionalists in China tend to be suspicious of the individualism, change, and "creative destruction" promised by the creativity discourse. The central government thus prefers to use the term "cultural industries" in its policy documents.

4 According to Chow (2019), these trivialized politics often unfold through the recognition of individual differences, the refusal of social, cultural, and political arrangements, and care for self and others.

5 Kuaishou is a popular Chinese social media platform on which users make, post, and monetize short videos.

6 Including both central and local provincial administrative bodies such as the State Council, the Ministry of Culture, the National Radio and Television Administration, the Cyberspace Administration of China, and the Ministry of Finance. These documents are publicly accessible through the official Chinese Cultural Policy Library database (http://e.cacanet.cn/cpll/index.aspx), established and maintained by the Chinese Central Academy of Culture and Tourism Administration. Most of these sources are also available on government websites.

7 I provide detailed descriptions of the methods used for each case study in its respective empirical chapter.

8 I collected textual and interview data through both online ethnography and semistructured interviews with content creators, algorithm engineers, and MCNs (multi-channel networks) managers. See chapter 5.

9 Films made by the state-owned studios for the state's political propaganda, such as *The Founding of a Republic* (2009) and *The Founding of an Army* (2017). Some commercial productions of recent years can also be categorized as "main melody" movies, given that their content is closely related to state ideology; examples include *Operation Mekong* (2016), *Wolf Warrior 2* (2017), and *The Wandering Earth* (2019).

1. UNDERSTANDING CHINA'S CULTURAL INDUSTRIES

1 Ever since the Mao era, Chinese cultural and media production has been fully sponsored by the state, and all cultural workers, including artists, journalists, writers, and musicians, are employed by state-controlled cultural units (*danwei* 单位). See chapter 2.

2 In the 1990s, record companies in Mainland China were dominated by regional competitors from Hong Kong and Taiwan such as Magic Stone. Only through joint ventures were international record companies allowed to set up offices in China. Only after the late 1990s did local record companies such as Modern Sky start to grow (de Kloet 2002).

3 As I will explain later in this chapter, however, most of these parks are far from profitable due to the complicated administrative system and the state-commerce relationship.

4 US Secretary of State John Foster Dulles first formulated the term "peaceful evolution" in the 1950s during the Cold War, referring to attempts to peacefully transform the socialist regimes into capitalist and democratic states. Since then, the Chinese state has believed that this theory is part of US foreign policy toward China (Ong 2007).

5 According to the "Regulations on Film Production" (State Council 2002) and the "Chinese Film Industry Promotion Law" (2016), foreign individuals and organizations are prohibited from producing films in China independently. But international (including from Hong Kong and Taiwan) film companies (neither individuals nor noncommercial organizations) are allowed to participate in film coproduction with Chinese film companies that have a special license issued by the Chinese government.

6 According to the Chinese nomenklatura system, the Central Committee of the Chinese Communist Party holds power in the appointment of senior cadres to leading positions of the party state's bureaucratic apparatus, including the CCP high command, the central party bureaucracy, state advisory organs, the National People's Congress, the State Council, state-owned banks, and state-owned media (Chan 2004).

7 Interview, Wang Hai, September 1, 2016, Beijing.

2. BEING CREATIVE FOR THE STATE

1 Some of these hosts have included Cui Yongyuan, Ma Dong, Li Yong, Chai Jing, Zhang Quanlin, Li Xiaomeng, Lang Yongchun, and Ha Wen.

2 This Chinese phrase refers to a permanent contracted job, which used to be a basic welfare benefit for those working in state-owned institutions. Most state-controlled companies have gradually abolished this tenured employment system since the launch of the "market economy reform" in the 1990s. See Hay et al. 1994; Benson and Zhu 1999.

3 See the previous section for a discussion of cultural-system reform.

4 As requested by the informant, I pseudonymized the name of this company, which is a very influential SOCE in China.

5 In China, this hierarchical familial relation is often used to describe a socially unequal power relationship. "Grandpa" refers to the powerful party, while "grandson" stands for the weak, often bullied side.

6 By using the term "private production," I do not assume it is a productive activity that is completely separate from the system. As I will show below, it is "private" in the sense that producers attach this form of production to a more individualized motif aligned with their personal cultural values.

3. FROM INDEPENDENT TO ART FILM AND BACK AGAIN

1 According to Zhang (2004) and Nakajima (2016), the function of cinema, as defined by the Chinese nation-state, has undergone a transformation from the Mao era, when "political propaganda and education" were its only missions, to the time following the "reform and opening-up" policy, when entertainment and commercial success gained importance. "Main melody" films, which uphold political propaganda and education missions, and commercial films, which aim to achieve high box office sales, now constitute mainstream film production in China.

2 Independent cinema in China includes both fiction films and documentaries (see Zhang 2006).

3 Examples of such films include Jia Zhangke's *Mountains May Depart* (2015) and *Ash Is Purest White* (2018) and Lou Ye's *The Shadow Play* (2018).

4 According to Deleuze and Guattari (1987), lines of flight are "not themselves constituted/imprisoned in specific identities" (Todd 2005, 137) but "provid[e] the resources (material) for erasing and redrawing boundaries, for fleeing a particular territory for another one, and, under certain conditions, for imploding the territory itself" (2005, 139).

5 In his political theory of "exodus," Paolo Virno (1996, 191) conceives it as a massive defection from the state in order to institute "a non-state run public sphere" and to achieve a "radically new form of democracy."

6 In China, the term "left-behind children" refers to children whose parents work as migrant workers in the cities while their children stay in their rural hometowns with their grandparents or other relatives. In this case, four "left-behind" children were reportedly found dead from drinking pesticide after being abandoned by their parents. No sufficient food or other help had been offered by the local authorities before the suicides happened (Lin 2015).

7 As reported by various scholars and media, Jia Zhangke's recent films—including *The World* (2004), *24 City* (2008), *A Touch of Sin* (2013), and *Mountains May Depart* (2015)—were all approved by the state Film Bureau and received substantial financial support from both international and domestic film companies (Callahan 2014; Nakajima 2016).

8 In 2009, Zhao Liang was commissioned by the Ministry of Health to make the documentary *Together* (2010), which is about the social discrimination of people with HIV and AIDS in Chinese society.

9 *Kaili Blues* (*Lu Bian Ye Can*) tells the story of Chen's dreamlike experiences on a journey as he searches for his nephew. Chen is a physician in Kaili, a small county of Guizhou Province. In the film, the director Bi Gan uses various symbolic and visual elements to build up a surreal time-space continuum in which Chen encounters his past memories and lost love in a very emotional and poetic way. *Crosscurrent* (*Chang Jiang Tu*) depicts the magical love story of a couple on a trip along the Yangtze River in a nonlinear way. Similarly to Bi Gan, its director, Yang Chao, seems more interested in conveying emotions through poetic visual symbols than in presenting clear story lines with a political message.

10 Thanks to timely treatment and the financial support of his filmmaking friends, the operation was successful, and Cong Feng eventually returned all donations from fans.

11 According to Zhu, his aggressive approach consisted of selecting films critical of the Chinese government, which brought political risks for the festival (Sniadecki 2013, 172).

4. (UN-)BECOMING CHINESE CREATIVES

1 Among those with Western passports, more participants from the Netherlands were interviewed because of my own social network.

2 In early 2019, the Institute of Provocation moved to the 798 Art Zone due to rent increases.

5. THE UNLIKELY CREATIVE CLASS

1 In rapper culture, "MC" stands for "microphone controller" or "master of ceremonies"; the abbreviation is often used as a title for skilled rappers. Tian You chose this title to identify himself as a Chinese rapper.

2 *Hanmai* literally means "shouting with a microphone." Chinese online rappers such as Tian You created and popularized this form. They shout out rhythmical lyrics, usually rephrased in classical Chinese combined with popular online slang, to up-tempo music.

3 All are private companies that receive financial investment from Chinese internet giants such as Baidu, Tencent, and Alibaba. The headquarters of the Kuaishou company are in Beijing, and the company receives investments from Baidu, Tencent, and several other venture capital firms.

4 The notion of "grassroots individuals" (*caogen* 草根) resonates with the frequently used term "common people" (*laobaixin* 老百姓). While I use these terms because of their prevalence in Chinese discourses, I have placed them in parentheses to show my awareness that they are highly problematic terms that obscure rather than clarify, and they produce a binary division between the "people" and the "elite" that ignores further stratifications and more subtle class differences.

5 See https://www.kuaishou.com/.

6 Accessed in 2018.

7 Kuaishou does not sell advertising space for financial or medical products, or for other social media platforms.

8 It is quite ironic that a China-based platform includes both Facebook and Google in its registration interface, underscoring how censorship of both is anything but clear cut or univocal.

9 The "Nearby" tab was replaced by "Selection" in 2020. The new Selection tab becomes the default tab when entering the app, and it has a similar interface design as TikTok; only one video is shown on the screen, and users need to scroll down to view the next.

10 https://www.Kuaishou.com/about/policy.

11 According to Jarvis and Pratt (2006), contemporary media and cultural industries lead to an increasing "extensification" of work, referring to the distribution or exporting of work across divergent spaces/scales and times.

REFERENCES

Abidin, Crystal. 2016. "Visibility Labour: Engaging with Influencers' Fashion Brands and #OOTD Advertorial Campaigns on Instagram." *Media International Australia* 161 (1): 86–100.

Alacovska, Ana. 2017. "The Gendering Power of Genres: How Female Scandinavian Crime Fiction Writers Experience Professional Authorship." *Organization* 24 (3): 377–96.

Alacovska, Ana, and Rosalind Gill. 2019. "De-Westernizing Creative Labour Studies: The Informality of Creative Work from an Ex-Centric Perspective." *International Journal of Cultural Studies* 22 (2): 195–212.

Alitech. April 28, 2017. "Alibaba Announces the Luban Smart Design Platform" (阿里发布鲁班智能设计平台). https://mp.weixin.qq.com/s/4MnThBmwpj9CtbofTkZFvg.

Appiah, Kwame Anthony. 2010. *The Ethics of Identity*. Princeton: Princeton University Press.

Arcbering. 2017. "Hanmai, a Chinese Rap-Like Performance, Symbolizes a Cultural Interest in Rural China." *Medium*. https://medium.com/@arcbering/.

Bai Ruoyun and Song Geng. 2014. "'Clean Up the Screen': Regulating Television Entertainment in the 2000s." In *Chinese Television in the Twenty-First Century*, edited by Bai Ruoyun and Song Geng, 89–106. London: Routledge.

Bakhshi, Hasan, Jonathan M. Downing, Michael A. Osborne, and Philippe Schneider. 2017. *The Future of Skills: Employment in 2030*. London: Pearson.

Banks, Mark. 2007. *The Politics of Cultural Work*. Basingstoke: Palgrave Macmillan.

Banks, Mark. 2010. "Autonomy Guaranteed? Cultural Work and the 'Art–Commerce Relation.'" *Journal for Cultural Research* 14 (3): 251–69.

Banks, Mark. 2017. *Creative Justice: Cultural Industries, Work and Inequality*. London: Rowman & Littlefield International.

Banks, Mark, Rosalind Gill, and Stephanie Taylor, eds. 2013. *Theorizing Cultural Work: Labour, Continuity and Change in the Cultural and Creative Industries*. London: Routledge.

Banks, Mark, and David Hesmondhalgh. 2009. "Looking for Work in Creative Industries Policy." *International Journal of Cultural Policy* 15 (4): 415–30.

Beck, Ulrich. 2006. *Cosmopolitan Vision*. Cambridge: Polity.

Beijing Institute of Culture Innovation and Communication (BICIC). 2020. "Evaluating the Impact of the Pandemic on the Cultural Industries" (评估疫情对文化产业的影响). https://mp.weixin.qq.com/.

Benson, John, and Zhu Ying. 1999. "Markets, Firms and Workers in Chinese State-Owned Enterprises." *Human Resource Management Journal* 9 (4): 58–74.

Berlant, Lauren. 1997. *The Queen of America Goes to Washington City: Essays on Sex and Citizenship*. Durham, NC: Duke University Press.

Berrio-Zapata, Cristian, Fábio Mosso Moreira, and Ricardo César Gonçalves Sant'Ana. 2015. "Barthes' Rhetorical Machine: Mythology and Connotation in the Digital Networks." *Bakhtiniana* 10 (2): 147–70.

Berry, Chris. 2006. "Independently Chinese: Duan Jinchuan, Jiang Yue, and Chinese Documentary." In *From Underground to Independent: Alternative Film Culture in Contemporary China*, edited by Paul G. Pickowicz and Zhang Yingjin, 109–22. Washington, DC: Rowman & Littlefield.

Berry, Chris, and Lisa Rofel. 2010. "Alternative Archive: China's Independent Documentary Culture." In *The New Chinese Documentary Film Movement: For the Public Record*, edited by Chris Berry, Lisa Rofel, and Lu Xinyu, 135–54. Hong Kong: University of Hong Kong Press.

Berry, Chris, and Mary Ann Farquhar. 2006. *China on Screen: Cinema and Nation*. New York City: Columbia University Press.

Biddle, Sam, Paulo Victor Ribeiro, and Tatiana Dias. March 16, 2021. "Invisible Censorship: TikTok Told Moderators to Suppress Posts by 'Ugly' People and the Poor to Attract New Users." *Intercept*. https://theintercept.com/2020/03/16/tiktok-app-moderators-users-discrimination/.

Bodomo, Adams. 2012. *Africans in China: A Sociocultural Study and Its Implications for African–Chinese Relations*. Amherst, NY: Cambria Press.

Boix, Rafael, Francesco Capone, Lisa de Propris, Luciana Lazzeretti, and Daniel Sanchez. 2016. "Comparing Creative Industries in Europe." *European Urban and Regional Studies* 23 (4): 935–40.

Borak, Masha. July 15, 2021. "Alibaba, Tencent, ByteDance and 30 Other Big Tech Firms Sign Voluntary Antitrust 'Self-Discipline' Pledge at Event." *South China Morning Post*. https://www.scmp.com/.

Bork-Hüffer, Tabea, and Yuan Yuan-Ihle. 2014. "The Management of Foreigners in China: Changes to the Migration Law and Regulations during the Late Hu-Wen and Early Xi-Li Eras and Their Potential Effects." *International Journal of China Studies* 5 (3): 571.

Breslin, Shaun. 2012. "Government–Industry Relations in China: A Review of the Art of the State." In *East Asian Capitalism: Diversity, Continuity, and Change*, edited by Andrew Walter and Zhang Xiaoke, 29–45. Oxford: Oxford University Press.

Brown, Kerry. 2012. "The Communist Party of China and Ideology." *China: An International Journal* 10 (2): 52–68.

Brown, Phillip, Hugh Lauder, and David Ashton. 2010. *The Global Auction: The Broken Promises of Education, Jobs, and Incomes*. Oxford: Oxford University Press.

Bulhões, Gabriela. April 23, 2021. "Kwai Grows in Brazil and Debuts in Argentina, Colombia, and Mexico." (Translated from Portuguese.) *Olhar Digital*. https://olhardigital.com.br/.

Burgess, Jean. 2006. "Hearing Ordinary Voices: Cultural Studies, Vernacular Creativity and Digital Storytelling." *Continuum* 20 (2): 201–14.

Business Insider. December 27, 2019. "Top Ten Most Downloaded Apps in India." *Business Insider*. https://www.businessinsider.in.

Butler, Judith. 2009. *Frames of War: When Is Life Grievable?* New York: Verso Books.

Callahan, William A. 2014. "Citizen Ai: Warrior, Jester, and Middleman." *Journal of Asian Studies* 73 (4): 899–920.

Castells, Manuel. 2005. "Space of Flows, Space of Places: Materials for a Theory of Urbanism in the Information Age." In *Comparative Planning Cultures*, edited by Bishwapriya Sanyal, 69–88. London: Routledge.

Castillo, Roberto. 2014. "Feeling at Home in the 'Chocolate City': An Exploration of Place-Making Practices and Structures of Belonging amongst Africans in Guangzhou." *Inter-Asia Cultural Studies* 15 (2): 235–57.

Castillo, Roberto. 2016. "'Homing' Guangzhou: Emplacement, Belonging and Precarity among Africans in China." *International Journal of Cultural Studies* 19 (3): 287–306.

Central Committee of the Chinese Community Party (CCP). 2011. "Decisions on Deepening Cultural-System Reform" (中央关于深化文化体制改革若干重大问题的决定). http://www.gov.cn/.

Central Committee of the Chinese Community Party (CCP) and State Council. 2005. "Instructions on Deepening Cultural-System Reform" (中共中央 国务院关于深化文化体制改革的若干意见). http://www.chuban.cc/.

Central Committee of the Chinese Community Party (CCP) and State Council. 2015. "Instructions on Promoting State-Owned Cultural Enterprises to Prioritize Social Benefits and Balance Social and Economic Benefits" (关于推动国有文化企业把社会效益放在首位，实现社会效益和经济效益相统一的指导意见). http://politics.people.com.cn/.

Chan, Hon S. 2004. "Cadre Personnel Management in China: The Nomenklatura System, 1990–1998." *China Quarterly* 179 (September): 703–34. https://doi.org/10.1017/S0305741004000554.

Chan, Kam Wing, and Will Buckingham. 2008. "Is China Abolishing the *Hukou* System?" *China Quarterly* 195 (September): 582–606.

Cheah Pheng. 2006. "Cosmopolitanism." *Theory, Culture & Society* 23 (2–3): 486–96.

Chen Kuan-Hsing. 2010. *Asia as Method: Toward Deimperialization*. Durham, NC: Duke University Press.

Chen Pei'ai. January 12, 2011. "Chinese Television Advertising in 30 Years Since the Reform and Opening Up" (改革开放三十年我国电视商业广告回顾). http://www.mediaresearch.cn/.

Chen Xiaoli. 2018. "Live-Streaming Star Banned over 'Offensive' Content." *Shine*. https://www.shine.cn/.

Chen Xu, D. Bondy Valdovinos Kaye, and Jing Zeng. 2021. "#PositiveEnergy Douyin: Constructing 'Playful Patriotism' in a Chinese Short-Video Application." *Chinese Journal of Communication* 14 (1): 97–117.

Cheng Qi. April 7, 2021. "What Has the Pandemic Brought to the Cultural Industries?" (疫情给文化产业带来了哪些影响？) *Chinese Economy*. http://m.ahcid.com/.

Cheung, Esther M. K. 2007. "Dialogues with Critics on Chinese Independent Cinemas." *Jump Cut: A Review of Contemporary Media* 49. https://www.ejumpcut.org/.

China Academy of Information and Communications Technology (CAICT). 2019. "White Paper on the Chinese Digital Economy 2019" (中国数字经济发展白皮书). http://www.caict.ac.cn/.

China Internet Network Information Center (CINIC). 2019. "Forty-Fourth Survey Report—Statistical Report on Internet Development" (第四十四次中国互联网络发展状况统计报告).http://www.cac.gov.cn/pdf/20190829/44.pdf.

Choi Ching Yan. 1975. *Chinese Migration and Settlement in Australia*. Sydney: Sydney University Press.

Chong, Gladys Pak Lei. 2011. "Volunteers as the 'New' Model Citizens: Governing Citizens through Soft Power." *China Information* 25 (1): 33–59.

Chorzempa, Martin. August 3, 2021. "China's Campaign to Regulate Big Tech Is More Than Just Retaliation." *Nikkei Asia*. https://asia.nikkei.com/.

Choudhury, Saheli Roy. 2020. "Bytedance Douyin Has 600 Million Daily Active Users." *CNBC*. https://www.cnbc.com/.

Chow Yiu Fai. 2011. "Hope against Hopes: Diana Zhu and the Transnational Politics of Chinese Popular Music." *Cultural Studies* 25 (6): 783–808. https://doi.org/10.1080/09502386.2011.576766.

Chow Yiu Fai. 2017. "Exploring Creative Class Mobility: Hong Kong Creative Workers in Shanghai and Beijing." *Eurasian Geography and Economics* 58 (4): 361–85.

Chow Yiu Fai. 2019. *Caring in Times of Precarity: A Study of Single Women Doing Creative Work in Shanghai*. Cham: Palgrave Macmillan.

chyxx. 2016. October 26, 2016. "The Distribution of Chinese Cultural-Industry Parks in 2016" (2016 年中国文化创意产业园区分布及关注格局现状回顾). http://www.chyxx.com/.

City of Beijing. 2014. "Plan for the Construction of the Creative Industries Functional Zone in Beijing (2014–2020)" (北京市文化创意产业功能区建设发展规划 [2014–2020]年). http://www.bjdch.gov.cn/n1683657/n3782513/c4006280/content.html.

City of Shanghai. 2017. "Thirteenth Five-Year Plan for the Development of the Creative and Design Industries in Shanghai" (上海创意与设计产业发展 "十三五"规划). http://www.shanghai.gov.cn/.

City of Shenzhen. 2016. "Thirteenth Five-Year Plan for Cultural Development in Shenzhen" (深圳市文化发展 "十三五" 规划). http://www.sz.gov.cn/.

Collie, Natalie, and Caroline Wilson-Barnao. 2020. "Playing with TikTok: Algorithmic Culture and the Future of Creative Work." In *The Future of Creative Work: Creativity and Digital Disruption*, edited by Greg Hearn. Cheltenham and Northampton: Edward Elgar.

Comunian, Roberta, and Lauren England. 2020. "Creative and Cultural Work without Filters: COVID-19 and Exposed Precarity in the Creative Economy." *Cultural Trends* 29 (2): 112–28.

Conor, Bridget. 2015. "'Egotist,' 'Masochist,' 'Supplicant': Charlie and Donald Kaufman and the Gendered Screenwriter as Creative Worker." *Sociological Review* 63:113–27.

Conor, Bridget, Rosalind Gill, and Stephanie Taylor. 2015. "Gender and Creative Labour." *Sociological Review* 63 (S1): 1–22.

Conradson, David, and Alan Latham. 2005. "Transnational Urbanism: Attending to Everyday Practices and Mobilities." *Journal of Ethnic and Migration Studies* 31 (2): 227–33.

Craig, David, Jian Lin, and Stuart Cunningham. 2021. *Wanghong as Social Media Entertainment in China*. Cham: Palgrave McMillan.

Cresswell, Tim. 2006. *On the Move: Mobility in the Modern Western World*. Milton Park, UK: Taylor & Francis.

Culp, Robert. 2006. "Rethinking Governmentality: Training, Cultivation, and Cultural Citizenship in Nationalist China." *Journal of Asian Studies* 65 (3): 529–54.

Cunningham, Stuart. 2009. "Trojan Horse or Rorschach Blot? Creative Industries Discourse around the World." *International Journal of Cultural Policy* 15 (4): 375–86.

Cunningham, Stuart, and David Craig. 2019. *Social Media Entertainment*. New York: New York University Press.

Cunningham, Stuart, David Craig, and Junyi Lv. 2019. "China's Livestreaming Industry: Platforms, Politics, and Precarity." *International Journal of Cultural Studies* 22 (6): 719–36.

Curtin, Michael, and Kevin Sanson, eds. 2016. *Precarious Creativity: Global Media, Local Labor*. Oakland: University of California Press.

Cyberspace Administration of China (CAC). 2017. "Detailed Regulations on the Administration of Internet News Service" (互联网新闻信息服务许可管理实施细则). http://www.cac.gov.cn/.

Cyberspace Administration of China (CAC). August 27, 2021. "Regulations on the Management of Recommendation Algorithms in Internet Information Service (Tentative)" (互联网信息服务算法推荐管理规定 [征求意见稿]). http://www.cac.gov.cn/2021-08/27/c_1631652502874117.htm.

Dai Jinhua. 2000. *Chinese Film Culture: 1978–1998* (雾中风景 1978–1998: 中国电影文化). Beijing: Peking University Press.

Davis, Aeron. 2008. "Investigating Cultural Producers." In *Research Methods for Cultural Studies*, edited by Michael Pickering, 53–67. Edinburgh: Edinburgh University Press.

de Kloet, Jeroen. 2002. "Rock in a Hard Place: Commercial Fantasies in China's Music Industry." In *Media in China: Consumption, Content and Crisis*, edited by Stephanie Hemelryk Donlad, Michael Keane, and Yin Hong, 93–104. London: Routledge.

de Kloet, Jeroen. 2010. *China with a Cut: Globalisation, Urban Youth and Popular Music*. Amsterdam: Amsterdam University Press.

Deleuze, Gilles, and Félix Guattari. 1983. *Anti-Oedipus: Capitalism and Schizophrenia*. Minneapolis: University of Minnesota Press.

Deleuze, Gilles, and Félix Guattari. 1987. *A Thousand Plateaus: Capitalism and Schizophrenia*. Minneapolis: University of Minnesota Press.

Deuze, Mark. 2009. "Media Industries, Work and Life." *European Journal of Communication* 24 (4): 467–80.

Dickson, Bruce J. 2003. *Red Capitalists in China: The Party, Private Entrepreneurs, and Prospects for Political Change*. Cambridge: Cambridge University Press.

Duan Qian Qian. 2020. "Driven by the Housing Economy, Tiger Tooth's First-Quarter Revenue Grew Nearly 50% Year-on-Year" (受宅经济推动, 虎牙一季度营收同比增长近五成). *Yicai*. https://www.yicai.com/news/.

Duffy, Brooke Erin. 2016. "The Romance of Work: Gender and Aspirational Labour in the Digital Culture Industries." *International Journal of Cultural Studies* 19 (4): 441–57.

Dunn, Kevin. 2010. "Embodied Transnationalism: Bodies in Transnational Spaces." *Population, Space and Place* 16 (1): 1–9.

Edensor, Timothy J. 2009. "Introduction: Rethinking Creativity: Critiquing the Creative Class Thesis." In *Spaces of Vernacular Creativity*, edited by Tim Edensor, Deborah Leslie, Steve Millington, and Norma Rantisi, 15–30. London: Routledge.

Elliott, Anthony, and John Urry. 2010. *Mobile Lives*. London: Routledge.

Finkel, Rebecca, Deborah Jones, Katherine Sang, and Dimitrinka Stoyanova Russell. 2017. "Diversifying the Creative: Creative Work, Creative Industries, Creative Identities." *Organization* 24 (3): 281–88.

Flew, Terry. 2012. *The Creative Industries: Culture and Policy*. London: Sage.

Flew, Terry. 2013. *Global Creative Industries*. Cambridge: Polity.

Flew, Terry, Xiang Ren, and Yi Wang. 2019. "Creative Industries in China: The Digital Turn." In *A Research Agenda for Creative Industries*, edited by Stuart Cunningham and Terry Flew, 164–78. Cheltenham: Edward Elgar Publishing.

Florida, Richard. 2002. *The Rise of the Creative Class: And How It's Transforming Work, Leisure, Community, and Everyday Life*. New York: Basic Books.

Florida, Richard. 2012. *The Rise of the Creative Class—Revisited: Revised and Expanded*. New York: Basic Books.

Foucault, Michel, Paul Rabinow, and James D. Faubion. 1997. *The Essential Works of Foucault, 1954–1984*. New York: New Press.

Friedman, Andrew L. 1977. *Industry and Labour: Class Struggle at Work and Monopoly Capitalism*. Basingstoke: Palgrave.

Fuchs, Christian. 2010. "Labor in Informational Capitalism and on the Internet." *Information Society* 26 (3): 179–96.

Fung, Anthony. 2016. "Redefining Creative Labor: East Asian Comparisons." In *Precarious Creativity: Global Media, Local Labor*, edited by Michael Curtin and Kevin Sanson, 200–214. Oakland: University of California Press.

Fung, Anthony, and Zhang Xiaoxiao. 2011. "The Chinese *Ugly Betty*: TV Cloning and Local Modernity." *International Journal of Cultural Studies* 14 (3): 265–76.

Galloway, Susan, and Stewart Dunlop. 2007. "A Critique of Definitions of the Cultural and Creative Industries in Public Policy." *International Journal of Cultural Policy* 13 (1): 17–31.

Gan Xiong. January 7, 2019. "Tencent-Designed Robot Can Write Thousands of Articles per Day" (腾讯机器人日均写稿过千篇). *Shenzhen Daily*. http://gd.sina.cn/.

Garnham, Nicholas. 2005. "From Cultural to Creative Industries: An Analysis of the Implications of the 'Creative Industries' Approach to Arts and Media Policy Making in the United Kingdom." *International Journal of Cultural Policy* 11 (1): 15–29.

George, Alexander L., and Andrew Bennett. 2004. *Case Studies and Theory Development in the Social Sciences*. Cambridge: MIT Press.

Gill, Rosalind. 2011. "Sexism Reloaded, Or, It's Time to Get Angry Again!" *Feminist Media Studies* 11 (1): 61–71.

Gill, Rosalind. 2014. "Unspeakable Inequalities: Post Feminism, Entrepreneurial Subjectivity, and the Repudiation of Sexism among Cultural Workers." *Social Politics: International Studies in Gender, State & Society* 21 (4): 509–28.

Gill, Rosalind, and Andy Pratt. 2008. "In the Social Factory? Immaterial Labour, Precariousness and Cultural Work." *Theory, Culture and Society* 25 (7–8): 1–30. https://doi.org/10.1177/0263276408097794.

Gillespie, Tarleton. 2014. "The Relevance of Algorithms." In *Media Technologies: Essays on Communication, Materiality, and Society*, edited by Tarleton Gillespie, Pablo J. Boczkowski, and Kirsten A. Foot, 167–94. Cambridge: MIT Press.

Gong Ting. 2006. "Corruption and Local Governance: The Double Identity of Chinese Local Governments in Market Reform." *Pacific Review* 19 (1): 85–102.

Gregg, Melissa. 2013. *Work's Intimacy*. Cambridge: Polity.

Guangming Daily. 2015. "China's Cultural Industries in 10 Years" (我国文化产业10年发展对比分析报告). http://cpc.people.com.cn/.

Hammersley, Martyn, and Paul Atkinson. 2007. *Ethnography: Principles in Practice*. 3rd ed. London: Routledge.

Hansen, Høgni Kalsø, and Thomas Niedomysl. 2009. "Migration of the Creative Class: Evidence from Sweden." *Journal of Economic Geography* 9 (2): 191–206.

Han Xiao. 2021. "Historicising Wanghong Economy: Connecting Platforms through Wanghong and Wanghong Incubators." *Celebrity Studies* 12 (2): 317–25.

Havens, Timothy, Amanda D. Lotz, and Serra Tinic. 2009. "Critical Media Industry Studies: A Research Approach." *Communication, Culture & Critique* 2 (2): 234–53.

Hay, Donald, Derek Morris, Guy Liu, and Yao Shujie. 1994. *Economic Reform and State-Owned Enterprises in China 1979–87*. Oxford: Clarendon Press.

Heilmann, Sebastian, and Elizabeth J. Perry, eds. 2011. *Mao's Invisible Hand: The Political Foundations of Adaptive Governance in China*. Cambridge, MA: Harvard University Press.

Helmond, Anne. 2015. "The Platformization of the Web: Making Web Data Platform Ready." *Social Media + Society* 1 (2): 1–11.

Hernández, Javier. September 15, 2017. "Ranting and Rapping Online in China, and Raking in Millions." *New York Times*. https://www.nytimes.com/.

Hesmondhalgh, David. 2008. "Cultural and Creative Industries." In *The Sage Handbook of Cultural Analysis*, edited by Tony Bennett and John Frow, 552–69. London: Sage.

Hesmondhalgh, David. 2010. "Normativity and Social Justice in the Analysis of Creative Labour." *Journal for Cultural Research* 14 (3): 231–49.

Hesmondhalgh, David. 2019. *The Cultural Industries*. 4th ed. London: Sage.

Hesmondhalgh, David, and Sarah Baker. 2011. *Creative Labour: Media Work in Three Cultural Industries*. New York: Routledge.

Hickey-Moody, Anna, and Peta Malins, eds. 2007. *Deleuzian Encounters: Studies in Contemporary Social Issues*. New York: Palgrave Macmillan.

Hoffman, Lisa. 2006. "Autonomous Choices and Patriotic Professionalism: On Governmentality in Late-Socialist China." *Economy and Society* 35 (4): 550–70.

Holford, W. David. 2019. "The Future of Human Creative Knowledge Work within the Digital Economy." *Futures* 105:143–54.

Holt, Fabian, and Francesco Lapenta. 2010. "Introduction: Autonomy and Creative Labour." *Journal for Cultural Research* 14 (3): 223–29.

Hong Yu. 2017a. *Networking China: The Digital Transformation of the Chinese Economy*. Urbana: University of Illinois Press.

Hong Yu. 2017b. "Pivot to Internet Plus: Molding China's Digital Economy for Economic Restructuring?" *International Journal of Communication* 11.

Howkins, John. 2002. *The Creative Economy: How People Make Money from Ideas*. London: Penguin UK.

Huashangbao. 2014. "The Average Monthly Salary of CCTV Employees Is Only 8161 Yuan" (央视员工月薪平均8161元). http://ent.sina.com.cn/.

Hu Huilin. 2005. *On National Cultural Security* (中国国家文化安全论). Shanghai: Shanghai People's Press.

Hu Xiaohan and Dan Wang. May 22, 2021. "The Recovery of Chinese Cinema after the Pandemic" (风景缘何这边独好？中国电影在疫情后复苏的经验、价值与启示). *Chinese Cinema*. https://www.163.com/dy/article/GAKK8N7B0517DKB7.html.

Huang Tianran. January 8, 2020. "This Smart Technology Can Design 100 Million Posters in One Day" (这款人工智能可以一天设计10亿张海报). *Sohu*. https://www.sohu.com.

Huang Yasheng. 2008. *Capitalism with Chinese Characteristics: Entrepreneurship and the State*. Cambridge: Cambridge University Press.

Huo Qiming. June 8, 2016. "The Cruel Bottom Class: Chinese Rural Society in a Video App" (残酷底层物语：一个视频软件的中国农村). *Tencent News*. https://xw.qq.com/.

Iqbal, Mansoor. August 4, 2021. "TikTok Revenue and Usage Statistics (2021)." *Business of Apps*. https://www.businessofapps.com/.

Jarvis, Helen, and Andy C. Pratt. 2006. "Bringing It All Back Home: The Extensification and 'Overflowing' of Work: The Case of San Francisco's New Media Households." *Geoforum* 37 (3): 331–39.

Jeffcutt, Paul, and Andrew Pratt. 2002. "Managing Creativity in the Cultural Industries." *Creativity and Innovation Management* 11 (4): 225–33.

Jeffreys, Elaine, and Gary Sigley. 2009. "Governmentality, Governance, and China." In *China's Governmentalities*, edited by Elaine Jeffreys, 13–35. London: Routledge.

Jenkins, Henry, Sam Ford, and Joshua Green. 2013. *Spreadable Media*. New York: New York University Press.

Jia Lianrui and Fan Liang. 2021. "The Globalization of TikTok: Strategies, Governance and Geopolitics." *Journal of Digital Media & Policy* 12 (2): 273–92.

Jiang Juan. 2012. *Subject, Viewpoint, and Expression: Studies on Chinese Independent Documentary* (主体·视点·表达: 中国独立纪录片研究). Beijing: Chinese University of Communication Press.

Jiang Zemin. 1992. "Jiang Zemin's Speech at the Fourteenth National Congress of the Chinese Communist Party" (江泽民在中国共产党第十四次全国代表大会上的报告). *China Daily*. http://www.chinadaily.com.cn/.

Jiu Xing. 2016. "Lonely Hero" (一人饮酒醉). *Tianya BBS*. http://bbs.tianya.cn/post-641-31626-1.shtml.

Johnson, Matthew David. 2006. "A Scene beyond Our Line of Sight: Wu Wenguang and New Documentary Cinema's Politics of Independence." In *From Underground to Independent: Alternative Film Culture in Contemporary China*, edited by Paul G. Pickowicz and Zhang Yingjin, 47–76. Washington, DC: Rowman & Littlefield.

Jones, Deborah, and Judith K. Pringle. 2015. "Unmanageable Inequalities: Sexism in the Film Industry." *Sociological Review* 63:37–49.

Kalleberg, Arne L. 2009. "Precarious Work, Insecure Workers: Employment Relations in Transition." *American Sociological Review* 74 (1): 1–22.

Kaye, D. Bondy Valdovinos, Jing Zeng, and Patrik Wikström. Forthcoming. *TikTok: Creativity and Culture in Short Video*. Cambridge: Polity.

Kaye, D. Bondy Valdovinos, Xu Chen, and Jing Zeng. 2021. "The Co-Evolution of Two Chinese Mobile Short Video Apps: Parallel Platformization of Douyin and TikTok." *Mobile Media & Communication* 9 (2): 229–53.

Keane, Michael. 1998. "Television and Moral Development in China." *Asian Studies Review* 22 (4): 475–503.

Keane, Michael. 2001. "Broadcasting Policy, Creative Compliance and the Myth of Civil Society in China." *Media, Culture & Society* 23 (6): 783–98.

Keane, Michael. 2006. "From made in China to created in China." *International journal of cultural studies* 9 (3): 285-296.

Keane, Michael. 2009. "Creative Industries in China: Four Perspectives on Social Transformation." *International Journal of Cultural Policy* 15 (4): 431–43.

Keane, Michael. 2010. "Keeping Up with the Neighbors: China's Soft Power Ambitions." *Cinema Journal* 49 (3): 130–35.

Keane, Michael. 2013. *Creative Industries in China: Art, Design and Media*. Cambridge: Polity.

Keane, Michael. 2016. "Unbundling Precarious Creativity in China." In *Precarious Creativity: Global Media, Local Labor*, edited by Michael Curtin and Kevin Sanson, 215–30. Oakland: University of California Press.

Keane, Michael, and Ying Chen. 2017. "Entrepreneurial Solutionism, Characteristic Cultural Industries and the Chinese Dream." *International Journal of Cultural Policy*. DOI: 10.1080/10286632.2017.1374382.

Kennedy, John James. 2013. "Finance and Rural Governance: Centralization and Local Challenges." *Journal of Peasant Studies* 40 (6): 1009–26.

Kharpal, Arjun. September 3, 2021. "China's Tech Giants Pour Billions into Xi's Vision of 'Common Prosperity.'" CNBC. https://www.cnbc.com.

Kleinman, Arthur, Yunxiang Yan, Jing Jun, Sing Lee, and Everett Zhang. 2011. *Deep China: The Moral Life of the Person*. Berkeley: University of California Press.

Kohrman, Matthew. 2004. "Should I Quit? Tobacco, Fraught Identity, and the Risks of Governmentality in Urban China." *Urban Anthropology* 33 (2/4): 211–45.

Kong, Lily. 2014. "Transnational Mobilities and the Making of Creative Cities." *Theory, Culture & Society* 31 (7–8): 273–89.

Kraus, Richard Curt. 2004. *The Party and the Arty in China: The New Politics of Culture*. Lanham: Rowman & Littlefield.

Lan Shanshan. 2017. *Mapping the New African Diaspora in China: Race and the Cultural Politics of Belonging*. London: Routledge.

Larkin, Brian. 2013. "The Politics and Poetics of Infrastructure." *Annual Review of Anthropology* 42:327–43.

Leadbeater, Charles, and Kate Oakley. 1999. *The Independents: Britain's New Cultural Entrepreneurs*. London: Demos.

Lee Ching Kwan. 2016. "Precarization or Empowerment? Reflections on Recent Labor Unrest in China." *Journal of Asian Studies* 75 (2): 317–33.

Lee, David. 2011. "Networks, Cultural Capital and Creative Labour in the British Independent Television Industry." *Media, Culture & Society* 33 (4): 549–65.

Lee Hye-Kyung. 2016. "Politics of the 'Creative Industries' Discourse and Its Variants." *International Journal of Cultural Policy* 22 (3): 438–55.

Leonardo, Zeus. 2004. "The Color of Supremacy: Beyond the Discourse of 'White Privilege.'" *Educational Philosophy and Theory* 36 (2): 137–52.

Leung, Wing-Fai, and Alberto Cossu. 2019. "Digital Entrepreneurship in Taiwan and Thailand: Embracing Precarity as a Personal Response to Political and Economic Change." *International Journal of Cultural Studies* 22 (2): 264–80.

Leung, Wing-Fai, Rosalind Gill, and Keith Randle. 2015. "Getting In, Getting On, Getting Out? Women as Career Scramblers in the UK Film and Television Industries." *Sociological Review* 63:50–65.

Ley, David. 2004. "Transnational Spaces and Everyday Lives." *Transactions of the Institute of British Geographers* 29 (2): 151–64.

Li Han Lin and Wang Qi. 1996. *Research on the Chinese Work Unit Society*. Frankfurt: Peter Lang.

Li Keqiang. 2018. "'Internet+' Has Provided a Wide Stage for Mass Entrepreneurship" ("互联网+"为大众创业、万众创新提供了广阔的舞台). People.com. http://lianghui.people.com.cn.

Li Miao, Chris KK Tan, and Yuting Yang. 2020. "Shehui Ren: Cultural Production and Rural Youths' Use of the Kuaishou Video-Sharing App in Eastern China." *Information, Communication & Society* 23 (10): 1499–1514.

Li Xueqin. January 1, 2020. "Why Can Li Ziqi Attract So Many Fans Overseas?" (李子柒为啥能在海外"圈粉"?). *People's Daily*, overseas edition. http://media.people.com.cn.

Lieberthal, Kenneth, and David M. Lampton, eds. 1992. *Bureaucracy, Politics, and Decision Making in Post-Mao China*. Berkeley: University of California Press.

Liew Leong. 2005. "China's Engagement with Neo-Liberalism: Path Dependency, Geography and Party Self-Reinvention." *Journal of Development Studies* 41 (2): 331–52.

Light, Ben, Jean Burgess, and Stefanie Duguay. 2018. "The Walkthrough Method: An Approach to the Study of Apps." *New Media and Society* 20 (3): 881–900.

Lin, Luna. 2015. "Four 'Left-Behind' Children in China Die of Poisoning After Being Abandoned." *Guardian*. https://www.theguardian.com/.

Liu Danru. 2017. "After Staying Five Days in the Countryside, I Finally Understand Why Kuaishou Can Attract 400 Million Chinese People" (过年在农村待了5天，我终于知道为什么快手能横扫4亿中国人). *36KR*. https://36kr.com/.

Liu Guofu. 2009. "Changing Chinese Migration Law: From Restriction to Relaxation." *Journal of International Migration and Integration* 10 (3): 311–33.

Liu Jin. 2018. "Kuaishou and Toutiao Got Interviewed" (快手、今日头条、火山小视频被约谈). *People's Daily*. http://gongyi.people.com.cn/.

Liu Lian. 2020. "From a Brand to IP: Let's Talk about the 15-Year-Old One Way Space" (从书店品牌到文化 IP: 我们和 15 岁的单向空间聊了聊它未来的可能性). https://socialbeta.com/t/interview-brand-danxiang-2020-11.

Lloyd, Richard D. 2010. *Neo-Bohemia: Art and Commerce in the Postindustrial City*. 2nd ed. New York: Routledge.

Lorey, Isabell. 2015. *State of Insecurity: Government of the Precarious*. London: Verso Books.

Lu Xinyu. 2003. *Documenting China: The Contemporary Chinese New Documentary Movement* (纪录中国: 当代中国新纪录运动). Shanghai: SDX Joint Publishing Company.

Mao Zedong. 1967. *Talks at the Yenan Forum on Literature and Art*. Beijing: Foreign Languages Press.

Marcus, George E. 1995. "Ethnography in/of the World System: The Emergence of Multi-Sited Ethnography." *Annual Review of Anthropology* 24 (1): 95–117.

Martin, Fran. 2017. "Rethinking Network Capital: Hospitality Work and Parallel Trading among Chinese Students in Melbourne." *Mobilities* 12 (6): 890–907.

Matei, Adrienne. January 28, 2020. "Country Life: The Young Female Farmer Who Is Now a Top Influencer in China." *Guardian*. https://www.theguardian.com.

Matthews, Graham J. 2017. "Framing Risk in China: Precarity and Instability in the Stories of Li Yiyun." *Textual Practice* 31 (3): 505–21.

May, Todd. 2005. *Gilles Deleuze: An Introduction*. Cambridge: Cambridge University Press.

McGuigan, Jim. 2004. *Rethinking Cultural Policy*. Maidenhead, UK: Open University Press.

McGuigan, Jim. 2009. "Doing a Florida Thing: The Creative Class Thesis and Cultural Policy." *International Journal of Cultural Policy* 15 (3): 291–300.

McGuigan, Jim. 2010. "Creative Labour, Cultural Work and Individualisation." *International Journal of Cultural Policy* 16 (3): 323–35.

McIntyre, David P., and Arati Srinivasan. 2017. "Networks, Platforms, and Strategy: Emerging Views and Next Steps." *Strategic Management Journal* 38 (1): 141–60.

McIntosh, Peggy. 1988. *White Privilege and Male Privilege: A Personal Account of Coming to See Correspondences through Work in Women's Studies*. London: Routledge.

McIntosh, Peggy. 2018. "White Privilege and Male Privilege." In *Privilege: A Reader*, edited by Michael S. Kimmel and Abby L. Ferber, 28–40. London: Routledge.

McRobbie, Angela. 2002. "From Holloway to Hollywood: Happiness at Work in the New Cultural Economy." In *Cultural Economy*, edited by Paul du Gay and Michael Pryke, 87–114. Thousand Oaks, CA: Sage.

McRobbie, Angela. 2009. *The Aftermath of Feminism: Gender, Culture and Social Change*. Thousand Oaks, CA: Sage.

McRobbie, Angela. 2016. *Be Creative: Making a Living in the New Culture Industries*. Cambridge: Polity.

Mezzadra, Sandro, and Brett Neilson. 2013. *Border as Method, or, the Multiplication of Labor*. Durham: Duke University Press.

Mertha, Andrew. 2009. "'Fragmented Authoritarianism 2.0': Political Pluralization in the Chinese Policy Process." *China Quarterly* 200:995–1012.

Ministry of Commerce. 2006. "China's WTO accession commitments" (中国入世承诺). http://www.mofcom.gov.cn/

Ministry of Culture (MoC). 1987. "Interim Provisions on the Administration of Cultural Institutions Conducting Commercial Service and Activities" (文化事业单位开展有偿服务和经营活动的暂行办法). http://www.110.com/.

Ministry of Culture (MoC). 2003. "Opinions on Promoting the Cultural Industries" (文化部关于支持和促进文化产业发展的若干意见). http://www.chinalawedu.com/.

Ministry of Culture and Tourism (MCT). 2017. "Temporary Provisions on the Administration of Internet Culture" (互联网文化管理暂行规定). http://jinbao.people.cn/.

Ministry of Finance (MoF). 2016. "Annual Report on State-Owned Cultural Enterprises" (国有文化企业发展报告 2016). http://wzb.mof.gov.cn/.

Minyinzhiku. 2017. "Analysis of the Development of the Cultural Industries" (文化产业发展趋势及业务机会分析). http://www.sohu.com/.

Moorkens, Joss. 2020. "'A Tiny Cog in a Large Machine': Digital Taylorism in the Translation Industry." *Translation Spaces* 9 (1): 12–34.

Mouna, Thomas. 2017. "In Close Quarters." *ArtAsiaPacific* 103:63–64.

Munck, Ronaldo. 2013. "The Precariat: A View from the South." *Third World Quarterly* 34 (5): 747–62.

Murdock, Graham, and Peter Golding. 2005. "Culture, Communications and Political Economy." In *Mass Media and Society*, 4th ed., edited by James Curran and Michael Gurevitch, 60–83. London: Hodder Arnold.

Murphy, Enda, and Declan Redmond. 2009. "The Role of 'Hard' and 'Soft' Factors for Accommodating Creative Knowledge: Insights from Dublin's 'Creative Class.'" *Irish Geography* 42 (1): 69–84.

Myers, Steven Lee. July 17, 2017. "A Cleanup of 'Holes in the Wall' in China's Capital." *New York Times*. https://www.nytimes.com/.

Nakafuji, Rei. August 9, 2021. "TikTok Overtakes Facebook as World's Most Downloaded App." *Nikkei Asia*. https://asia.nikkei.com/.

Nakajima, Seio. 2012. Prosumption in Art. *American Behavioral Scientist* 56 (4): 550–69.

Nakajima, Seio. 2016. "The Genesis, Structure and Transformation of the Contemporary Chinese Cinematic Field: Global Linkages and National Refractions." *Global Media and Communication* 12 (1): 85–108.

Nation. July 21, 2020. "Pakistan Warns TikTok over 'Obscene, Immoral' Content." *Nation*. https://nation.com.pk/.

National Bureau of Statistics (NBS). 2018. "China's Cultural Industries in 2017" (2017年我国文化及相关产业增加值). http://www.stats.gov.cn/.

National Development and Reform Commission (NDRC). 2016. "Thirteenth Five-Year Plan for China's National Economic and Social Development" (中华人民共和国国民经济和社会发展第十三个五年规划). https://www.ndrc.gov.cn/.

National Development and Reform Commission (NDRC). 2021. "Fourteenth Five-Year Plan for China's National Economic and Social Development" (中华人民共和国国民经济和社会发展第十四个五年规划). https://www.ndrc.gov.cn/.

National Development and Reform Commission and Ministry of Commerce (NDRC and MoC). 2017. "Guidance on Foreign Investment in Chinese Industries" (外商投资产业指导目录). http://www.gov.cn/.

National People's Congress of the PRC (NPC). 2016. "Chinese Film Promotion Law" (中华人民共和国电影产业促进法). http://www.npc.gov.cn/.

Naughton, Barry J., and Dali L. Yang. 2004. *Holding China Together: Diversity and National Integration in the Post-Deng Era*. Cambridge: Cambridge University Press.

Nauta, Arjen. 2018. "Localizing Korean Reality Shows in China: The Practice of Production and Censorship." In *Willing Collaborators: Foreign Partners in Chinese Media*, edited by Michael Keane, Brian Yecies, and Terry Flew, 171–86. London: Rowman & Littlefield.

Neilson, Brett, and Ned Rossiter. 2008. "Precarity as a Political Concept, Or, Fordism as Exception." *Theory, Culture & Society* 25 (7–8): 51–72.

Nieborg, David, and Thomas Poell. 2018. "The Platformization of Cultural Production: Theorizing the Contingent Cultural Commodity." *New Media & Society* 20 (11): 4275–92.

Niewenhuis, Lucas. August 17, 2021. "China Steps Up Antitrust Campaign with New Draft Rules Targeting Internet Companies." *SupChina*. https://supchina.com/.

Nixon, Sean, and Ben Crewe. 2004. "Pleasure at Work? Gender, Consumption and Work-Based Identities in the Creative Industries." *Consumption Markets and Culture* 7 (2): 129–47.

Nowicka, Magdalena, and Maria Rovisco, eds. 2016. *Cosmopolitanism in Practice*. London: Routledge.

Nowicka, Magdalena, and Ramin Kaweh. 2016. "Looking at the Practice of UN Professionals: Strategies for Managing Differences and the Emergence of a Cosmopolitan Identity." In *Cosmopolitanism in Practice*, edited by Magdalena Nowicka and Maria Rovisco, 51–71. London: Routledge.

Nye, Joseph S. 2005. *Soft Power: The Means to Success in World Politics*. New York: Public Affairs.

O'Connor, Justin. 2010. *The Cultural and Creative Industries: A Literature Review*. Newcastle: Creativity, Culture and Education.

O'Connor, Justin, and Xin Gu. 2006. "A New Modernity? The Arrival of 'Creative Industries' in China." *International Journal of Cultural Studies* 9 (3): 271–83.

O'Connor, Justin, and Xin Gu. 2020. *Red Creative: Culture and Modernity in China*. Chicago: Intellect Books.

Ong, Lynette. 2006. "The Political Economy of Township Government Debt, Township Enterprises and Rural Financial Institutions in China." *China Quarterly* 186:377–400.

Ong, Russell. 2007. "'Peaceful Evolution,' 'Regime Change' and China's Political Security." *Journal of Contemporary China* 16 (53): 717–27.

People's Daily. 2019. "Guiding the Development of the Platform Economy" (引导平台经济健康发展).http://www.gov.cn/zhengce/2019-08/09/content_5419951.htm.

Pickowicz, Paul. 2006. "Social and Political Dynamics of Underground Filmmaking in China." In *From Underground to Independent: Alternative Film Culture in Contemporary China*, edited by Paul G. Pickowicz and Zhang Yingjin, 1–22. Washington, DC: Rowman & Littlefield.

Pickowicz, Paul, and Zhang Yingjin, eds. 2006. *From Underground to Independent: Alternative Film Culture in Contemporary China*. Washington, DC: Rowman & Littlefield.

Pieke, Frank N. 2012. "The Communist Party and Social Management in China." *China Information* 26 (2): 149–65.

Powell, Jason, and Ian Cook. 2000. "'A Tiger Behind, and Coming Up Fast': Governmentality and the Politics of Population Control in China." *Journal of Aging and Identity* 5 (2): 79–89.

Pulido, Laura. 2000. "Rethinking Environmental Racism: White Privilege and Urban Development in Southern California." *Annals of the Association of American Geographers* 90 (1): 12–40.

Qirui. 2017. "Kuaishou Video Advertisement" (快手视频广告). http://www.qiruiwangluo.com/.

Qu, Sandy Q., and John Dumay. 2011. "The Qualitative Research Interview." *Qualitative Research in Accounting and Management* 8 (3): 238–64.

Reckwitz, Andreas. 2017. *The Invention of Creativity: Modern Society and the Culture of the New*. Translated by Steven Black. Cambridge: Polity.

Ricoeur, Paul. 1976. *Interpretation Theory: Discourse and the Surplus of Meaning*. Fort Worth: Texas Christian University Press.

Ritzer, George, and Nathan Jurgenson. 2010. "Production, Consumption, Prosumption: The Nature of Capitalism in the Age of the Digital 'Prosumer.'" *Journal of Consumer Culture* 10 (1): 13–36.

Robinson, Luke. 2013. *Independent Chinese Documentary: From the Studio to the Street*. Basingstoke: Palgrave Macmillan.

Rose, Nikolas, Pat O'Malley, and Mariana Valverde. 2006. "Governmentality." *Annual Review of Law and Social Science* 2 (1): 83–104.

Rosen, Stanley. 2012. "Film and Society in China." In *A Companion to Chinese Cinema*, edited by Zhang Yingjin, 197–217. Chichester: Wiley-Blackwell.

Ross, Andrew. 2009. *Nice Work if You Can Get It: Life and Labor in Precarious Times*. New York: New York University Press.

Rossiter, Ned. 2016. *Software, Infrastructure, Labor: A Media Theory of Logistical Nightmares*. London: Routledge.

Rossiter, Ned. 2017. "Imperial Infrastructures and Asia Beyond Asia: Data Centres, State Formation and the Territoriality of Logistical Media." *Fibreculture Journal* 29:1–20.

Saich, Tony. 2009. *The Blind Man and Elephant: Analysing the Local State in China*. London: Routledge.

Saich, Tony. 2011. *Governance and Politics of China*. 3rd ed. Basingstoke: Palgrave Macmillan.

Scharff, Christina. 2017. *Gender, Subjectivity, and Cultural Work: The Classical Music Profession*. London: Routledge.

Scott, Allen J., Stefano Lucarelli, Michael A. Peters, and Carlo Vercellone. 2013. "Cognitive-Cultural Production, Digital Labour and the New Frontiers of Knowledge: A Conversation with Allen J. Scott." *Knowledge Cultures* 1 (4): 167–78.

Selmer, Jan. 2006. "Cultural Novelty and Adjustment: Western Business Expatriates in China." *International Journal of Human Resource Management* 17 (7): 1209–22.

Shanghai Association of Creative and Cultural Industry (SACCI). 2016. "Three-Year Planning of the Cultural Creative Industries in Shanghai: 2016–2018" (上海市文化创意产业发展三年行动计划 2016–2018 年). http://www.shcia.org/.

Shao Dong. 2016. "Bi Gan and Kaili Blues" (毕赣与《路边野餐》：27岁的贵州导演和他的大师雏形之作). *The Papers*. http://www.thepaper.cn/.

Shaw, Victor N. 1996. *Social Control in China: A Study of Chinese Work Units*. Westport, CT: Greenwood Publishing Group.

Short Video Factory. 2018. "Top 20 List of the Most Viewed Short Videos in August 2018." http://www.sohu.com/.

Sniadecki, John Paul. 2013. "Digital Jianghu: Independent Documentary in a Beijing Art Village." PhD diss., Harvard University.

Standing, Guy. 2016. *The Precariat: The New Dangerous Class*. London: Bloomsbury.

State Administration for Industry and Commerce (SAIC). 1987. "Regulations on Advertising" (广告管理条例). http://home.saic.gov.cn/.

State Administration of Press and Publishing (SAPP) and State Administration for Industry and Commerce (SAIC). 1988. "Interim Provisions on the Administration of News, Journal, and Publishing Presses Conducting Commercial Service and Activities" (关于报社、期刊社、出版社开展有偿服务和经营活动的暂行办法). http://www.chinalawedu.com/.

State Administration of Press, Publication, Radio, Film and Television (SAPPRFT). 2015. "Provisions on the Administration of Electronic Publications" (电子出版物出版管理规定). http://www.mofcom.gov.cn/.

State Council. 2001. "Tenth Five-Year Plan on the Development of the National Economy and Society" (国民经济和社会发展第十个五年计划纲要). http://www.people.com.cn/.

State Council. 2002. "Regulations on Film Production" (电影管理条例). http://www.gov.cn/.

State Council. 2003. "Regulations on Supporting the Development of the Cultural Industries and the Enterprise Reform of Cultural Units" (文化体制改革试点中支持文化产业发展和经营性文化事业单位转制为企业的两个规定). http://www.lawxp.com.

State Council. 2005. "Decisions on Allowing Nonpublic Capital into the Cultural Industries" (国务院关于非公有资本进入文化产业的若干决定). http://www.gov.cn/.

State Council. 2008. "Regulations on Supporting the Development of the Cultural Industries and the Enterprise Reform of Cultural Units" (关于印发文化体制改革中经营性文化事业单位转制为企业和支持文化企业发展两个规定的通知). http://www.chinaacc.com/.

State Council. 2009. "The Planning of the Cultural Industries" (文化产业振兴规划). http://www.gov.cn/.

State Council. 2014. "Regulations on Further Promoting the Cultural Industries and Reforming Commercial Cultural Institutions in the Cultural-System Reform" (关于文化体制改革中经营性文化事业单位转制为企业和进一步支持文化企业发展两个规定的通知). http://www.gov.cn/.

State Council. 2015a. "Instructions on Constructing Platforms to Promote Mass Entrepreneurship" (国务院关于加快构建大众创业万众创新支撑平台的指导意见). http://www.gov.cn/.

State Council. 2015b. "Instructions on Promoting 'Internet+'" (国务院关于积极推进"互联网+"行动的指导意见). http://www.gov.cn/.

State Council. 2015c. "Instructions on Promoting the State-Owned Cultural Enterprises to Put Social Benefits First While Uniting the Social Benefits with Economic Benefits" (关于推动国有文化企业把社会效益放在首位、实现社会效益和经济效益相统一的指导意见). http://politics.people.com.cn/.

State Council. 2016. "From Made in China to Created in China" (从中国制造到中国创造). http://english.gov.cn/.

State Council. 2018a. "Regulations on Supporting the Development of the Cultural Industries and the Enterprise Reform of Cultural Units" (国务院办公厅关于印发文化体制改革中经营性文化事业单位转制为企业和进一步支持文化企业发展两个规定的通知). http://www.gov.cn/.

State Council. 2018b. "Specifications on the Reform of the State Council" (关于国务院机构改革方案的说明). http://www.xinhuanet.com/.

Stokel-Walker, Chris. February 20, 2020. "TikTok Influencers Are Telling People to Stop Using the App." *Input*. https://www.inputmag.com/.

Su, Wendy. 2015. "From Culture for the People to Culture for Profit: The PRC's Journey toward a Cultural Industries Approach." *International Journal of Cultural Policy* 21 (5): 513–28. DOI: 10.1080/10286632.2014.931382.

Su Xiaochen. May 8, 2020. "The Trouble with TikTok's Global Rise." *New Lens*. https://international.thenewslens.com/.

Sun Baoguo. 2011. "Five Layers of Television Commission" (试析推进电视台制播分离改革的路径). *Shitingjie* 1:77–79.

Sun Wanning. 2005. "Media and the Chinese Diaspora: Community, Consumption, and Transnational Imagination." *Journal of Chinese Overseas* 1 (1): 65–86. DOI: 10.1163/179325405788639373.

Sun Wanning. 2009. "Mission Impossible? Soft Power, Communication Capacity, and the Globalization of Chinese Media." *International Journal of Communication* 4:54–72.

Tillich, Paul. 1999. *The Essential Tillich*. Chicago: University of Chicago Press.

Tong, Q. S., and Ruth Y. Y. Hung. 2012. "Cultural Policy between the State and the Market: Regulation, Creativity and Contradiction." *International Journal of Cultural Policy* 18 (3): 265–78.

Travel China Guide. 2018. "China Work Visa (Z)." https://www.travelchinaguide.com/.

Tse, Tommy, Vivienne Leung, Kimmy Cheng, and Joey Chan. 2018. "A Clown, a Political Messiah or a Punching Bag? Rethinking the Performative Identity Construction of Celebrity through Social Media." *Global Media and China* 3 (3): 141–57.

Tzioumakis, Yannis. 2006. *American Independent Cinema*. Edinburgh: Edinburgh University Press.

Urry, John. 2012. *Sociology beyond Societies: Mobilities for the Twenty-First Century*. London: Routledge.

Ursell, Gillian. 2000. "Television Production: Issues of Exploitation, Commodification and Subjectivity in UK Television Labour Markets." *Media, Culture & Society* 22 (6): 805–25. DOI: 10.1177/016344300022006006.

van der Kamp, Denise, Peter Lorentzen, and Daniel Mattingly. 2017. "Racing to the Bottom or to the Top? Decentralization, Revenue Pressures, and Governance Reform in China." *World Development* 95:164–76.

van Dijck, Josè. 2014. Datafication, Dataism and Dataveillance: Big Data between Scientific Paradigm and Ideology." *Surveillance & Society* 12 (2): 197–208.

van Doorn, Niels. 2017. "Platform Labor: On the Gendered and Racialized Exploitation of Low-Income Service Work in the 'On-Demand' Economy." *Information, Communication & Society* 20 (6): 898–914.

Virno, Paolo. 1996. "Virtuosity and Revolution: The Political Theory of Exodus." In *Radical Thought in Italy: A Potential Politics*, edited by Michael Hardt and Paolo Virno, 189–210. Minneapolis: University of Minnesota Press.

WallStreetCn. 2018. "Stones of Other Mountains: How Has the Overseas Game Market Been Regulated?" (他山之石：海外游戏市场是如何监管的?) *WallStreetCn*. https://wallstreetcn.com/.

Wang Jing. 2001. "The State Question in Chinese Popular Cultural Studies." *Inter-Asia Cultural Studies* 2 (1): 35–52.

Wang Jing. 2003. "Framing Policy Research on Chinese 'Culture Industry': Cultural Goods, Market–State Relations, and the International Free Trade Regime." In *Workshop on Critical Policy Studies*, 15–16. Cambridge, MA.

Wang Jing. 2004. "The Global Reach of a New Discourse: How Far Can 'Creative Industries' Travel?" *International Journal of Cultural Studies* 7 (1): 9–19. DOI: 10.1177/1367877904040601.

Wang Lingjie. 2006. *Analyzing the Dynamics between Organizational Culture and Change: A Case Study of China Central Television (CCTV) in Transition*. PhD diss., University of Warwick.

Wang Qi. 2014. *Memory, Subjectivity and Independent Chinese Cinema*. Edinburgh: Edinburgh University Press.

Wang Weijia. 2011. *Communication as Labor* (作为劳动的传播). Beijing: Chinese Communication University Press.

Wang Yongzhang. 2007. "Can Creative Industries Replace Cultural Industries?" (创意产业能替代文化产业？) http://www.techweb.com.cn/.

Wang Yuhua. 2016. "Beyond Local Protectionism: China's State–Business Relations in the Last Two Decades." *China Quarterly* 226 (June): 319–41.

Womack, Mari. 2005. *Symbols and Meaning: A Concise Introduction*. New York: Altamira Press.

Xi Jinping. 2014. "Talk at the Forum on Arts and Culture" (习近平在文艺工作座谈会上的讲话). http://www.xinhuanet.com/.

Xi Jinping. 2015. "On National Cultural Soft Power" (习近平谈国家文化软实力). http://www.xinhuanet.com/.

Xi Jinping. 2017. "Speech at the Nineteenth National Congress of the Chinese Communist Party" (在中国共产党第十九次全国代表大会上的报告). http://www.gov.cn/.

Xie Yixuan. 2017. "Interview with Rong Guangrong: Despair and Madness" (专访荣光荣-在影像里:绝望与疯癫). *Cinephilia*. http://chuansong.me/.

Xing Fang. 1995. "The Chinese Cultural System: Implications for Cross-Cultural Management." *SAM Advanced Management Journal* 60 (1): 14–21.

Xingjue. 2017. March 27, 2017. "Chinese Art Cinema: Film Always Needs an Audience, However Good It Is" (中国艺术电影现状解读：再好的电影，也需要找到自己的观众). *Ifeng*. http://wemedia.ifeng.com/.

Xu Chenggang. 2011. "The Fundamental Institutions of China's Reforms and Development." *Journal of Economic Literature* 49 (4): 1076–1151.

Xu, Lianlian. 2020. "Douyu's Rapid Increase of Revenue in the Q1 of 2020" (2020 年Q1净利润同比激增 742% 斗鱼直播,带货瞄准直男市场). *meijingwang*. http://www.nbd.com.cn/.

Yang, Jisheng, 2000. *A Study of Chinese Social Classes.* (中國社會各階層分析). Hong Kong: Joint Publishing HK (三聯書店香港).

Yang, Jisheng, 2004. *Chinese Politics in the Time of Reform.* (中國改革年代的政治鬥爭). Hong Kong: Excellent Culture Press.

Yang, Jisheng, 2008. *The Gravestone: A Documentary of the Great Famine in 1960s China.* (墓碑:中国六十年代大饥荒纪实). Hong Kong: Excellent Culture Press.

Yang Zhenjie. 2013. "'Fragmented Authoritarianism'—The Facilitator behind the Chinese Reform Miracle: A Case Study in Central China." *China Journal of Social Work* 6 (1): 4–13.

Yeoh, S. A. Brenda, and Katie Willis. 2005. "Singaporean and British Transmigrants in China and the Cultural Politics of 'Contact Zones.'" *Journal of Ethnic and Migration Studies* 31 (2): 269–85.

Yin Hong and Sun Yanbin. 2017. "Report on the Development of the Chinese Film Industry in 2015" (2015 年中国电影产业发展报告). http://guoqing.china.com.cn/.

Youmshajekian, Lori. 2019. "The $24 Billion Chinese Industry You've Never Heard of". *UNSW Newsroom*. https://newsroom.unsw.edu.au/.

Youwenyouda. 2020. "How will the rise of Wanghong economy impact the restructuring of national economy during the Covid- 19?" (新冠肺炎疫情下,网红经济的"异军突起"对我国产 业结构的主动性调整有何重大影响?). https://zhuanlan.zhihu.com/p/109357506.

Yu Xiaoqing. July 13, 2017. "Renovating the Hutong, Bringing Back the Vintage Look of Beijing as the Ancient Capital" (北京东城整治百街千巷彰显古都风貌). *China Daily*. http://bj.chinadaily.com.cn/.

Yúdice, George. 2018. "Innovations in Cultural Policy and Development in Latin America." *International Journal of Cultural Policy* 24 (5): 647–63.

Zhang Li. 2001. *Strangers in the City: Reconfigurations of Space, Power, and Social Networks within China's Floating Population*. Redwood: Stanford University Press.

Zhang Xiaorong and Ya Su. April 22, 2016. "2016 Chinese Wanghong Year-Zero Report" 2016 (年中国网红元年报告：TA为什么那么红). *The Paper*. https://www.thepaper.cn/.

Zhang Yingjin. 2006. "My Camera Doesn't Lie? Truth, Subjectivity, and Audience in Chinese Independent Film and Video." In *From Underground to Independent: Alternative Film Culture in Contemporary China*, edited by Paul G. Pickowicz and Zhang Yingjin, 23–45. Washington, DC: Rowman & Littlefield.

Zhang Yingjin. 2007. "Rebel without a Cause? China's New Urban Generation and Postsocialist Filmmaking." In *The Urban Generation: Chinese Cinema and Society at the Turn of the Twenty-First Century*, edited by Zhen Zhang, 49–81. Durham, NC: Duke University Press.

Zhang Yunan. May 28, 2020. "Chinese Rival Launches US App to Challenge TikTok." *The Information*. https://www.theinformation.com/.

Zhao Shena and Li Mingxuan. 2009. "The Four Dimensions of Cultural Soft Power" (文化软实力的四个层面内涵及其培育). http://www.shszx.gov.cn/.

Zhu Ying. 2012. *Two Billion Eyes: The Story of China Central Television*. New York: New Press.

INDEX

Page numbers in *italics* indicate Figures

ABOUT THE AUTHOR

Jian Lin is a 100-Talent Young Professor at Zhejiang University. He worked as an assistant professor at the University of Groningen and obtained his PhD in media studies from the University of Amsterdam (jointly awarded by Western Sydney University). He is the coauthor of *Wanghong as Social Media Entertainment in China.*